P9-DUS-484

Absalom and Achitophel

CONTEXTS 3

Absalom and Achitophel

Robert W. McHenry Jr.

ARCHON BOOKS
1986

© 1986 The Shoe String Press, Inc. All rights reserved
First published 1986 as an Archon Book, an imprint of
The Shoe String Press, Inc., Hamden, CT 06514

Printed in the United States of America

The paper in this book meets the guidelines for permanence
and durability of the Committee on Production Guidelines
for Book Longevity of the Council on Library Resources.

I am grateful to the Oxford University Press for permission
to reproduce a selection, vol. 4, pp. 173–76, from John Evelyn's
Diary, edited by E. S. de Beer (Clarendon Press, 1955).

Library of Congress Cataloging in Publication Data
Main entry under title:
Absalom and Achitophel.
Contexts—selected literary works in their
historical settings; 3)
Bibliography: p.
Includes index.
1. Dryden, John, 1631–1700. Absalom and Achitophel—
Sources.   2. Popish Plot, 1678.   3. Great Britain—
History—Charles II, 1660-1685 —Sources.   I. McHenry,
Robert W.   II. Series.
PR3416.A23A27   1986   821'.4   84–24160
ISBN 0–208–01845–X

Notes to Frontispiece

Illustration of
"A Representation of the Popish Plot
in Twenty-nine Figures"

This rendering, published as a broadside in 1681, provides a vivid if somewhat disorganized panorama of the Popish Plot as seen by a believer in Oates and the other Plot witnesses. The first two scenes in the first row concern the preliminaries — the Pope's planning, with Satan under the table (fig. 1), the Great Fire of London in 1666, blamed on the Papists (fig. 2). The next two scenes show Titus Oates revealing the Plot to Sir Edmund Berry Godfrey (fig. 3) and to the king and his council (fig. 4). The next six scenes (row 1, fig. 5 through fig. 5) concern Godfrey's murder — the Papists stab and strangle him in Somerset House, then move his body to Primrose Hill, where it was discovered. In the second row (fig. 4) Miles Prance is shown testifying that Green, Berry, and Hill committed the murder, and figure 5 in this row shows their execution. Many of the following scenes show the activities of the Plotters, as recounted in Oates's *True Narrative,* particularly the attempts to kill the king: by Irish ruffians (row 3, fig. 1), by Pickering (row 3, fig. 2) whose gun jams, and by Sir George Wakeman (row 4, fig. 3), who is to use poison. The scene of Whitebread's being made provincial of the English Jesuits (row 5, fig. 5) is also from Oates's Narrative, where Whitebread is a major character. Considerable attention is given also to Edward Coleman, whose letters to Father La Chaise seemed to confirm Oates's tales: he is paying the ruffians (row 2, fig. 6) for their assassination attempt; in row 3, fig. 3, he is writing to La Chaise, and in row 4, fig. 5, he is drawn to his execution. Other Plot witnesses who appear include William Bedloe, (row 3, fig. 4) seen riding in foreign parts, collecting information; the next two panels disclose Nathaniel Reading trying to currupt him and then being punished for the attempt. Also shown is Stephen Dugdale (row 5, fig. 4), the chief witness against Lord Stafford, reading letters — doubtless incriminating ones — in Staffordshire. The other panels are mostly executions of convicted Papists — Stafford (row 5, fig. 6), the five Jesuits (row 4, fig. 2), Ireland and Grove (row 4, fig. 4), and Pickering (row 5, fig. 1) — all had been named by Oates.

In addition there are four panel representing miscellaneous incidents connected with the Plot — Sir William Waller, a zealously anti-Catholic magistrate, burning Papist books (row 4, fig. 6), Edmund Everard languishing in the Tower (row 4, fig. 1) for distributing an Exclusionist pamphlet, Captain Berry and Alderman Brooks (row 5, fig. 3) trying to throw the blame for the Plot on the Protestants, and Morrice Gifford and Nicholas Stubbs arranging with Elizabeth Oxby to burn London in 1666 (row 5, fig. 2).

CONTEXTS: SELECTED LITERARY WORKS
IN THEIR HISTORICAL SETTINGS

Maynard Mack, General Editor

CONTEXTS 1: *The Beggar's Opera*
J. V. Guerinot and Rodney D. Jilg

CONTEXTS 2: *The Rape of the Lock*
William Kinsley

Contents

Illustrations   ix

Abbreviations   xi

Preface   xiii

Introduction   1

I An Harbinger of Fear

Andrew Marvell's *An Account of the Growth of Popery, and*   17
Arbitrary Government in England (1678)

II The First Evidence of the Plot

Titus Oates's *A True Narrative of the Horrid Plot and Conspiracy*   27
of the Popish Party . . . (1679)

A True and Perfect Narrative of the Late Terrible and Bloody   47
Murther of Sir Edmundberry Godfrey (1678)

The Second Letter of Mr. Coleman's to the French Kings   57
Confessor, Monsieur L'Chaise (1679)

III Public Hysteria and Its Fomenters

Roger North's *Examen* on Godfrey's Funeral and Oates (1740)   66

"The Proceedings Against William Staley" in Henry Care's *The*   72
History of the Damnable Popish Plot (1680)

Gilbert Burnet's *History of My Own Time* on the Trials of Lang-   79
horn and the Five Jesuits (June 13-14, 1679)   85

Charles Blount's *An Appeal from the Country to the City* (1679)

IV The Plot Trials: The Case of Sir George Wakeman

The Trial of Sir George Wakeman (July 18, 1679)   99

John Evelyn's *Diary* (July 18, 1679)   115

Henry Care's *The Weekly Pacquet of Advice from Rome —*   119
The Popish Courant (July 25, 1679)

V The Exclusion Crisis

Anchitell Grey's *Debates in the House of Commons* 125
(November 4, 9, 11, 1680)

Shaftesbury's "Speech upon the Bill of Exclusion and the Popish 147
Plot" (December 23, 1680)

An Address to the Honourable City of London (1681) 155

Vox Populi (1681) 162

VI Countermeasures

Richard Langhorn's *Memoires* (1679) 171

Sir Roger L'Estrange's *A Further Discovery of the Plot* (1680) 186
and *The Observator* (July 20, 1681)

His Majesties Declaration (April 8, 1681) 205

The Trial of Stephen College (August 17, 1681) 214

The History of the Association (1682) 221

VII Some Characters

George Villiers, Duke of Buckingham (1707) 229

James, Duke of Monmouth: 231

   *A True Narrative of the Duke of Monmouth's Late Journey
   into the West* (1680)

   His Grace the Duke of Monmouth Honoured in His Progress
   (1681)

James, Duke of York 239

Slingsby Bethel: 240

   *A Seasonable Answer To a Late Pamphlet, Entituled The
   Vindication of Slingsby Bethel Esq.* (1681)

VIII Literary Antecedents

Absalom's Conspiracy; or, The Tragedy of Treason (1680) 255

John Caryll's *Naboth's Vinyard: or the Innocent Traytor* (1679) 258

Suggested Readings 279

Index 281

Illustrations

"A Representation of the Popish Plot in Twenty-nine Figures" — frontispiece

Portrait of Titus Oates — 26

"The Solemn Mock Procession of the Pope" — 64

Portrait of the Earl of Shaftesbury — 146

Portrait of King Charles II — 204

Portrait of George Villiers, Duke of Buckingham — 228

Portrait of James, Duke of Monmouth — 230

Portrait of James, Duke of York — 238

Abbreviations

Burnet	Gilbert Burnet, *History of My Own Time*, vol. 2, ed. by Osmund Airy (Oxford: Clarendon Press, 1900).
Haley	K. H. D. Haley, *The First Earl of Shaftesbury* (Oxford: Clarendon Press, 1968).
Kenyon	John Kenyon, *The Popish Plot* (London: Heinemann, 1972).
Luttrell	Narcissus Luttrell, *A Brief Historical Relation of State Affairs (Oxford: Oxford University Press, 1857).*
Miller	*John Miller, Popery and Politics in England, 1660-1688* (Cambridge: Cambridge University Press, 1973).
Ogg	David Ogg, *England in the Reign of Charles II*, 2nd. ed. (Oxford: Clarendon Press, 1956).
Reresby	Sir John Reresby, *Memoirs and Travels of Sir John Reresby,* ed. A. Ivatt (London: Kegan Paul & Co., 1904).

Preface

The sheer bulk of existing material on the Popish Plot and the Exclusion Crisis has made the choosing of these selections difficult. Therefore, I decided to concentrate on materials not available in other editions. This policy led me to omit the "answers" to *Absalom and Achitophel* and to include only two of the poem's literary antecedents.

For excellent advice and assistance, I am indebted to Thomas H. Fujimura and Roger Whitlock, my colleagues at the University of Hawaii, and to Rudolph J. Schork of the University of Massachusetts, Boston. I am also grateful to Philip Harth, of the University of Wisconsin, and Alan Roper, of the University of California, Los Angeles, for suggestions that improved my introduction. Maynard Mack generously gave me good advice about every part of this project. And I wish to thank my wife Patricia for all her help, which was immeasurable and invaluable.

This book could not have been completed without research grants from the University of Hawaii and from the William Andrews Clark Memorial Library, where I worked on these materials under the best possible conditions. I also owe much to the Houghton Library, Harvard University, and the Beinecke Library, Yale University, for providing photographs of materials from their collections and for granting permission to reprint them here.

Introduction

Dryden wrote *Absalom and Achitophel,* his masterpiece, in 1681, in the time of the political turmoil ignited by the Popish Plot. This poem is his most complete expression of the political themes that had become important to him during his career as poet, critic, and playwright. In earlier poems, notably *Annus Mirabilis* (1667), which explored the moral and political significance of the Second Dutch War and London's Great Fire of 1666, he had addressed recent historical events. Since his appointment as poet laureate (1667), he had written a number of plays whose plots centered on political passions and values, with particular emphasis on freedom and rebellion. Both *The Conquest of Granada* and *Aurenge-Zebe,* for example, concern weak or corrupt but rightful monarchs threatened by rebellious subjects. By 1681 his long-standing concern with political affairs had been profoundly intensified for several years by the concatenation of events that today is usually called the Exclusion Crisis. This was the struggle by both Establishment and dissenting Protestants to deny to Charles II's brother James, the Roman Catholic duke of York, right of succession to the throne and to substitute a Protestant; Charles's illegitimate son, the duke of Monmouth, became a prominent candidate. Because of the Popish Plot hysteria (discussed below), this struggle seriously threatened for a time the conservative and royalist values Dryden cherished.

At the core of Dryden's design for the poem is a Biblical parallel to Monmouth's threat, the story of Absalom and David in 2 Samuel, chapters 13–19. A beloved but rebellious son (Absalom/Monmouth) is seduced by an evil counselor (Achitophel/Shaftesbury) to attempt to overthrow his father, the rightful king (David/Charles II). Giving a compact exposition of the main elements of the conflict, Dryden shapes the myriad events of the topical situation and their causes—the king's lack of a legitimate heir among his children and the popular fear that a papist king would join with other papists (the Jebusites) to exterminate English Protestantism—into a confrontation of forces that "bubbles o'r" into the threat of civil war. The poem's only "action" follows in three dramatic scenes: a long temptation scene where Achitophel, Satan-like, persuades Absalom to rebel; a brief representation of "Deluded Absalom" speaking, with theatrical sentimentality, to a crowd of supporters; and finally an impressive monologue in which King David, in a *fiat* seconded by heavenly thunder, reaffirms his authority and restores peace.

Though this design has seemed anticlimactic to some critics, it has the virtue of ordering a multitude of confusing historical events in a pattern long familiar: the plot of a restoration or return to peace after disorders and dislocations. This plot, which may be seen in both the *Odyssey* and the *Aeneid,* constantly informs Dryden's earlier writings. For example, *Astrea Redux,* his celebration of the restoration of the king in 1660, employs this pattern and concludes with the prophecy, "And now Time's whiter series is begun"; in *Annus Mirabilis,* the chronicle of war and fire is resolved with an image of trade winds that "gently lay us on the spicy shore." *Absalom and Achitophel* concludes with a similar statement: "Henceforth a series of new time began."

The poem reaches out to a universal meaning in depicting the struggle between David and Achitophel as an instance of the eternal conflict between disorder and order, between selfish madness and lawful stability, here enhanced by generational conflict as well. Through these Biblical analogies, Dryden can interpret in terms favorable to his party the emotions and values that the Exclusion Crisis aroused, while at the same time suggesting general political, social, and psychic issues that make his poem, as Aristotle might have said, "more philosophic and of graver import than history."[1] The political myth of restoration becomes a religious one, as the trio of David, Absalom, and Achitophel is seen to prefigure that of God, Adam, and Satan, and both threesomes become associated with Charles II, Monmouth and Shaftesbury—an interaction Dryden reinforces with frequent allusions to *Paradise Lost,* where the motifs of rebellion and restoration reflect the analogy yet again.

Dryden uses the Biblical material for two additional purposes. One of these is to accommodate the awkward fact of King Charles's promiscuity; despite David's godlike role as a symbol of authority, Dryden must stress Monmouth's illegitimacy to justify his father's refusal to make him his heir. Therefore, he wittily commends the king's sexual "warmth"—associating it with ideal values of "nature" and heavenly guidance belonging to the polygamous "pious times" of the Old Testament. The other purpose is to provide a warning to young Monmouth. His ultimate fate is left in doubt, yet despite Dryden's hope, expressed in the preface, that a reconciliation may still be possible, the poet expects his readers to recall, without his mentioning it, the account of Absalom's defeat and grisly death that is such a memorable part of the Biblical story (2 Sam. 18:9–17).[2]

With its clear sense of the dangers of innovation and its firm use of Christian and heroic imagery to justify the king against the exclusionists, *Absalom and Achitophel* is something of a miracle. To be sure, it makes sense of the contemporary political situation in the way that Dryden and other conservatives wanted to make sense of it. What is astounding is that so much and such compelling sense could be made

2

from the lies, ambiguities, and uncertainties that constituted the realities of the time. To these "realities" we must now turn.

On November 14, 1678, William Staley, the son of a wealthy Roman Catholic banker, engaged in a passionate conversation with a Frenchman called Fromante in the Black Lion, a London eating house. Perhaps excited by the rumors of plots to assassinate King Charles, Staley referred to him as "a great heretic" and exclaimed "I would kill him myself."[3] His words, spoken in French, were overheard; the following day he found himself under arrest. Tried for treason for "compassing" or "imagining" the king's death, convicted within a week, he was executed at Tyburn on November 26—only twelve days after his offense. He was the first to lose his life as a result of the hysteria generated by the Popish Plot, whose terrible nature his case exemplifies, for his conviction and punishment undoubtedly derived their momentum from the widespread public feeling that horrible events were imminent. Chief Justice Sir William Scroggs, presiding at Staley's trial, stressed the need for severity, with "our king in so great danger, and religion at stake."[4] Since most of the public had by this time been terrorized with rumors of Roman Catholic plots, put forward by Titus Oates and his collaborators, it was easy to imagine that the king would be murdered, all good Protestants put to the stake, and London burned again as in 1666.

In this atmosphere, more than thirty of Staley's coreligionists were to be executed. Yet that Staley should be the first is ironic; no plotter, he had not been one of the many Roman Catholics whom Oates accused. And there is reason to doubt his guilt. Bishop Burnet, a stout supporter of the Protestant establishment, believed the two witnesses against him to be "profligate wretches" who were lying to serve their own interests. When, however, he tried to stop the trial, he found to his dismay that his efforts were received with indignation. The earl of Shaftesbury (Achitophel), a skilled manipulator of mob feeling, told him that "we must support the evidence, and that all those who undermined the credit of the witnesses were to be looked on as public enemies."[5] This ruthless argument was to become frequent in the later trials. Nonetheless, it is an index of the difficulties of judgment facing a student of this period that the latest historian of the Popish Plot, John Kenyon, has argued that Burnet is "not to be trusted" in this matter and that Staley was indeed guilty by the standards of the day.[6]

One final episode in Staley's short history also attests to the hatreds aroused by the plot. Because the condemned man had behaved well in prison, the king allowed his body to be returned to his family for burial. But his friends proved tactless; they mourned too publicly by arranging several masses for Staley together with a "pompous and great" funeral that included a public procession to St. Paul's, Covent Garden, where he was interred. Affronted, the Privy Council ordered that the body be removed from its grave and exposed to the usual treatment given traitors; as John Pollock sardonically writes, "to vindicate the majesty of justice his quarters were affixed to the city gates and his head set up to rot on London Bridge."[7]

If the depositions of Oates and his fellow witnesses William Bedloe, Israel Tonge, and others were the immediate cause of many such ferocious deeds during the years 1678 to 1681, the events of the previous two decades had opened the way for their success. In the words of David Ogg, "England was ripe for a plot."[8] Since the Restoration of 1660, English Protestants had been subject to numerous fears of plots to introduce "popery and slavery"—that is, Roman Catholicism and absolute monarchy—into England. Usually they regarded the two evils as inherently connected and assumed that the means of achieving them could only be through plots involving armed uprisings, assassination of the king, and a lurid series of executions of the Protestant populace. The papists, always in the popular view led by traitorous Jesuits, were supposed to believe that their triumph could come only through fire and sword, never by rational persuasion. And of course English history was invoked to verify these fears. One could read in Foxe's *Book of Martyrs* (1563) of the sufferings of the Protestants sent to the stake by "Bloody Mary." No one bothered to recall the sufferings of the Catholics under Elizabeth and Edward VI. And then, in addition, there was the Gunpowder Plot of 1605, the nation's deliverance from which was celebrated on each November 5, together with London's Great Fire of 1666. Protestants regularly blamed this last disaster on the papists, and while subsequent investigations never uncovered any evidence, this deficiency did not prevent papist guilt from being regarded as an article of faith.

Protestant apprehensions fed also on actions of the royal family. It had not escaped notice that Charles II had spent his youth in Catholic France, that his brother James, the duke of York, his heir, had become an open convert to Rome, and that each had taken a Roman Catholic as his wife. Indeed, James's marriage to Mary of Modena in 1673 occasioned a considerable outcry in public and Parliament. Additionally, the intermittent and ineffective enforcement of the existing laws against Roman Catholic recusants and of the Test Act (an oath requiring papists to repudiate the papacy as a condition for holding any position of authority and thus effectively denying them the right to civil and military office) made for greater suspicions that the monarchy was partial to the feared Roman Church.

The international situation appeared ominous as well. Until 1677, England had been frequently at war with the Protestant Dutch because of trade and naval rivalries, but especially after the Treaty of Nijmegen of 1678, solidifying the military gains of Louis XIV, France came to be regarded as the more formidable threat. Charles's willingness to resist French interests appeared questionable. In fact, as a result of a secret clause in the Treaty of Dover (1670), he had received a clandestine French subsidy in return for his promise to declare, as soon as possible, his conversion to Catholicism and to join with France in military efforts against Holland. Despite this, however, he did agree under popular pressure in 1678 to form an army to engage the French. When the Nijmegen treaty relieved him of that obligation and the army became unnecessary, Parliament immediately voted £200,000 to disband it. The following autumn, it remained intact. Since a standing army was usually associated with arbitrary power, opponents of the government feared that the king had retained it to suppress dissent at home. The best known expression of all the accumulated Protestant fears is Andrew Marvell's *An Account of the Growth of Popery, and Arbitrary Government in England,* issued anonymously in 1677; it denounced a royalist conspiracy to bring into England "Absolute Tyranny" and "down-right Popery."[9]

Titus Oates, the Corah of Dryden's poem, a man of many vices and monumental assurance, began his career as an informer against the papists in 1678. He was then twenty-nine years old, a lapsed Anglican clergyman who could look back upon a dismal life of richly deserved failure and humiliation. Dismissed from two public schools, as well as from Gonville and Caius College, Cambridge, rejected by his parishioners in Kent, and expelled from the chaplaincy of a frigate in the Royal Navy, he had already sought revenge against certain of his enemies by charging them with treason and sodomy—only to find his evidence rejected. He had just managed to escape his intended victims' action for perjury by signing aboard the *Adventure* in 1675. By 1677 he had lost yet another chaplaincy in the household of the earl of Norwich, and so, on March 3 of that year became a Roman Catholic. The Jesuits arranged for him to go to the English College at Valladolid for study, but as Oates was no scholar, the authorities there soon sent him back to England. Then he was sent to the College of St. Omers in France, where he lasted, not very happily, for seven months before being expelled once more.

Thus in the summer of 1678, Oates was again in London, without any means of support and full of hatred for the Jesuits, who had found him out. He quickly became associated with Israel Tonge, another clergyman who, as Kenyon writes, had become "permanently unhinged" by the loss of his church in the Great Fire of London.[10] Obsessed by popery, Tonge dwelt especially upon the notion that London was to be

5

burnt again and that the papists had singled him out, along with other prominent enemies of their religion, for assassination. His zeal and Oates's detailed knowledge of the Jesuits proved a powerful combination. Before the end of the summer, Oates had drawn up an indictment of his enemies in forty-three articles (later expanded to eighty-one). He alluded to various conspiracies to kill the king and to root out Protestantism in England, and asserted that a great Jesuit Consult had been held in London during the April just past to plan assassinations. About the means of unveiling their accusations the two informers were quite uncertain, since they could not be sure of their reception at court. Tonge's previous alarms had been rejected with scorn. In the end they entrusted a friend and fellow fanatic, Christopher Kirkby, with the honor of informing the king of his danger. On August 13 he did so.

Although Oates's circumstantial account conformed too well with popular prejudices to be dismissed out of hand, several blunders almost destroyed its credibility. Desperate for independent evidence, the informers next forged five letters that verified Oates's narrative and had them sent to Thomas Bedingfield, the duke of York's confessor. But the Council soon discredited them, and on September 29, the king himself, interviewing Oates in Council, caught him in a number of errors, notably his inaccurate description of Don John of Austria, whom he claimed to have met. Before skepticism could result in the dismissal of his allegations, however, two dramatic events seemed to confirm them so thoroughly that further expressions of doubt became politically impossible.

First came the exposure of Edward Coleman, for a time secretary to the duchess of York, James's wife, and to James himself. He promptly burned his papers on learning that Oates had named him, but the authorities discovered in his lodgings a number of letters to M. La Chaise, Louis XIV's confessor. Although containing nothing that specifically supported Oates's charges, they appeared treasonable, for Coleman had formulated schemes to bribe Charles with French money to dissolve Parliament and to bribe members of the Parliament as well. When the Council saw these letters, he was arrested. Sent to Newgate, he was soon convicted of treason, and on December 3, about two months later, executed.

The other event that seemed to confirm the existence of a plot was a murder, one of the most famous and mysterious of the century. Thinking it prudent to set his depositions before a justice of the peace, Oates swore, on September 28, to the truth of his narrative before Sir Edmund Berry Godfrey, who recorded his oath and kept a copy of the depositions. Then on October 12, Godfrey was reported missing, and after five days of search, his body was discovered on Primrose Hill; he had been strangled and run through with his own sword. Instantly everyone suspected that the papists had done the deed in an attempt to suppress Oates's revelations. A flood of sermons, pamphlets, songs, and portrait medals poured forth, eulogizing Godfrey and damning the papists. For most contemporaries, his death proved the existence of the plot, and, as Parliament met just as the body was discovered, a terrible witch-hunt began. Oates, demanding body guards, addressed Parliament, and those he named, including five Roman Catholic lords, were arrested.

During the following year, the nation witnessed a series of well-reported trials of Roman Catholics accused by Oates, and by other informers who now flocked to London seeking their portion of fame or wealth, or some personal revenge on Catholic enemies. One of these, William Bedloe, proved willing to confirm many of Oates's accusations, thus providing the second witness legally required for a verdict of treason. Three Jesuit priests—William Ireland, Thomas Pickering, and John Grove—were tried on December 16, 1678. Despite the obvious frailties of the prosecution's case and the evidence of poor character given against Oates and Bedloe, Chief Justice Scroggs, himself violently anti-Catholic, had little difficulty in extracting from the jury a verdict of guilty and a sentence of death. Ireland and Grove were executed about five weeks later; Pickering followed in May 1679. That February, three unfortunates connected with Somerset House, the queen's residence—Robert Green, Henry Berry, and Lawrence Hill—were tried for murdering Godfrey; they were convicted on the testimony of Miles Prance, a Roman Catholic silversmith who denounced them after being arrested himself on suspicion of complicity in the murder. Though he recanted twice, he was finally persuaded, through imprisonment and short rations, to return to his original story, and these three men were hurried off to execution within the month. June of the same year brought the trials of five more Jesuit priests accused by Oates, Bedloe, Prance, and others, and of Richard Langhorn, a Roman Catholic attorney. All were soon executed, although Langhorn was held in close confinement for a time, apparently in the hope that he would confess and implicate others. Like the other victims of these judicial murders, he steadfastly reiterated his innocence and went bravely to his death. His meditations in prison and the narrative of his ordeal before and after the trial, as well as his fervent denials of guilt, were published, and, along with the other gallows literature of this time, may have helped eventually to turn the tide of public opinion against Oates and the other prosecutors of the plot.

Anti-Catholic passion remained strong, however, partly because leaders of the opposition fanned the flames as a means of achieving their goal of excluding James—Charles's brother and heir—from any title to the royal succession. Anthony Ashley Cooper, the first earl of Shaftesbury (Dryden's Achitophel, as we have seen), became the leader of the exclusionist forces and the "impresario" of the informers and pamphleteers who inflamed public opinion against the papists.[11] He adopted Oates and other informers and supported their revelations, no matter how outrageous or incredible. As a member of several committees established by the House of Lords to investigate the plot, he bullied and threatened suspects in such an extreme way that many claimed he had attempted to suborn them. The choice offered to the accused was an unequal one: they could unavailingly maintain their innocence and face execution, or they could "confess" and receive a pardon and a reward. Miles Prance did just this, at the cost of sending three innocent men to the hangman. Shaftesbury's tactics extended to the writing or sponsoring of inflammatory pamphlets designed to increase fears of popery. He also gave private encouragement and advice to the duke of Monmouth, Charles's illegitimate son (the Absalom of the poem), who sought to establish himself as the Protestant alternative to James. Aware that many exclusionists favored the succession of James's Protestant daughter, Mary, and her husband, William of Orange, Monmouth appealed to public opinion by his "progresses" through the country and by appearances in London in defiance of the king's commands. His supporters even circulated rumors of a mysterious "Black Box" containing the marriage license of Charles and Monmouth's mother, and thus legitimizing his claims.

These efforts to manipulate public opinion aimed also to manipulate Parliament, where the struggle for exclusion had its center. During these three years of crisis four Parliaments convened. The first, which assembled on October 21, 1678, just in time to hear Oates's story and to react to the news of Godfrey's murder, was the Cavalier Long Parliament (the second of Charles's reign) which had been operative since 1661. Its first major reaction was to pass the second Test Act, which excluded Roman Catholics from sitting in either House of Parliament. Though several Roman Catholic lords were in this way forced to retire from Parliament, the duke of York managed to be exempted from its strictures, thus leaving open the central issue of the succession. The most dramatic event of the session was Ralph Montagu's revelation of letters written by the earl of Danby, the lord treasurer, that revealed his secret negotiations earlier in 1678 with Louis XIV. Opponents of the court were quick to take them as evidence that Danby too was part of a popish plot; the Commons at once impeached him, but before the Lords were willing to bring him to trial, the king prorogued Parliament, and subsequently dissolved it.

Charles apparently hoped that new elections would bring in a more tractable Parliament, but the results were exactly the reverse. The elections took place at the height of the plot scare, and those opposed to the government made substantial gains. The new Parliament, which first met on March 6, 1679, is known as the first exclusion or Whig Parliament, for this period saw the beginnings of modern political parties. The Whigs, initially known as the "country" party, consisting mainly of commercial and dissenting segments of society, sought to reduce the royal prerogative and to exclude James from the succession. The Tories, or the "court" party, characteristically landowners and Anglicans, supported the king's prerogative and the succession as already established. Both names, incidentally, came from derisive terms that each group used against the other.

During this session, the court made some attempts to accommodate the opposition by creating an enlarged Privy Council that included Lord Shaftesbury and other opposition leaders and by offering a compromise proposal on the succession whereby James's powers would be restricted should he become king. Neither effort succeeded. Parliament, after imprisoning Danby in the Tower, began debate upon the first Exclusion Bill in May 1679. Riding high on the fears excited by the Popish Plot, it passed two readings in the House of Commons; its supporters argued that the mere existence of a Roman Catholic heir provided an inevitable inducement to papist conspiracies (in spite of Oates's care to omit any imputations against James in his original depositions) and that a popish monarch would necessarily become a tyrant and a zealot to convert his Protestant subjects. The king killed this bill by proroguing Parliament on May 27 and, later, dissolving it and ordering new elections. This Parliament had not progressed very far in investigating the plot, for procedural dissensions between the two houses had prevented the trial of Danby and the five imprisoned Roman Catholic lords; it has, however, obtained a place in history by its passage of the Habeas Corpus Amendment Act, which strengthened the rights of the accused to a speedy trial.

The second Whig Parliament, assembled in October 1679, was immediately prorogued, and did not meet again for a year. Clearly the court hoped to allow the fires of exclusionist zeal to burn out, and to some degree they did so. The public grew sated with revelations and alarms. Bedloe had died, and accusations against the opponents of the crown began to be heard, especially in the writings of Sir Roger L'Estrange, the chief Tory propagandist. Certain papists attempted to create fears of Protestant treason by inventing the Meal Tub Plot, but it was exposed as a fraud and thus backfired. Nevertheless, no new convictions occurred for some sixteen months, and a few of those imprisoned, thanks to the king's influence, obtained release. It was during this year of parliamentary recess that the public debate began to rage between the "petitioners" who called upon the king to assemble Parliament—that is, those who wished to get on with exclusion—and their opponents, the "abhorrers," who denounced the petitions and supported the royal prerogative.

When this Parliament at last met, it proved to be just as hostile to the court as its predecessor and immediately turned to the great topic of exclusion. A second Exclusion Bill was approved by the Commons on November 11. But in the Lords, it encountered defeat, owing principally to the presence of the king during the debates and the brilliant argumentation of Lord Halifax against it. Its aims thwarted, the Commons turned to the cases of the five Roman Catholic lords, still awaiting trial in the Tower. The elderly and unpopular Lord Stafford was selected to be the first to face his accusers. He was tried before the Lords between November 30 and December 7, 1680. Oates and a long string of newly unearthed informers duly gave their evidence, and Stafford was convicted by a vote of fifty-five to thirty-one. The Tory majority in the Lords had rejected exclusion by a similar majority, but it was not prepared to reject the plot itself. Stafford was executed on December 29. The remainder of this session was occupied with various measures against the duke of York and those of the king's advisors who had worked against exclusion; its final resolution was to affirm that the Great Fire of London had been set by the papists, thus giving validity of a sort to Israel Tonge's obsessive conviction, as well as providing a grim release for the frustrations of the exclusionists. On January 10, the king brought this Parliament to an end.

The third and last Whig Parliament was a brief affair. Because Charles wished to remove it from the environs of the strongly exclusionist city of London, he ordered it to assemble in Oxford, where his guards could more easily maintain order. The sessions, which began on March 21, 1681, were expected to be the scene of another struggle between the forces of exclusion and those advocating the court's proposed compromise. But with anti-Catholic sentiment continuing high, the Commons was intransigent. Immediately the Whigs introduced a third exclusion bill, only to see the proceedings interrupted within a week by a royal order of dissolution. Always clustered around Parliament, the exclusionist forces now disbanded. They could not have known that this short session was to be King Charles's last Parliament. A few days earlier he had concluded yet another secret agreement with Louis XIV, which guaranteed him a subsidy obviating the need for parliamentary appropriations for the remainder of his reign. In the Lords shortly before, Shafestbury had offered the king a proposal by which Monmouth would succeed him on the throne. But Charles's reply indicated his awareness of the strength of his position: "Let there be no delusion," he answered, "I will not yield, nor will I be bullied."[12] In fact, the Whigs had underestimated Charles's firmness throughout the crisis. Known to be amiable and amatory, the king was widely expected to yield to the immense political pressure in favor of exclusion, especially since he was quite fond of the young Monmouth. But his determination to keep the succession unchanged never wavered. When Burnet told him of rumors that Monmouth would be declared his heir, "he answered quick, that, as well as he loved him, he had rather see him hanged."[13]

Despite Charles's tactical victory, the plot did fasten on another important victim in May, when Oliver Plunkett, titular archbishop of Armagh, a sick old man, was condemned on the evidence of disreputable Irish informers brought over and encouraged by Shaftesbury. Plunkett was the last Roman Catholic to be executed (July 1, 1681) because of the Popish Plot.

Before his dissolution of Parliament in March, the king was on the defensive, and the royalists' efforts against Oates and the exclusionists were cautious. Charles could prorogue or dissolve Parliament when it displeased him, but to do so deprived him of the opportunity of raising revenue, and the Whigs filled the parliamentary recesses with clamors for new legislative sessions, public spectacles such as the massive pope-burning processions held in London on November 17 (the anniversary of Queen Elizabeth's accession) in 1679, 1680, and 1681, and a steady stream of inflammatory pamphlets and newspapers spreading fears and hatred. Despite efforts to discredit Oates, revealing much of his unsavory past, he remained as powerful as ever. Nonetheless, as the embattled and prolific L'Estrange continued his attacks, and as the papists' professions of innocence written on the eve of their executions were published, often together with harrowing accounts of the pressures exerted by Shaftesbury and others to force them to confess, the climate slowly changed. The trials, fully reported in print, frequently contained matter embarrassing to the exclusionists, and indeed, in two cases, the accused managed to be acquitted. Samuel Atkins, a clerk employed by Samuel Pepys, charged with aiding in Godfrey's murder, was able to prove an alibi, and had the good luck to come to trial three days after Green, Berry, and Hill had been convicted for the same murder. A more important reverse befell the informers when Sir George Wakeman, the queen's physician, came to trial, with three co-defendants, on July 18, 1679. He was accused by Oates, Bedloe, and others of agreeing to poison the king. But Wakeman's questions embarrassed the prosecution, particularly when he demanded to know why Oates had claimed to know nothing against him when they had first met at the Privy Council. Oates had no convincing answer. He was accustomed to "remembering" additional facts when the need arose. Chief Justice Scroggs openly derided the witnesses and instructed the jury that, although the plot as a whole must be true, it was not necessary to regard these four defendants as guilty. Taking the hint, the jury returned verdicts of "not guilty" for all of them. Though the popular reaction against Scroggs, widely assumed to have been bribed, was furious, he escaped his enemies, and the published account of the trial made troubling reading for anyone who had accepted Oates's veracity.

After March 1681, the government began to move aggressively against its opponents. One would-be informer, Edward Fitzharris, was successfully rushed to execution for treason on July 1, before the Whigs could make use of his allegations in the fight for exclusion. Another of the first Whig victims was Stephen College, "the Protestant Joiner," who was arraigned in London for seditious actions during the Oxford Parliament. The London grand jury, packed with Whigs by the two sheriffs, Henry Cornish and Slingsby Bethel, refused to indict him; the government, however, managed to bring him to trial in Oxford, where Tories packed the juries, and there, despite the testimony of Oates in his defense, he was convicted. He was executed on August 31. In the meantime, the government had accused Shaftesbury himself of treason; he was arrested the day after Fitzharris's execution in July, and kept in the Tower for five months before his case was brought before the London grand jury in November. The Whigs, however, had again succeeded in electing sheriffs loyal to themselves, and the packed jury's verdict was *Ignoramus*. The victory was short-lived; the following year, the government was able, by none-too-honest means, to replace the Whig sheriffs with Tory ones, thus ensuring the impaneling of Tory juries. When their term of office began in September, Shaftesbury went immediately into hiding, and soon fled to Holland, where he died a few months later in 1683.

Besides pursuing the lives of the exclusionist leaders and plot informers, the government now mounted a broad attack upon the independence of the cities, particularly London, which had been strongly Whig. Writs of *quo warranto* were issued to seize the cities' charters. London lost its charter in 1683, and the new one devised by the government provided that "no mayor, sheriff, recorder, or town clerk was to be appointed without the royal approval."[14] Soon after, Oates was arrested for perjury. He came to trial on February 8, 1685, two days after Charles had died and James had succeeded to the throne, and was, of course, convicted. His judges sentenced him to life imprisonment, a huge fine, and a severe course of pillorying, five times a year, beginning immediately with a series of public whippings. They expressed regret that the law did not provide for capital punishment. Incredibly, Oates survived this sentence; indeed, he lived to secure release from prison and, eventually, to receive a pardon and a pension from William III.

What finally undermined the Whig cause toward the close of Charles's reign was the discovery of the Rye House Plot in 1683, a Whig conspiracy to assassinate the king and the duke of York. Again, informers gave the plotters away, punishment came swiftly, and public fears of regicide and revolution were turned against the Whigs. The country had to wait until 1688 before its fears of a popish monarch were removed by the "Glorious Revolution."

The Popish Plot and the Exclusion Crisis occasioned a large volume of literature in various genres by writers of all levels of ability and political persuasions. Many of them introduced historical or Biblical parallels to illuminate the events of the day. The greatest of these literary productions is *Absalom and Achitophel*. Published shortly before Shaftesbury was to stand trial, it seems to have been designed to contribute to the Tory propaganda assailing the Whig leader and the whole scheme of exclusion. But Dryden achieved more than that. Whether or not one may credit *Absalom and Achitopel*, as David Ogg does, with returning the public mind to sanity,[15] it remains one of the great statements of the conservative spirit in English literature, and is certainly one of the most engrossing political poems ever written. In it Dryden shows, not faded tapestries of forgotten politics, but the intensity of a humanist committed to Christian values and the rule of law in a time when "peace itself is war in masquerade."

Notes

1. *The Basic Works of Aristotle*, ed. Richard McKeon (New York: Random House, 1941), p. 1464. On the "restoration" mythos, cf. Northrop Frye, *The Educated Imagination* (Bloomington: Indiana University Press, 1964), p. 55 and *passim*.

2. Cf. Michael McKeon, *Politics and Poetry in Restoration England: The Case of Dryden's "Annus Mirabilis"* (Cambridge: Harvard University Press, 1975), p. 186.

3. Kenyon, p. 98.

4. Ibid., p. 99.

5. Burnett, II, 171–72.

6. Kenyon, p. 99.

7. John Pollock, *The Popish Plot: A Study in the History of the Reign of Charles II* (London: Duckworth and Co., 1903), p. 326.

8. Ogg, II, 561.

9. Reprinted in *The Complete Works of Andrew Marvell*, ed. Alexander B. Grosart (1872–75; rpt. New York: AMS Press, 1966), IV, 248. See the selection in this volume.

10. Kenyon, p. 45.

11. Haley, p. 462.

12. Ogg, II, 618.
13. Burnet, II, 179.
14. Ogg, II, 639.
15. Ibid., pp. 630–31.

PART ONE

An Harbinger of Fear

Andrew Marvell's
An Account of the Growth of Popery, and Arbitrary Government in England (1678)

Andrew Marvell's *An Account of the Growth of Popery, and Arbitrary Government in England* was published late in 1677; a second edition (much better printed) appeared in 1678, after the poet's death that August. Though both editions were anonymous and carried an Amsterdam imprint, the author's identity was known immediately, a circumstance that might have lead to Marvell's prosecution had he lived. His final tract made a great impression, one that grew during the following years, for in it Marvell seemed to anticipate the revelations delivered later in 1678 by Titus Oates.

Marvell's thesis appears, with vivid directness, in his first sentence; there is a plot to convert the government into an "absolute tyranny" and the nation's religion into "downright popery." The essay is mainly devoted to a detailed account (of some forty-eight pages in the second edition given here) of the parliamentary disputes of the past two years, interlarded with copies of the acts and petitions that figured in them. This narrative leads Marvell to a conclusion filled with menace. The play is almost over: "It is now come to the fourth act, and the next scene that opens may be in Rome or Paris, yet men sit by, like idle spectators, and still give money towards their own tragedy."

Even though Marvell disclaimed any "sinister surmise" about the king, it is not difficult to see why the government regarded this as a seditious document. Even as late as 1683, Sir Roger L'Estrange was insisting that Marvell had been in league with Oates. Modern commentators have taken the milder view that the tract was a moderate, even patient, though extremely bigoted attempt to preserve England's constitution. If at the time it seemed explosive, it was because, as K. H. D. Haley comments, "it put into epigrammatic expression what many were already obscurely feeling; and if the names of the alleged conspirators were not given, the reader could supply them for himself" (Haley, p. 438).

In the introductory section that follows, Marvell seeks to distinguish the English limited monarchy from the "arbitrary power" wielded by monarchs abroad—specifically by Louis XIV. He wishes to make it clear that he is not a republican; his arguments are directed only against tyrannical power, not against the English monarchy itself. Then he launches into a violent attack on Catholicism as irrational, idolatrous, and absurd.

AN ACCOUNT

Of the Growth of

POPERY,

And Arbitrary GOVERNMENT in

ENGLAND, &c.

THere has now for divers Years, a Defign been carried on, to change the Lawful Government of *England* into an Abfolute Tyranny, and to Convert the Eftablifhed *Proteftant Religion* into down-right *Popery*: than both which, nothing can be more Deftructive or contrary to the Intereft and Happinefs, to the Conftitution and Being of the King and Kingdom.

For if we firft confider the State, the Kings of *England* Rule not upon the fame terms with thofe of our Neighbour Nations, who, having by Force or by Addrefs Ufurped that due fhare which there People had in the Government, are now for fome Ages in poffeffion of an Arbitrary Power (which yet no Prefcription can make Legal) and Exercife it over their Perfons and Eftates in a moft Tyrannical manner. But here the Subjects retain their proportion in the Legiflature; the very meaneft Commoner of *England* is reprefented in *Parliament*, and is a party to thofe Laws by which the Prince is Sworn to Govern himfelf and his People. No Money is to be Levied but by the common confent. No man is for *Life, Limb, Goods, or Liberty* at the Sovereigns Difcretion: But we have the fame Right (modeftly underftood) *in our Propriety* that the Prince hath *in his Regality*; and in all Cafes where the King is concerned, we have our juft Remedy as againft any private Perfon of the Neighbour-hood, in the Courts of *Weftminfter*-Hall, or in the High Court of *Parliament*. His very Prerogative is no more than what the Law has determined. His Broad Seal, which is the Legitimate ftamp of his Pleafure, yet is no longer currant, than upon the Tryal it is found to be Legal. He cannot commit any Perfon by his particular Warrant. He cannot himfelf be Witnefs in any Caufe: The Balance of Publick Juftice being fo delicate, that not the head only, but even the breath of the Prince would turn the Scale. Nothing is left to the Kings will, but all is Subjected to his Authority: by which means it follows that he can do no wrong, nor can he receive wrong; and a King of *England*, keeping to thefe meafures, may without arrogance be faid to remain the onely Intelligent Ruler over a Rational people. In recompenfe therefore and acknowledgment of fo good a Government under his Influence, his Perfon is moft Sacred and Inviolable; and whatfoever Exceffes are committed againft fo High a Truft, nothing of them is imputed to him, as being free from the Neceffity or Temptation, but his Minifters

A 2   only

only are Accountable for all, and muſt anſwer it their perils. He hath a vaſt Revenue conſtantly ariſing from the Hearth of the Houſhoulder, the Sweat of the Labourers, the Rent of the Farmer, the Induſtry of the Merchant, and conſequently out of the Eſtate of the Gentleman . a large competence to defray the ordinary expenſe of the Crown, and maintain its luſtre. And if any extraordinary Occaſion happen, or be but with any probable decency pretended, the whole Land at whatſoever Seaſon of the Year does yield him a plentiful Harveſt. So forward are his Peoples Affectiōs to give, even to ſuperfluity, that a Forainer (or *Engliſh-man* that hath been long abroad) would think they could neither will nor chuſe, but that the asking of a Supply, were a meer formality, it is ſo readily granted. He is the Fountain of all Honours, and has moreover the diſtribution of ſo many profitable Offices, of the Houſhold, of the Revenue, of State, of Law, of Religion, of the Navy (and, ſince his preſent *Majeſties* time, of the Army) that it ſeems as if the Nation could ſcarce furniſh honeſt Men enow to ſupply all thoſe Imployments. So that the Kings of *England* are in nothing Inferiour to other Princes, ſave in being more abridged from Injuring their own Subjects: But have as large a Field as any of external Felicity, wherein to exerciſe their own Vertue, and ſo reward and incourage it in others. In ſhort, there is nothing that comes nearer in Government to the Divine perfection, than where the Monarch, as with us, enjoys a capacity of doing all the good imaginable to mankind, under a diſability to all that is evil.

And as we are thus happy in the Conſtitution of our State, ſo are we yet more bleſſed in that of our Church; being free from that *Romiſh Yoak*, which ſo great a part of Chriſtendome do yet draw and labour under, That *Popery* is ſuch a thing as cannot, but for want of a word to expreſs it, be called *a Religion*: nor is it to be mentioned with what civility which is otherwiſe decent to be uſed, in ſpeaking of the differences of humane Opinion about Divine Matters. Were it either open Judaiſm, or plain Turkery, or honeſt Paganiſm, there is yet a certain *Bona fides* in the moſt extravagant Belief, and the ſincerity of an erroneous Profeſſion may render it more pardonable : but this is a compound of all the three, an extract of whatſoever is moſt ridiculous and impious in them, incorporated with more peculiar abſurdities of its own, in which thoſe were deficient; and all this deliberately contrived, knowingly carried on by the bold Impoſture of Prieſts under the Name of Chriſtianity. The wiſdom of this fifth Religion, this laſt and Inſolenteſt attempt upon the credulity of mankind ſeems to me (though not ignorant otherwiſe of the times, degrees and methods of its progreſs) principally to have conſiſted in their owning the Scriptures to be the Word of God, and the Rule of Faith and Manners, but in prohibiting at the ſame time their common uſe, or the reading of them in publick Churches but in a *Latine* Tranſlation to the Vulgar : there being no better or more rational way to fruſtrate the very Deſign of the great Inſtitutor of Chriſtianity, who firſt planted it by the extraordinary gift of Tongues, than to forbid the uſe even of the ordinary Languages. For having thus a Book which is univerſally avowed to be of Divine Authority, but ſequeſtring it only into ſuch hands as were intruſted in the Cheat, they had the opportunity to vitiate, ſuppreſs, or interpret to their own profit thoſe Records by which the poor people hold their Salvation. And this neceſſary point being once gained, there was thence-forward nothing ſo Monſtrous to Reaſon, ſo abhorring from Morality, or ſo contrary to Scripture which they might not in prudence adventure on. The Idolatry (for alas, it is neither better nor worſe) of adoring and praying to Saints and Angels, of Worſhipping Pictures, Images, and Reliques, Incredible Miracles, and palpable Fables to promote that Veneration. The whole Liturgy and Worſhip of the Bleſſed Virgin. The ſaying of *Pater Noſters* and Creeds, to the honour of Saints, and of *Ave Mary's* too, not to her honour, but of others. The Publick Service, which

which they can spare to God among so many Competitors, in an unknown tongue; and intangled with such Vestments, *Consecrations*, *Exorcismes*, *Whisperings*, *Sprinklings*, *Censings*, *and Phantastical Rites*, *Gesticulations*, and Removals, so unbeseeming a Christian Office, that it represents rather the pranks and Ceremonies of *Juglers* and *Coujurers*. The Refusal of the *Cup* to the *Laity*. The Necessity of the Priests Intention to make any of their Sacraments effectual. Debarring their Clergy from Marriage. Interdicting of *Meats*, *Auricular Confession and Absolution*, as with them practised. *Penances*, *Pilgrimages*, *Purgatory, and Prayer for the Dead*. But above all their other Devices, that *Transubstantial solacism*, whereby that glorified Body, which at the same time they allow to be in Heaven, is *is sold again*, and *Crucified daily* upon all the *Altars* of their Communion. For God indeed may now and then do a *Miracle*, but a *Romish Priest* can, it seems, work in one moment *a thousand Impossibilities*. Thus by a new and Anti-scriptural Belief, compiled of Terrours to the Phansy, Contradictions to Sense, and Impositions on the Understanding, *their Laity* have *turned Tenants for their Souls*, and in consequence Tributary for their Estates to a more *than Omnipotent Priest-hood*.

I must indeed do them that right, to avow, that out of an equitable consideration and recompense of so faithful a Slavery, they have discharged the People from all other Services and dependance, infranchised them *from all Duty to God or Man*; insomuch that their severer and more Learned Divines, their *Governours of Conscience*, have so well Instructed them in all the Arts of Circumventing their Neighbour, and of colluding with Heaven, that, were the Scholars as apt as their Teachers, there would have been long since an end of all, either true Piety, or common Honesty; and nothing left among them but *Authorized Hypocrisie, Licentiousness*, and *Knavery*; had not the Natural worth of the better sort, and the Good simplicity of the meaner, in great measure preserved them. For nothing indeed but an extraordinary temper and Ingenuity of Spirit, and that too assisted by a Diviner influence, could possibly restrain those within any the termes or Laws of Humanity, who at the same time own the Doctrine of their Casuists, or the Authority of the Pope, as it is by him claimed and exercised. He by his Indulgences delivers Souls out of the pains of the other World: So that who would refuse to be *vicious here*, upon so good *Security*. He by his Dispensation annuls Contracts betwixt Man and Man, dissolves *Oaths between Princes*, or *betwixt them and their People*, and gives allowance in cases which God and Nature prohibits. He, as Clerk of the Spiritual Market, hath set a rate upon all Crimes: the more flagitious they are and *abominable*, the *better Commodities*, and men pay only an *higher price*, as for *greater Rarities*. So that it seems as if the commands of God had been invented meerly to erect an Office for the Pope; the *worse Christians men are*, the *better Customers*; and this *Rome* does by the same policy people its Church, as the Pagan *Rome* did the City, by *opening a Sanctuary* to all *Malefactors*. And why not, if his power be indeed of such virtue and extent as is by him challenged? That he is the Ruler over 1
Angels, Purgatory, and Hell. That his Tribunal and Gods are all one. That all that God, he can do, *Clave non errante*, and what he does is as God and not 2
as Man. That he is the *Universal Head* of the *Church*, The *sole Interpreter of Scripture*, and Judge of Controversie. That he is *above General Councils*. That his power is Absolute, and his Decrees *Infallible*. That he can change the very Nature of things, making what is *Just* to be *Unjust*, and what is *Vice* to be *Virtue*. That all Laws are in the Cabinet of his Breast. That he can Dispence with the New Testament. That he is Monarch of this World, and that he can dispose of Kingdoms and Empires as he pleases.

---

1. *challenged:* asserted as a right.
2. *Clave non errante:* by means of a key that does not fail.

In this section, which leads directly into his main narrative, Marvell turns from denouncing the papists to describing their activities as threats to property—the possible confiscation of former Church lands—and to the government itself. The description of clandestine plots and references to the king's murder, secret conspirators, and intervention by France, all anticipate Oates's more specific depositions.

So that we may reckon the Reigns of our late Princes, by a Succeſſion of the *Popiſh Treaſons* againſt them.   And, if under His preſent Majeſty we have as yet ſeen no more viſible effects of the ſame Spirit than the *Firing of London* (acted by *Hubert*, Hired by *Pieddelon* two *French-men*) which remains a Controverſie, it is not to be attributed to the good Nature or better Principles of that Sect, but to the Wiſdom of his *Holyneſs*; who obſerves that we are not of late ſo dangerous *Proteſtants*, as to deſerve any ſpecial *mark* of his *Indignation*, but that we may be made better uſe of to the weakning of thoſe that are of our own Religion, and that if he do not diſturb us, there are thoſe among our ſelves, that are leading us into a fair way of Reconciliation with him.

But thoſe continued freſh Inſtances, in relation to the Crown, together with the *Popes* claim of the Temporal and immediate Dominion of the Kingdoms of *England* and *Ireland*, which he does ſo challenge, are a ſufficient caution to the Kings of *England*, and of the People, there is as little hopes to ſeduce them, the *Proteſtant Religion* being ſo interwoven as it is with their Secular Intereſt. For the Lands that were formerly given to Superſtitious Uſes, having firſt been applyed to the Publick Revenue, and afterwards by ſeveral Alienations and Contracts diſtributed into private poſſeſſion, the alteration of Religion would neceſſarily introduce a change of Property.   *Nullum tempus occurrit Eccleſiæ*, it   4 would make a general Earth-quake over the Nation, and even now the *Romiſh* Clergy on the other ſide of the Water, ſnuff up the ſavoury Odour of ſo many Rich *Abbies* and *Monaſteries* that belonged to their Predeceſſors.   Hereby no conſiderable Eſtate in *England* but muſt have a piece torn out of it upon the Title of Piety, and the reſt ſubject to be wholly forfeited upon the Account of *Hereſie*.   Another *Chimney-mony* of the old *Peter-pence* muſt again be payed, as   5   6 Tribute to the Pope, beſide that which is eſtabliſhed on His Majeſty : and the People, inſtead of thoſe moderate Tithes that are with too much difficulty payed to their Proteſtant Paſtors, will be expoſed to all the evactions of the Court of   7 *Rome*, and a thouſand Artifices by which in former times they were uſed to drain away the Wealth of ours more than any other Nation.   So that in concluſion, there is no *Engliſh-man* that hath *a Soul*, *a Body*, or an *Eſtate to ſave*, that *Loves* either *God*, his *King*, or his *Countrey*, but is by all thoſe *Tenures bound*, to the beſt of his *Power* and *Knowledge*, to maintain the Eſtabliſhed *Proteſtant Religion*.

And yet, all this notwithſtanding, there are thoſe Men among us, who have undertaken, and do make it their buſineſs, under ſo Legal and perfect a Government, to introduce a *French Slavery*, and inſtead of ſo pure a Religion, to eſtabliſh the *Roman Idolatry* : Both and either of which are crimes of the Higheſt Nature.   For, as to matter of Government, if to Murther the King be, as certainly it is, a Fact ſo Horrid, how much more hainous is it to aſſaſſinate the Kingdom? And as none will deny, that to alter our *Monarchy* into a *Commonwealth* were *Treaſon*; ſo by the ſame Fundamental Rule, the Crime is no leſs, to make that *Monarchy Abſolute*.

---

3. *Hubert:* A French Catholic who confessed to setting the Great Fire of London in 1666; he claimed that Pieddelon hired him. Despite a lack of other evidence of his guilt, he was convicted and hanged.

4. *Nullum tempus occurrit Ecclesiae:* No period of time blocks the Church.

5. *Chimney-money:* a tax imposed by Charles II of two shillings per annum on every fire-hearth in England and Wales.

6. *Peter-Pence:* an annual tax of a penny from each householder having land of a certain value, paid before the Reformation to the Papal See in Rome.

7. *evactions:* exactions (a misprint).

What is thus true, in regard of the State, holds as well in reference to our Religion, former Parliaments have made it Treason in whosoever shall attempt to seduce any one the meanest of the King's Subjects to the Church of *Rome*, and this Parliament, hath, to all Penalties by the Common or Statute Law, added incapacity for any man who shall presume to say that the King is a Papist or an Introducer of Popery. But what sawless and incapable miscreants then, what wicked Traytors are those wretched men, who endeavour to pervert our whole Church, and to bring that about in effect, which even to mention is penal, at one *Italian* stroke attempting to subvert the Government and Religion, to kill the Body and damn the Soul of our Nation.

Yet were these men honest old Cavaliers that had suffered in his late Majesties Service, it were allowable in them, as oft as their wounds brake out at Spring or Fall, to think of a more Arbitrary Government, as a soveraign Balsom for their Aches, or to imagine that no Weapon-Salve but of the Mofs that grows on an Enemies Skull could cure them. Should they mistake this Long *Parliament* also for Rebels, and that, although all Cir-   8
cumstances be altered, there were still the same necessity to fight it all over again in pure Loyalty, yet their Age and the Times they have lived in, might excuse them. But those worthy Gentlemen are too Generous, too good Christians and Subjects, too affectionate to the good *English* Government, to be capable of such an Impression. Whereas those Conspirators are such as have not one drop of *Cavalier Blood*, or no *Bowels* at least of a *Cavalier* in them; but have starved them, to Revel and Surfeit upon their Calamities, making their Persons, and the very Cause by pretending to it themselves, almost Ridiculous.

Or, were these *Conspirators* on the other side but avowed *Papists*, they were the more honest, the less dangerous, and the Religion were answerable for the Errors they might commit in order to promote it. Who is there but must acknowledge, if he do not commend the Ingenuity (or by what better Name I may call it) of Sir *Thomas Strickland*, Lord *Bellasis*, the late Lord *Clifford* and others, eminent in their several stations? These,   9
having so long appeared the most zealous Sons of our Church, yet, as soon as the late Test   10
against Popery was enacted, took up the Cross, quitted their present Imployments and all hopes of the future, rather than falsifie their opinion: though otherwise men for Quality, Estate and Abilities whether in War or Peace, as capable and well deserving (without disparagement) as others that have the art to continue in Offices. And above all, his Royal Highness is to be admired for his unparallelled magnanimity on the same account: there be-   11
ing in all history perhaps no Record of any Prince that ever changed his Religion in his circumstances. But these persons, that have since taken the work in hand, are such as lie under no temptation of Religion: secure men, that are above either Honour or Consciences; but obliged by all the most sacred tyes of Malice and Ambition to advance the ruine of the King and Kingdom, and qualified much better than others, under the name of good Protestants, to effect it.

And because it was yet difficult to find Complices enough at home, that were ripe for so black a design, but they wanted a Back for their Edge; therefore they applyed themselves to *France*, that King being indowed with all those qualities, which in a Prince, may pass   12
for Virtues; but in any private man, would be capital: and moreover so abounding in wealth that no man else could go to the price of their wickedness: To which Considerations, adding that he is Master of *Absolute Dominion*, the *Presumptive Monarch* of *Christendom*, the declared *Champion* of *Popery*, and the hereditary, natural, inveterate *Enemy* of our *King* and *Nation*, he was in all respects the most likely (of all Earthly Powers) to reward and support them in a Project every way suitable to his own Inclination and Interest.

---

8. *Long Parliament:* The Cavalier Long Parliament (1660–1678), compared to the Long Parliament of 1640–1653, which led the rebellion against Charles I.

9. *Strickland, Bellasis, Clifford:* Roman Catholics who resigned their posts because of the Test Act of 1673.

10. *Test:* The Test Act of 1673 sought to exclude Catholics from civil and military offices by requiring the oaths of Allegiance and Supremacy and a declaration against transubstantiation. Office holders had also to receive the sacrament in the Anglican Church.

11. *Royal Highness:* James, duke of York.

12. *King:* Louis XIV.

13. Page [9] is misnumbered [5].

PART TWO

The First Evidence of the Plot

Portrait of Titus Oates. Published with "A Poem upon Mr. Titus Oates" (1679); a broadside. The poem praises Oates, excuses his "crimes," and condemns the Jesuits.

Titus Oates's
A True Narrative of the Horrid Plot
and Conspiracy of the Popish Party (1679)

For six weeks after Titus Oates's revelations were given to the king, the government kept them quiet. Danby, the lord treasurer, hoped to use them to rally support for the king. Instead, Parliament blamed him for "keeping the plot so long in the dark" (Reresby, p. 180), the exclusionist leaders outmaneuvered him, with the aid of Ralph Montagu's accusations, and he spent the next five years in the Tower awaiting trial for high treason. After September 28, when Oates astonished the Privy Council by the confidence and readiness of his presentation, his "narrative" became a seven-days' wonder. By October 10, the news had already reached Sir John Reresby in York. "Nobody can conceive that was not a witness thereof," he wrote, "what a ferment this raised among all ranks and degrees" (Reresby, p. 179).

Indeed it might have made a powerful weapon in Danby's hands. John Miller argues that Oates may have had such a strategy in mind—and therefore avoided implicating York in the plot—until he alienated the king on November 28 by rashly accusing the queen before Parliament. In that instance his denunciations led to no action against his victim; instead, he was arrested and his papers seized. After that, his lot fell naturally to the exclusionists (Miller, p. 157).

The *True Narrative* is an arresting piece of propaganda, particularly as seen in its third and most elaborate version (excerpted here). Based at least in part upon "Habernfeld's Plot" of 1643, a scheme to assassinate Charles I and Laud, its eighty-one articles, in roughly chronological order, juxtapose trivial charges with serious accusations of plans for murder and mass executions in London. Yet the weight of the innumerable facts about the Jesuits makes itself felt, and the very artlessness of the plan lends it an air of authenticity.

This official edition, printed by parliamentary order in April 1679, begins with a dedication to Charles II—surely one of the most unwelcome in history—in which Oates lectures the king on the dangers of popery and declares that all anti-monarchical feelings have their basis in that religion. Then Oates addresses the reader, complaining about an unauthorized edition of his work and asserting that he has published his *Narrative* only because the papists were claiming that the plot was a Protestant trick. In the body of his work, the early "Items" concern conspiracies of the Jesuits in Scotland, examples of treasonable talk, and accounts of various plans for murdering the king, raising rebellions in England and Ireland, and even for a French invasion. Item 19 (reprinted here) is a startling account of Thomas Pickering's attempt to kill the king.

A TRUE

NARRATIVE

OF THE

Horrid PLOT

AND

CONSPIRACY

OF THE

POPISH PARTY

Againſt the LIFE of

His Sacred Majeſty,

THE

GOVERNMENT,

AND THE

𝕻roteſtant 𝕽eligion:

With a LIST of ſuch NOBLEMEN, GENTLEMEN, and others, as were the CONSPIRATORS:

And the HEAD-OFFICERS both Civil and Military, that were to Effect it.

Publiſhed by the Order of the Right Honourable the Lords Spiritual and Temporal in PARLIAMENT Aſſembled.

Humbly Preſented to His Moſt Excellent MAJESTY.

By TITVS OATES, D.D.

LONDON:

Printed for *Thomas Parkhurſt*, and *Thomas Cockerill*, at the Bible and Three Crowns in *Cheapſide* near *Mercers Chappel*, and at the Three Legs in the *Poultrey*. MDCLXXIX.

28

Item XIX.

That another Packet arrived at *Saint Omers* directed to 1
Richard Ashby, Rector of the English Seminary there: The
Date of which is not well remembred by the Deponent,
but as near as he doth remember, it was about the beginning of the Parliament, for there came the Speeches of the 2
King and Lord Chancellour, and the Votes of the Parliament, which were put into ridiculous phrases, in contempt
of the King and both Houses of Parliament, for the Fathers
and Scholers to laugh at, and then translated into the French
Tongue, and presented to the Governor of Saint *Omers,* who
sendeth them to the French King his Master: and in the Packet was contained an account of the attempt of one *Picker-*
ing, a lay Brother, that waits upon the Jesuits lying at *Somer-* 3
set house, to shoot the King as he was was walking in Saint
James's

---

1. *St. Omers:* the Jesuit college Oates had attended from December 10, 1677 to
June 1678.

2. *Parliament:* i.e., January 1678.

3. *Pickering:* Thomas Pickering—tried and convicted of high treason on December 17, 1678, executed May 9, 1679.

James park, when he was at some distance from his No-
bles and Attendants, but the *Flint* of his *Pistol* being somewhat loose, he did defer the action till another opportunity, and if he had done it and had suffered, he should have
had thirty thousand Masses said for the health of his soul:
Which Letters were signed by *Thomas White* alias *White-* 4
bread Provincial, which Letters, when read, the *Fathers*
in the English Seminary were in great trouble, for the
negligence of the said *Pickering*, and the Deponent saw
and read them in the latter part of *January*, and the Votes
put into such mock *Phrases*, as also the Speeches of
the King and Lord Chancellor in the moneth of *February*.

Item XX.

That the Deponent, went on the nine and twentieth of
January to know of his Confessarius, whether he might 5
keep the thirtieth of *January* as a fast, the Confessor replyed, that the account with them was on the ninth of
February, because the account of *England* did differ from 6
the account on that side the Water: The Deponent asked him, whether then he might keep the ninth of *February* as a day of Fasting? The Confessor asked him, why?
The Deponent replyed, because of the Martyrdome of the
late King, the Confessarius answered, that the late King
was no Martyr but an Heretick, and withal added, that
he was none of King *James* Son, but a Bastard begotten
upon the body of *Anne* of *Denmark* by her *Taylor*. This Confessarius is a Jesuit, and his name *Charles Peters*, Prefect of
the Sodality.

---

4. *White:* the Jesuit provincial for England; convicted of high treason on June
13, 1679, executed on June 20.
5. *Confessarius:* confessor.
6. *the account of England:* the difference in calendars; see the following note.

Items 28 to 30 contain the important account of the great Jesuit Consult to plan the king's assassination. In fact there had been a meeting, but simply one of the "regular Triennial business meetings" (Kenyon, p. 56) of the Jesuits, held, not at the White Horse Tavern as Oates claims, but at the duke of York's apartments at Whitehall. As James later remarked, "If Oates had but known, he would have cut out a fine spot of work for me" (Reresby, p. 260).

Item XXVIII.

That in order to this Command, on *April* 24. 1678. *Stylo Novo*, Father *Warren*, Rector of *Leige*, Sir *Thomas Preston*, Baronet, Father *Marsh*, Rector of *Ghent*, Father *Williams*, Rector of *Watton*, and Master of the *Novices*, Sir *John Warner* Baronet, (*Rich. Ashby*, Rector of the *English* Seminary at S. *Omers*, being sick of the Gout could not go) but out of the said Seminary went Sir *Robert Brett*, Baronet, Father *Poole*, *Edward Nevill*; there were in all with the *Deponent* about 9 or 10 who met in *London* in Consult with *Tho. Whitebread*, Father *Harcourt*, *senior*, and Father *Harcourt*, *junior*, *John Fenwick*, *Basil Langworth*, *William Morgan*, *John Keines*, Father *Lovell*, Father *Ireland*, Father *Blundell*, *Rich. Strange*, Father *Mico*, Father *Gray*, and others, to the number of Fifty *Jesuits*, met at the *White-horse Tavern*, in the *Strand*, where they plotted their Designs for the Society, and ordered Father *John Cary*, who was also there, to go *Procurator* for *Rome*: At which Consult, thus held in the Month of *May*, the Deponent was present to attend the *Consulters*, and delivered their *Concerns* from Company to Company; and then a little after they left the *White-horse Tavern*, and divided themselves into several *Clubs* or *Companies*. Some met at Mrs. *Saunders house*, in *Wild-street*; others at Mrs. *Fenwicks*, at *Ayre's* House, in *Drury-lane*; others at Mr. *Ireland's*, in *Russel-street* near *Covent-Garden*, and in other places; all which, though in several Companies, 5 or 6 in a Company, did contrive the death of the King: In order to which there were Papers sent from *Company* to *Company*, which the Deponent carried, containing the Opinions of the timeing their business, and the manner how it was to be done: And within 3 or 4 days after, the Deponent went to S. *Omers* with the Fathers that came from the other side of the Water.

7

8

Item

---

7. *Style Novo:* on the Continent, the Gregorian—New Style—calendar was ten days ahead of the Julian—Old Style— calendar still used in England. The new year began on March 25 in the English calendar of this period.
    8. *Society:* the Society of Jesus, the Jesuits.

Item XXIX.

That on the 10th of *June, Stylo Novo,* came *Thomas White* to S. *Omers,* in order to vifit his Colledges in *Flanders* and *Germany* ; and in his Chamber the 11th day, where the Deponent was prefent, together with *Rich. Aſhby,* Rector, he there told the *Deponent* and the faid *Aſhby, That he hoped to ſee the Fool at* White-hall *laid faſt enough* ; *and that the Society need not fear, for he* (that is the King) *was grown ſecure, and would hear no complaints againſt them, and if the Duke ſhould ſet his Face in the leaſt meaſure to follow his Brothers Foot-ſteps, his paſsport was made to lay him to ſleep.* 9

Item XXX.

That the faid *Thomas Whitebread,* on the 13th of *June,* did tell the Rector of S. *Omers, That a Miniſter of the Church of* England *had ſcandalouſly and baſely put out the* Jeſuits Morals *in* Engliſh, *and had endeavoured villanouſly* 10 *to render them odious to the people, and asked the faid Rector whether he thought the Deponent might poſſibly know him ?* and the Rector not knowing, called the Deponent, who heard theſe words as he ſtood at the Chamber door of the faid Provincial, and when the Deponent went into the Chamber of the faid Provincial, he asked him, *If he knew the Author of the* Jeſuits Morals? the Deponent anfwered, *his Perſon, but not his Name.* The faid *Thomas Whitebread* demanded then, *Whether he would undertake to poyſon or aſſaſſinate the Author ?* which the *Deponent* undertook to do, having 50l. reward promiſed him by the faid *Provincial,* and appointed to return to *England.* And the Deponent doth farther teſtifie, that at the ſame time the faid *Provincial* did in his Chamber ſay, *That he and the Society in* London *would procure Dr.* Stillingfleet *to be knockt* 11 *on the head, and alſo* Poole, *the Author of* Synopſis Criticorum, *for writing ſome things againſt them.* 12

---

9. *Duke:* York. As a Catholic and heir apparent, James might appear the beneficiary of the Jesuits' plots, but Oates cautiously paints him as a possible victim.

10. *Jesuits Morals:* Anti-Jesuit tracts by Nicholas Perrault, translated into English by Oates's confederate Israel Tonge (1621–1680) in 1670 (reprinted in 1679).

11. *Dr. Stillingfleet:* Edward Stillingfeet (1635–1699), eminent Anglican prelate and controversialist; he wrote several works against popery and nonconformity.

12. *Poole:* Matthew Poole (1624–1679), a Biblical commentator, whose *Synopsis Criticorum* appeared between 1669 and 1676; he had also published a tract against "the Romish Faith" in 1666.

33

Item 33 implicates Sir George Wakeman in the plot to poison the king. As he was the queen's physician, this charge seems to strike at her as well. Perhaps when Oates learned that Prance's and Bedloe's tales of Godfrey's murder implicated servants in Somerset House, the queen's residence, he thought that he might destroy her also. Such a plan would have suited the strategies of Lord Shaftesbury, who had long advocated the king's divorce and remarriage in order to produce a legitimate heir.

Item XXXIII.

That in the Month of *July*, *Rich. Ashby* came to *London* with Inſtructions from the ſaid *Thomas Whitebread*, or *White*, that the 10000*l.* procured by Father *Leſhee*, and then in the hands of the Society in *London*, ſhould be put into the hands of one *Worſly*, their Banker ; and that the ſaid *Rich. Ashby*, with other Fathers, ſhould treat and agree with Sir *George Wakeman* about the concern of poyſoning the King ; and that if he would undertake it he ſhould have the 10000*l.* which the ſaid *Rich. Ashby* told the Deponent, ſhewing him the ſaid Inſtructions by way of *Memorandum* in Writing. In which *Memorandum* was contained an *Item* given by the ſaid *Thomas Whitebread* for the procuring the Aſſaſſination of the Right Reverend Father in God *Herbert*, Lord Biſhop of *Hereford* ; for the ſaid Biſhop had been educated in the Popiſh Religion, and was fallen, and they were reſolved not to pity nor ſpare any Apoſtate from the *Roman Faith*. The ſaid *Rich. Ashby* asked the Deponent, whether the ſaid Biſhop were not a forward Man againſt *Catholicks* ? and the Deponent not knowing the ſaid Biſhop, told the ſaid *Ashby* he could not tell ; and the ſaid *Ashby* did ſay, *That times now being ready*

G   *to*

13. *Leshee:* Father François de La Chaise (1624–1709), Louis XIV's confessor from 1675 until 1709. See Coleman's letters to him.

14. *Herbert:* Herbert Croft, a Protestant extremist, known for his persecution of papists.

to change, they would be ready to give not only *Apostates*, but also those Hereticks that had obstinately opposed the proceedings of the Society, and their Agents, in propagating the Faith and Interest of the Church of Rome, a just Reward for their Apostacy and infamous obstinacy; and though the Parliament have taken away the Act for burning Hereticks, they should not escape the Vengeance of Catholicks.

Item XXXIV.

That in the Month of *July*, 1678. *Rich. Strange*, the last Provincial of the *Jesuits*, came to the Lodgings of Mr. *Rich. Ashby*, who, before he went down to the *Bath*, lay in the new Provincial's Lodgings, at Mrs. *Saunders* house, a part of *Wild-house* in *Wild Street*, and finding the Deponent with the said *Ashby*, did desire the Deponent to meet him at his Chamber, at Mr. *John Groves* in *York-Street* near *Covent-Garden*, and after a short stay at *Ashbies* Lodgings, took his leave of the said *Ashby*, and presently after the Deponent took his leave also of the said *Ashby*, and followed *Strange*, and got to his Chamber presently after him; where the said *Strange* did encourage the Deponent to go on in assisting the Society in carrying on the Design; And thereupon told the Deponent that they got 14000*l*. in the Fire of *London*, in the year 1666. The Deponent asked the said *Strange* how they came to effect that great and famous business? The said *Strange* replyed, That himself, and one *Gray*, and *Pennington*, and *Barton*, *Jesuits*, with some others, together with one *Keimash*, a *Dominican* Fryar, joyned with one *Green*, and met at one *William Wests* house, who kept the Green-Dragon in *Puddle-dock*: The said *West* was by Trade a Taylor, whom they employed to make them some Cloaths, and there they did debate about the manner of firing the City, and where they should begin, and did attempt it in *February* 166⅚. The *Thames* being frozen, they lost that good opportunity, and not being provided of assistance enough, and the Sickness coming on apace, they altered their purpose:

15

16

---

15. *Strange:* Richard Strange was the former Jesuit provincial (preceding White) who had sent Oates to Valladolid and St. Omers for study.

16. *firing the City:* the Great Fire of London (1666) was often blamed on the papists. The date 1665/66 reflects the differences between the old and new calendars. See the note on *stylo novo* above (p. 32).

Items 50 (the latter part given here) and 51 report characteristic instances of the Jesuits' treasonable talk, and their code. Item 60 gives more threats against the king, along with a vividly phrased wager on the king's death. It also indicated Oates's reluctance to implicate James in the plot; he is cast as one of the Jesuits' possible victims.

---

17. *God:* This continues a report on treasonable letters of August 1678, from Father Ireland at St. Omers.

18. *Fenwick:* John Fenwick, one of the five Jesuits tried and convicted of treason on June 13, 1679; executed on June 20.

19. *Forty Eight:* code word for King Charles II. See below.

20. *Lauderdale:* John Maitland, duke of Lauderdale (1616–1682), the high commissioner for Scotland and a known enemy of Catholicism.

21. *Prince of Orange:* William of Orange (1650–1702), later William III of England, a Protestant champion.

God had hitherto given them such a hopeful Prospect of
things, and that no Opportunity on his part was or should
be lost, and that they in *London* (if they thought it fit to
communicate these things) should have a care that they did
it to no more than to one at a time, left they should be
baffled in their Enterprise. Which Letter, when read by
the *Deponent*, the said *Fenwick*, to whom the Letter was directed, told the *Deponent* that it was his Duty to offer up a
Mass or two, that God would prosper those Holy Endeavours of the Fathers of the Society, in promoting *Catholick
Religion* and *Faith*; and told him further, That if he, the
Deponent lived till *Christmas*, he should see a good Change of
things, either that *Forty Eight* should be taken from the
World, or the World (especially the little he was concerned in) should be taken from him : And one that was a
Catholick should play such a Game, as never was playd since
the Conquest.   All which the said *Fenwick* told the *Deponent*
in his Chamber; and the *Deponent* asked the said *Fenwick*,
Who this Catholick was? And *Fenwick* said, It was the *Duke*
of *York*.   And the *Deponent* saith, the Ciphers 48 are put for
the King.

L I. *Item.*

That on the said 11th. of *August* in the Evening, the *De-
ponent* went to the Lodgings of *John Keines*, where he found
another Jesuit with him, whose Name the *Deponent* doth not
remember; in whose presence the said *John Keines* told the
Deponent that the *Provincial* had taken great care of Keeping
Alive the Difference betwixt the Disaffected *Scots* and Duke
Lauderdale, and that the Affairs in *Ireland* went on with great
Expedition, and that all means were now used to beget a
Difference betwixt the *Dutch* and the Prince of *Orange*, and
if that could be effected, there was no question to be made,
but that the *Protestant Interest* would fail in *Holland*, and that
Forty Eight would not last long in *England*, for it was high time
to hinder *Forty Nine* from being effected : That *Barly-Broth-
Trade* should grow dead, and *Twelve* would be Cut off,

K   and

and that *Mum* and *Chocolate* fhould be put down, and the *Order of Mag-Pies* fhould be turned into their Primitive Inftitution and Habit. Now the *Deponent* faith, that the words [hinder *Forty Nine* from being effected] is an Odd Expreffion, that is amongft them ufed for the *Cutting off the King*, that he may not live to be compleat *Forty Nine* Years of Age. And by *Barley-Broth*, is meant the Houfe of Commons, which fhall be turned out and Sit no more. And by *Mum* and *Chocolate*, is meant the Proteftant Peers ; which, if not deftroyed, fhall never have any Vote in the Houfe of Peers more, after the Death of this King. And by *Mag-Pies*, they underftand the Bifhops, whofe Habit in Parliament is Black and White, which fhall be changed into Purple. And by *Twelve*, is meant the Duke of *Monmouth*.

Whilft the faid *Keines* with the other Jefuit entertained the *Deponent* with thefe Treafonable Expreffions, Mr. *Jennifon* came to the faid *Keines*, and told him, that he had loft a Letter which he had received from *Tho. White*, the Provincial at St. *Omers*, in a Walk he took to *Iflington*, and would give ten pounds to any friend that would give it him, and was afraid that fome Inconvenience might follow, if found by fome Heretick : Which words put the faid *Keines* into fuch a Confternation, that he asked him, Whether he had a mind to ruine them all : But *Jennifon* bad the faid *Keines* be quiet, for none could underftand it ; which words the *Deponent* did likewife hear.

L X. Item.

That *John Keines* came to the Lodgings of the *Deponent*, on *Saturday, August* 17, and said it was endeavoured to dispatch *Forty Eight* at *Windsor*, if possible, (by which number the *Deponent* saith, they mean the King) and withal told the *Deponent*, That Mr. *Howard*, Prior of the *Benedictines*, and Mr. *Hitchcock* Subprior, and Mr. *Skinner*, Mr. *Corker*, and other *Benedictines*, had promised to assist them with 6000 *l.* in order to the design. The said Monks did then lye at or near the *Wardrobe* behind the *Savoy*; which report the *Deponent* did believe, because the said Mr. *Howard*, Prior of the *Benedictines*, and Mr. *Hitchcock* Subprior, told the Deponent in the morning, *August* 17, that they had promised such a sum, and withal that the securing of his Majesties person in his Flight from *Worcester* was the worst days work that ever simple *Jack Huddlestone* did in all his Life. But now it 22 was their business to get the *Stuarts* out of the way: which the *Deponent* related to *John Keines*, and then *Keines* did tell the *Deponent*, That if he would undertake to assist in the dispatching of the King, he should be well rewarded, if not here, in Heaven : and the *Deponent* replied, that he never shot off a Gun in his Life, and withal told *Keines*, that he could not be guilty of such a thing for the World. And then the said *Keines* did further inform the Deponent, that Mr. *Coniers* a Benedictine Monk was resolved to pursue the Design of dispatching the King, which did appear to be evidently true to the Deponent, because he did hear the said *Coniers* on the 14*th* of 23 *August* lay a Wager of 100 *l.* with a Gentleman not known to the *Deponent*, in the *Benedictine Convent* in the *Savoy* : ten Guinies were deposited in the hands of *Hitchcock* Subprior of the *Benedictines*. Now the Wager which *Coniers* did lay was, That the *Villain*, the *K I N G*, should not live to eat any more Christmas Pies ; and the other Gentleman did lay that he would : So that the *Deponent* saith, That *Keines* told him no more of the Concern of *Coniers*, than the *Deponent* had heard of the said *Coniers* before, on the 14*th*. of *August*.

But

---

22. *Huddlestone:* the Benedictine priest (1628–1698) who helped Charles escape after the Battle of Worcester (September 3, 1651).

23. *Coniers:* George Coniers—he escaped arrest.

But the *Deponent* before he parted from *Keines*, asked him, What news about the Town? *Keines* replyed, That all the news about the Town was, *War with the French*: and *Keines*, did say, that if that held true, then *Have at the Rogues of the House of Commons*, they should be remembred for all their Long Bills against the Catholicks. The *Deponent* replyed, that (with submission) he thought the Revenge proposed against them would not do the business, and therefore not a Resolution consistent with a Catholick Spirit, for the Enterprise must be more Noble: And withal the *Deponent* urged, that he feared the Death of the King would scarcely do the business and effect the Design, unless his R. Highness 24 would pardon those that did the business, and stand by them in it. To which the said *Keines* reply'd, that the Duke was not the strength of their Trust, for they had another way to effect the setting up the *Catholick Religion* : For when they had destroied the King, they had a List of 20000 *Catholicks* in *London*, that were substantial persons and fit for Arms, that would Rise in twenty four hours time and less :· And if *James* did not comply with them, to Pot he must go also.

It being late in the Night, the said *John Keines* prayed the *Deponent* to come to him the next morning, and he would have one hours discourse with him before he went to *Mass*, and being about to take leave of the *Deponent*, asked him, What he meant by those words [he could not be guilty of any such thing, as to assist in dispatching the King] there being no guilt in the Case ; the *Deponent* smiled and said, He could not be guilty of so much Courage. Besides the *Deponent* saith, That he told the said *Keines*, that it was his opinion, that it would be more safe to let Sir *George Wakeman* try his skill, and then the People would not apprehend it so much.

L 2   LXI.

---

24. *R. Highness:* James, duke of York.

In Item 64, Oates fatally mentions Coleman in telling of plans to hire four Irish ruffians to assassinate Charles. Item 68 presents George Coniers with a long knife designed to murder the king.

L X I V. Item.

That the said *Fogarthy* is a main Agent in this Hellish- 25
Plot, and hath promised, That if this Bishop *Talbot* will 26
make use of him, he will do all the service he can : which
the Deponent is ready to justify to the face of the said *Fo-*
garthy; who did tell the Deponent, that he and *Coleman* were
in the Consult, when *Wakeman* was contracted withal in order to Poyson the KING; and said, That if he had the
interest in the KING, as *Wakeman* had, he would have undertaken it himself. And all this was told the Deponent
on the *Twenty first* of *August*, in the Chamber of the said
Fogarthy. And furthermore, the said *Fogarthy* then and there
did tell the Deponent, That he had hired Four *Irish* Ruffians, whose Names he did neither tell the Consulters that
met on the *Twenty first* of *August*, nor the Deponent; and
these *Irish* Ruffians were to mind the KING's Postures at
Windsor : But the Deponent telling the said *Fogarthy*, that
he heard the KING was going to *Portsmouth*, he was wonderfully troubled at it, and said, It did very much im-
pede their Design, and nothing would be Attempted so
long as he was absent from *Windsor*.

M 2

25. *Fogarthy:* Dr. William Fogarty, Oates's physician.
26. *Talbot:* Peter Talbot, archbishop of Dublin, whose letters about plots in Ireland Oates had quoted; in October 1678, he was imprisoned in Dublin Castle, where
he remained until his death in November 1681.

LXVIII *Item*.

That the Deponent being to meet with Dr. *Tonge* on the 22*th* of *August*, at the Kings head in *Grays-Inne-lane*, about six of the Clock at night, accordingly went; and finding that the said Doctor was not there, he walked in *Grays-Inne-walks*, and there he met with *Coniers*, who was 27 supposed to be gone to *Windsor*. The Deponent asked him, how it happened that he did not go his Journey? he replied, that his horse fell so lame, that he could scarce carry him five miles on the way, and so was forced to return; and that he himself was taken ill with the Sciatica, which had given him great trouble for all the night before. The Deponent was then urgent with him to tell him how he would kill the King, seeing he did laugh at the means the Fathers intended to use, *viz.* by shooting him. Then the said *Coniers*, by reason of the Deponents importunity, shewed him a Dagger or Knife two-edged, with a very sharp point; and it was broader and broader towards the haft, which was of Buckhorn, and was a foot long in the blade, and neer half a foot in the haft. With this (said he) the Villain shall fall to the ground, if possible. *Coniers* demanded of the Deponent, what he thought it might cost him? the Deponent said, he could not tell: *Coniers* replied, Ten shillings, or thereabouts. The Deponent told him it was too dear: he replied, Nothing could be too dear for the King. The Deponent asked him where he bought it? *Coniers* replied, Of the old Cutler in *Russel-street*. The Deponent asked him why he would have it so long? he replied, That the Villain might fall by it. The Deponent asked, How? he replied, Through my Cloak will I stab him. The Deponent asked him, how he thought to escape? *Coniers* answered, that he doubted not but to obtain a Pardon, if he were not knockt on the head upon the place. The Deponent, after some discourse, went to the Kings head, where he met with Dr. *Tonge* between six and seven of the Clock. **LXIX**

---

27. *Coniers:* George Coniers; see p. 39.

Items 69 and 71 give plans for burning London once more; this idea was doubtless included because of Israel Tonge, who had been obsessed by it since he had lost his church in the flames of 1666.

LXIX *Item*.

That the Deponent did on the 22*th* of *August*, about nine of the Clock, meet with *Blundell* ; and feeing him have 28 a Bag, asked him what he had ? and he replied, *Tewxbury* Muftard-balls, a notable biting Sawce, and would furnish *Weftminfter* when he had enough of them. The Deponent faith, that by *Tewxbury* Muftard-balls, we are to underftand, Fire-balls.

LXX *Item*.

That on the 24*th* of *August*, *Blundell* told the Deponent in *Fenwick*'s Chamber, that it would be fo ordered by the Society, that the Catholicks of *England* would advance the defigne of fhortning the Kings days; and bad the Deponent be of good Cheer, for Proteftant Religion was on its laft legs.

LXXI *Item*.

That the Deponent met with *Blundell* on *August* the thirtieth, who told him, that he muft fhew him what *Weftminfter*, and the houfes on both fides the Water, were to be done withal ; and carried him to *Fenwick*'s Chamber, and there drew out of a Paper-Cafe a Paper, in which was the manner of Firing *Weftminfter* and *Wapping*, *Toolies - ftreet*, *Barnaby - ftreet* , and St. *Thomas* Apoftles. Firft for *Weftminfter*, if the wind blew nothernly , then they were to begin at the next houfe to the Palfgraves-head Tavern, where the Jefuits and their Agents were to carry on the Fire to the *Savoy* ; and then the Benedictines and they , to carry it on both fides to *Charing-Crofs* ; and

28. *Blundell:* Nicholas Blundell, a Jesuit priest; despite Oates's charges, he was released and allowed to return to St. Omers in 1679.

and then the Fire was by them and their Agents to be carried to *Whitehall:* and neer the end of the Stone-gallery 29
another Company is to begin and carry it on to *Kings-ftreet*
and *Channel-Row*; which was firft defigned to be acted in
the time of the great Froft, in the year 1676; but then
they were not affured of the French Kings affiftance, of
which they are now affured by *Lefhee*, the French Kings 30
Confeffor. At the fame time *Wapping,* and the Ships in
the River, were to be burnt: and the faid Fire (in cafe
the Wind blow up the River) is to begin at a place neer
Bugbies-hole or *Limehoufe-hole*, and is to be carried on by
four men (of whom they had made choice) to *Wapping* 31
middle-ftairs, and then four or five more were to carry it
up higher. And the Deponent found himfelf, with feven
more, ordered to ply about the *Armitage*; and his bufinefs was to encourage the feven men committed to his
care; and for his reward One thoufand pound was therein
promifed him, befides Eighty pound for his former fervi-
ces. But the Deponent faith, if the Wind ftood contrary,
they were to change the Commencement of the Fire. At
the fame time others were to have the Charge in *Barnaby-
ftreet*, *Toolies-ftreet*, and St. *Thomas* Apoftles on the other
fide of the Water, committed to them; and the Fire was
to begin at *Redriff* when it was begun on *Wapping*-fide: 32
And this is to be done when the Water is low, that the
Ships might not get off from the Keys. In order to the
Deponents managing that part of the Fire that was to be
begun about the *Armitage*, he was ordered to remove his
Lodging into *Wapping* as foon as order was given him,
and he fhould have a Prieft come and fay Mafs unto him in
his Chamber every day for a good fuccefs on the Defigne.
But the Deponent faith, he did not know he was to be an
Agent in the bufinefs, till he faw that Paper; which Paper
was figned by the Provincial *Tho.White*, in the name of the
whole Society.

O

29. *Whitehall:* the royal palace.
30. *Leshee:* see above, p. 34.
31. *Wapping:* a hamlet on the London side of the Thames, near the Tower.
32. *Redriff:* a shortening of Rotherhithe, a hamlet just across the river.

In the last items, Oates stresses the dangers facing himself during the summer of 1678, when he had turned informer. His appendix lists some hundred conspirators and contains Oates's oath before the late Justice Godfrey, along with "The General Design of the Pope" for gaining domination over Britain. This document stresses a strategy of conspiracies, fires, and even plans for "setting up pretended false Titles to the Succession of the Crown." In all of this, Oates has impressively imagined—and claimed as fact—the warnings formulated by Marvell of an imminent threat to England from the forces of tyranny and popery.

LXXVIII. 𝕴tem.

That on the *Sixth* of *September*, Mr. *Pickering* told the Deponent, that *Conyers* was gone for *Windsor*; and he said, that after *Ten* Days ſtay there, he would go to the Lord *Brudena's* Houſe.   33

LXXIX. 𝕴tem.

That at night the Deponent attending at the door of the Provincial, and about to go in, heard *White*, and ſome others (whom the Deponent ſuppoſed by their Voices to be Mr. *Mico*, and one Mr. *Poole*) conſulting about the diſpoſing of a Perſon, whom the Deponent ſuppoſes to be himſelf. Their Words were theſe:

This Man hath Betrayed us, and therefore we *will give a Coach-man* Twenty Pound *to take him up, and Carry him directly to* Rocheſter *to Eſquire* Lees Houſe*, who lives near the* Town*; and from thence to* Dover*, by ſome By-way, becauſe he is acquainted at* Sittingburn*; and ſaid, that if they could but get him on the other Side of the Water, they would torment him till he had confeſſed to them, who it* was *that had been* with *the* KING*, and Informed Him of the buſineſs.*

When the Deponent heard theſe Words, he went down the Stairs with all the ſpeed he could make, and durſt not return to his lodgings that night, but lay in another place.

P 2

---

33. *Brudenal:* Francis Brudenell; he was imprisoned in 1679.

A True and Perfect Narrative
of the Late Terrible and Bloody Murther
of Sir Edmundberry Godfrey (1678)

The murder of Sir Edmund Berry Godfrey remains one of the great puzzles in the history of the Popish Plot. When his body was found, the news spread rapidly throughout London, and, as Burnet reported, "men's spirits were so sharpened upon it, that we all looked on it as a very great happiness that the people did not vent their fury upon the papists about the town" (Burnet, II, 165). His death made Oates's story seem incontestable as he himself grew into a martyr and a symbol of papist malice. And since the question of who killed him became bound to the whole issue of the reality of the plot itself, the mystery has continued to provoke passionate controversy among historians.

Godfrey had been a well-known and esteemed justice of the peace for the county of Middlesex and the city of Westminster. He received his knighthood in 1666 for bravely staying at his post during the plague. He was notable too for his religious toleration and had a number of important Catholic friends, including Edward Coleman, whose fatal letters were also to confirm the plot in the public's mind.

After Godfrey had taken Oates's oath on his "narrative," on September 6, 1678, he was understandably depressed and apprehensive—the secrets he held were obviously explosive, especially for his Catholic friends. He undoubtedly warned Coleman of his danger, and he told Burnet that he expected to be "knocked on the head" (Burnet, II, 163).

He was last seen on October 12. Five days later his body was discovered at Primrose Hill. The spectacular circumstances were bound to make a strong impression, as the *Narrative* demonstrates. His own sword had been thrust through his body after he had been strangled; his corpse had been moved to the place where it was found; yet despite his murderers' evident planning, they had taken neither his money nor his valuables.

All was blamed on the papists, who were allegedly hoping to suppress Oates's evidence against them. A reward of £500 was offered for the discovery of the murderers, and soon "witnesses" emerged to claim it. William Bedloe, an experienced criminal, came forward with elaborate tales of papist plots. Claiming to have seen Godfrey's body at Somerset House, he implicated two men, one a servant of Lord Belasyse and the other Samuel Atkins, a servant of Samuel Pepys, secretary to the Admiralty Commission, who had close connections to the duke of York. As evidence these charges carried little weight; Atkins, for example, proved to be an able defender of his innocence and with Pepys's help constructed a solid alibi. But then Bedloe saw Miles Prance, a Catholic silversmith who had been arrested because he was reported to be absent from home during the time of Godfrey's disappearance. Bedloe claimed to recognize Prance as one of those he had seen with Godfrey's corpse in Somerset House. After two days in an especially cold cell in Newgate, Prance confessed and agreed to testify against others in return for a pardon. He denounced Green, Berry, and Hill as the murderers. According to Prance, they had lured Godfrey into Somerset House on the twelfth, strangled him, concealed the body there until the sixteenth, then taken it to Primrose Hill and impaled it with the sword. Though Prance recanted this story on two occasions, threats and imprisonment convinced him to return to it each time. Later, when James II was on the throne, Prance denied it all again. But in 1678 it saved his life, provided the government with the convictions it needed to show that it was combating the popish menace, and supplied the exclusionists with evidence to bolster Oates's accusations.

Later generations have never regarded Green, Berry, and Hill as guilty, and the search for the real murderers has continued in histories and even in novels. The most difficult issue is the question of motive. Since Oates was giving his evidence to the Privy Council, the papists could have had no reasonable hope of suppressing his charges by killing Godfrey. Though Sir John Pollock did conclude that the papists were responsible in his *Popish Plot* (London: Duckworth, 1903), his analysis of their motives was based on conjectures about what Godfrey may have learned from Coleman. Another theory is that of Sir Roger L'Estrange, who believed that Godfrey, known to be of a melancholy disposition, had committed suicide. Others have found this explanation attractive, including David Ogg, who has speculated that after the suicide, Oates or his associates may have found the body and arranged the circumstances to make the deed look like murder (Ogg, II, 579–84). This theory is conjectural, but it does bring into relief the fact that the person who benefited most from Godfrey's murder was Oates, as it seemed to prove his testimony beyond doubt. And indeed others have suggested that Oates himself might have murdered Godfrey. While no crime seems beyond Oates's reach, in this instance no direct evidence against him has ever been unearthed.

Other theories suggest that Godfrey was murdered for causes totally unrelated to the plot or the papists. Some have argued that the villain could have been the earl of Pembroke. A quarrelsome lord, he killed at least two men and injured many more in various brawls, and Godfrey had been involved in one of the proceedings against him. But again, the evidence is merely conjectural. Indeed the elaborate planning evident in Godfrey's murder would not be characteristic of the impetuous Pembroke. Finally, as John Kenyon has noted, Godfrey may have been the victim of a totally unknown hand which has left no trace in history (Kenyon, pp. 264–70).

All of these theories leave open the possibility that Oates or his allies may have stage-managed the corpse to suggest a papist murder, but that too remains only a surmise. Only the perjured Bedloe and Prance came forward at the time to collect the £500 reward. Despite enormous effort, no one solved the mystery, and probably no one ever will.

It remains to ask how important a solution would be. That is, what effect would it have upon our interpretation of the plot? Pollock was convinced that it would be fundamental, for if the papists were guilty, the contemporary belief in Oates might be justified and "much of the censure which has been poured on the Protestant Party misses the mark" (*The Popish Plot,* p. 83). But is this true? The menaces described by Oates were after all not directly related to Godfrey, and many were clearly lies, as were the depositions of Bedloe and Prance. Even if the Papists had committed the murder, it would prove only an immensely foolish effort to suppress Oates's charges. It would not prove that the charges were true; they were, after all, dangerous whether they were true or not. And no real evidence has ever emerged to support Oates's claims of a papist plot to kill the king and subvert Protestantism by fire and sword. During the fearful times of 1678–1681 such a connection between Godfrey's murder and the entire fabric of Oates's plot seemed natural enough, but now it would be impossible to defend.

A True and perfect

N A R R A T I V E

Of the late Terrible and Bloody
Murther of Sir *Edmondberry Godfrey* ;

Who was found Murthered on *Thurs-*
day the 17th. of this Inftant *October* , in a Field
near *Primrofe-Hill.*

WITH

A full Accompt of the manner of his
being Murthered , and in what manner he
was found.

ALSO,

The full Proceedings of the Coroner , who fat
upon the Inqueft, &c.

―――――――――――――――――――

With Allowance.

―――――――――――――――――――

E D I N B U R G H,
Re-printed by the *Heir* of *Andrew Anderfon* , Printer to
the Kings moft Sacred Majefty, *Anno Dom.* 1678.

❋❋❋❋❋❋❋❋❋❋❋❋❋❋❋❋❋❋❋❋❋❋❋❋❋❋❋❋❋❋❋❋❋❋❋
❋❋❋❋❋❋❋❋❋❋❋❋❋❋❋❋❋❋❋❋❋❋❋❋❋❋❋❋❋❋❋❋❋❋❋

A true and perfect Relation of that Horrid and Bloody Murder committed upon the Body of Sir Edmondberry Godfrey.

SIR *Edmundberry Godfrey's* Death being the sad occasion of this Narrative, and the Subject of most peoples Discourse: I shall (to prevent any false or surreptitious Stories that are usually carried abroad about things of this nature) give the Reader this true and impartial account thereof.

On the 12*th*. of this instant *October*, being Saturday, about Nine of the Clock in the Morning, Sir *Edmundberry Godfrey* went out of his own House in *Greens-lane* in the *Strand* about his Occasions: And was seen not long after near *Marybone*, but then supposed to be going home; and was at one of the Church-Wardens of the Parish of St. *Martins in the Fields* about some business at twelve of the Clock the same day: But so it was, that he came not to his own House that night, according to his usual Custom, nor gave any notice to his Servants of

A 2   any

51

any bufinefs that he had to hinder his returning that night. And from that time till Thurfday the 17*th* of the fame Moneth about fix a Clock at night, no tydings could be heard of him (although all earneft and diligent Inquiries and Searches were made for him) At which time his Dead Body was found dead in a Ditch upon the South fide of *Primerofe-hill* near *Hampftead*. The occafion of his being found was this: One *Promley* a Baker, and *Waters* a Farrier, both of the Parifh of St. *Giles in the Fields* , having an occafion to go to the Houfe, commonly called the *Whitehoufe* near *Primerofe-hill*; and going over the Field where the Body of Sr. *Edmundberry* lay, faw, as they thought, a fword and Belt, and a ftick and a pair of Gloves lying together hard by the Hedge fide , but they went not near to meddle with them, fuppofing they had belong'd to fome perfon that was gone into the Ditch to eafe himfelf. And when they came to the *White-houfe* , they told *John Rawfon* (the man of the faid Houfe) that they had feen a Sword and belt, and a Pair of Gloves and Stick lye in that place: Whereupon *John Rawfon* asked them , why they did not bring them thi her : They told him they did not know but there might be fome Body hard by to own them : *Rawfon* told them again; That there ha been feveral Soldiers thereabout this Week a Hedghog hunting, and it may be (faid he) fome of them ma have left them behind them.

After fome further Difcourfe, *Rawfon* agreed to g with the two men to the place, and if they found t things there, then, *Rawfon* was to give them a Shillin to Drink, and was to take the things to his own Houſe, till ſome body came thither to own them : and thereupon they went together to the place : When they came there, they found only a Belt and a Scabbard, and a Stick, and a pair of Gloves, but no Sword: which as *Rawſon* was ſtooping to take up, he thought he ſaw ſome thing like a Man in the Ditch hard by, and ſo going to the Ditch, there they ſaw a Man lying, as they ſuppos'd upon his Belly, with a Sword run thorow him, and the point appearing about Seven or Eight Inches above his back : Upon this, they went immediatly to the Church-Warden of the Pariſh, to give him an account of it; but he being Sick, ſent them to Mr. *Brown's* the Conſtable, who preſently taking with him ſeveral Neighbours and Houſe-keepers, went to the place where the Body lay : Which was in a dry Ditch upon the South ſide of *Primeroſe-hill*, about two Fields diſtant from the *White-houſe* : The Poſture in which he lay was this, he had a Sword run into him juſt under his left Pap, which came out upon the Right ſide of his back, about Seven or Eight Inches, one of his Hands being doubled under, on which he ſeemed to Lean, the other Hand lying upon the bank, his Hair Chamlet Coat being turned up over his [1] Head; his Hat and Perriwig being among the Buſhes over his Head, but no Band nor Cravat could be found [2] [3] about him; although when he went from Home, he had a large Lac'd Band on.

The Conſtable and the reſt that were with him, being about a dozen, having taken good notice of the manner of his lying, cauſed him to be removed, the

Sword

---

1. *Chamlet:* a fabric originally made with camel's hair and silk; in the seventeenth century, often made with hair of the Angora goat.
2. *Band:* a collar or ruff worn round the neck.
3. *Cravat:* necktie (a bow with long, flowing ends).

Sword drawn out of his Body ; concerning which Sword it is obfervable, that the point of it which came out at his back was covered all over with blood, and that part which was in his Body was black, without any blood upon it.

The Conftable having caus'd the Body to be removed to the *White Houfe*, and knowing it to be the Body of Sir *Edmondberry Godfrey* , he caufed his Pockets to be fearched, and found in one of them , in one Paper fix Guineys, and in another paper four broad pieces of Gold, and a half Crown ; and in the other Pocket two Rings, whereof one was a Diamond , one Guiney , and four pound in Silver , and two fmall pieces of Gold, and one Ring he had upon one of his fingers : His Pocket Book (in which he ufed to take notes of Examination) being only miffing.

One *Friday* the 18th of this inftant , Mr. *Cooper* the Coronor of *Midlefex* , impannel'd a Jury at the *White-Houfe* to inquire about the occafion of the death of the faid Sir *Edmondberry* : and two Chyrurgions, (having been firft Sworn) viewed the Body in the prefence of the Coronor and the Jury ; and found two wounds about it , which one of the Chyrurgions fearched with his   4 Probe ; and found one of them not above an inch deep, the Probe going againft one of his Ribs ; but the other being a little below the left Pap , went quite thorow the Body : his Face was of a frefh colour , though in his life time very pale, fomewhat fwell'd, and a green circle about his Neck, as if he had been ftrangled, his blood be-ing fettled about his Neck, Throat, and the upper part of
his

4. *Chyrurgions:* surgeons.

hisBreſt : The Chyrurgions having viewed the Body, delivered their Judgements, That the wounds they found about him, were not the cauſe of his death , but that he was ſuffocated before the wounds were made. And that which may fully perſwade any perſon of the truth thereof, is, That there was not one drop of blood to be found in the place where he lay , nor the leaſt appearance of any ſuch thing ; though the Ditch was dry, and it might have been eaſily ſeen, if there had been any. Another thing was , that the very bottom of the ſoles of his Shoes were as clean as if he had but juſt come out of his own Chamber , which was an evident ſign that he was carried thither.

A third thing very remarkable , is , That one of the Jury affirmed , That a Servant of his Mothers (who is owner of the ground where the Body lay) with a Butcher and two Boys , made a very ſtrict and narrow ſearch in all parts of that ground for a Calf that was miſſing, upon *Munday* and *Tueſday* laſt , and at that time there lay no dead Body, Belt, Gloves, Stick , or other things there.

Now becauſe ſeveral falſe Reports have gone abroad, tending to the Diſhonour of this worthy Deceaſed Knight , as though he had been diſcontented about ſome Moneys owing by him to the Pariſh , and upon that account ſhould make himſelf away : The Relator thinks good to teſtifie to the World, That to his own knowledge Sir *Edmondberry* lent to the Pariſh above 300 *l.* without Intereſt , a good part of which is yet unpaid, ſo palpable

pable an untruth it is , that some wicked persons have spread abroad about him. But it is no wonder that those inhumane Wretches that have taken away his life, should go also about to blast his Reputation.

One thing more I cannot omit to mention , having received it from the mouth of one of the Church-Wardens of the Parish where he lived, which is, That Sir *Edmondsberry* not long ago gave him an hundred pound to bestow upon such poor People in the Parish as he knew were in want: Neither was that the first time that Sir *Edmondsberry* had imployed him in works of that nature, having often made him the distributer of his Charity, because he did not desire the applause of men for it. This without all doubt proceeded from so remarkable and so sincere a piety, That though it may be commended, I am afraid it will scarce be imitated.

F I N I S.

The Second Letter of Mr. Coleman's to the French Kings Confessor, Monsieur L'Chaise (1679)

Edward Coleman was a zealous convert to Roman Catholicism who served as secretary to the future James II in 1670, and became his wife's servant in 1674. Much of this time he was an energetic conspirator, carrying on a considerable correspondence with various agents of the French court. Convinced that Catholic interests could be furthered by preventing Parliament from meeting, he succeeded from time to time in securing small sums of money intended as bribes to further this purpose—though he claimed at his trial that he merely kept the money. Indiscreet and politically naive, "he was," as Sir Robert Southwell declared, "a man who would certainly run himself into the briars" (quoted by Kenyon, p. 38). When his two letters to Father La Chaise were found in 1678, he entangled his patron in the briars also, for they seemed to prove that James knew and approved of his subversive activities. Yet, as James had allied himself with Danby's anti-French parliamentary policy during this period, there may be some truth to his claim that Coleman was not speaking for him. Though, at best, Coleman's serpentine intrigues were insignificant, once revealed they raised serious questions about James's role in plot. In Parliament, his enemies loudly demanded that he be exiled or at least denied access to the court. As a result, on November 3, the king felt obligated to order his brother out of the Privy Council.

Coleman came to trial for high treason on November 27. His was the first trial in which Oates and Bedloe were the chief witnesses, and Oates in particular had a difficult time, for Coleman exposed his inconsistencies and demanded to know why Oates had failed to recognize him when he had first appeared before the Privy Council. Oates's excuses—he blamed eyestrain and poor light—met with some skepticism; yet the letters remained, and they were damning enough. Although they actually confirmed none of the informers' particular accusations, this disparity did not seem to strike observers at the time, as one can see in Narcissus Luttrell's account:

> The tryall lasted from nine in the morning till five in the afternoon. The witnesses against him were Dr. Oates and Capt. Bedloe, who spoke very fully; as also his own writings and papers, which were undeniable proof: so that the jury in a little time brought him in guilty; and the next morning he

57

was brought to the kings bench barr again, and there received sentence to be drawn, hang'd, and quartered." (Luttrell, I, 4)

While awaiting execution, his behavior was noble. Although he hoped, quite unrealistically, for a royal pardon, he steadfastly refused to save himself by a false confession. His execution took place on December 3, 1678.

The exclusionists had the letters used against Coleman at his trial printed, illegally, within a few days of his conviction. This tract also included a letter from James to Father La Chaise described on the title page as showing that *"what Mr. Coleman wrote to him was by his special command and appointment"* (quoted in Kenyon, p. 124).

The second letter, given here, is the briefer and more dramatic, with its recommendation of invisible writing with lemon juice. Like the first, it discusses obscure and elaborate plots for the advancement of Catholicism.

THE

SECOND LETTER

O F

Mr. Coleman's

To the *French* Kings Confeffor,

MONSIEUR L CHAISE.

I Sent your Reverence a tedious Letter on our 29th. of
September, to inform you of the progrefs of our Affaires
for thefe two or three laft years.   I have now again the opportunity of a very fure hand to conveigh this by.   I have
fent you a *Cypher*, becaufe our Parliament now drawing on,
I may poffibly have occafion to fend you fomething which
*You may be vvilling enough to knovv, and may be neceffary for us
that you should,* when I may want the conveniency of a Meffenger.   When any thing occurs of more concern than
other, which may not be fit to be trufted to a *Cypher* alone,
I will, to make fuch a thing more fecure, write in *Lemon,*
between the Lines of a Letter which fhall have nothing in it
vifible, but what I care not who fees, but dried by a warm
fire fhall difcover what is written, fo that if the Letter comes
to your hands, and upon drying it any thing appears more
than did before, you may be fure no body has feen it by the
way.

I will

I will not trouble you with that way of writing but upon special occasions, and then I will give you a hint to direct you to look for it, by concluding my visible Letter with something of *Fire* or *Burning*, by which mark you may please to know that there is something underneath, and how my Letter is to be used to find it out.

We have here a mighty work upon our hands, no less than *The Conversion of three Kingdoms, and by that perhaps the subduing a pestilent Heresy, vvhich has domineer'd over part of this Northern World a long time.* There was never such hopes of Success since the Death of our *Q. MARY,* as now in our dayes, when God has given us a *PRINCE* who is become (may I say by Miracle) *Zealous of being the Author and Instrument of so glorious a Work* : But the opposition we are sure to meet with, is also like to be great : So that it imports us to get all the Aid and Assistance. *For the Harvest is great and the Labourers are fevv.*

What we rely upon most, next to God Almighties *Providence,* and the Fervor of my *Master the Duke,* is the mighty mind of his *Christian Majesty,* [1] whose generous Soul inclines him to great undertakings, which being managed by your *Reverences* exemplary *Piety* and *Prudence,* will certainly make him look upon this, as most suitable to himself, and best becoming his power and thoughts ; so that I hope you will pardon me, if I be troublesom too upon this occasion, from whom we expect the greatest help we can hope for.

And I confess I think his *Christian Majesties* temporal interest is so much attracted to that of his *R. H.* [2] which can never be considerable but upon the advancement of the *Catholik Religion,* that his Ministers cannot give him better Advice even in a politick sence abstracted from the Considerations of the next world, then that of our dear Lord, *To seek first the Kingdom of Heaven, and the Righteousness thereof, that all other things may be added.*

Yet

---

1. *Christian Majesty:* Louis XIV.
2. *R.H.* his Royal Highness, James, duke of York.

Yet *I* know his moſt *Chriſtian Majeſty* has more power-
full motives ſuggeſted to him by his own Devotion, and
your R*everences* Zeal for Gods Glory, to engage himſelf to
afford us the beſt help he can in our preſent Circumſtances:
but we are a little unhappy in this, That we cannot preſs his
Majeſties preſent *Miniſter* here, upon theſe latter Arguments, which are moſt ſtrong, but only upon the firſt, *Mon-
ſieur Ravigny's* fence and ours differing very much upon 3
theſe, though we agree perfectly upon the reſt; And indeed
though he be a very able man, as to his Majeſties ſervice, in
things where Religion is not concern'd, yet *I* do believe
it were much more happy, conſidering the Poſt he is in, that
his temper vvere of ſuch a ſort that vve might deall clearly
vvith him throughout and not be forced to ſtop ſhort in a
diſcourſe of conſequence, and leave the moſt material part
out, becauſe vve knovv it vvill ſhake his particular opinion,
and ſo perhaps meet vvith diſlike, and oppoſition though
never ſo neceſſary to the main concern.

   I am afraid we ſhall find too much reaſon for this Com-
plaint this next Seſſions of Parliament, for had we one here
for his Chriſtian Majeſty who had taken the whole buſineſs
to heart, and who would have repreſented the ſtate of our
caſe truly as it is, to his Maſter, *I* do not doubt but his Chriſtian Majſtey would have engaged himſelf farther in the affair then at preſent I fear he has done, and by his approbation have given ſuch counſells *(as have been offered his*
R. H. *by thoſe fevv Catholicks vvho have acceſſe to him and
are bent to ſerve him, and advance the Catholick Religion, vvith
all their might*) more credit with his R. H. Then *I* fear
they have found; And have aſſiſted him alſo with his purſe
as far as 100000. Crovvns or ſome ſuch ſumme *(* vvhich
to him is very inconſiderable but vvould have been to them
of greater uſe then can be imagined) tovvards gaining o-
thers to help him, or at leaſt not to oppoſe him, if vve had
t een ſo happy as to have had his moſt Chriſtian Majeſty
                                                    vvith

---

3. *Monsieur Ravigny:* Henri de Massue Ruvigny (1610–1689), the French ambassador to London at that time, i.e., 1674–1675.

vvith us to this degree, *I vvould have anſvvered vvith my life for ſuch ſucceſs this Seſſions, as vvould have put the intereſt of the Catholick Religion in his R. H. And his moſt Chriſtian Majeſty out of all danger for the time to come.*

But vvanting thoſe hopes of recommending thoſe neceſſary councells vvhich have been given his Royall Highneſs in ſuch a manner as to make him think them vvorthy of his accepting, and fit to govern himſelf by, and of thoſe advantages, vvhich a little money vvell managed vvould certainly have gained us, *I* am affraid vve ſhall not be much better at the end of this Seſſion then vve are novv : *I* pray God vve do not looſe ground. By my next, vvhich ſhall be ere long, *I* ſhall be able to tell your Reverence more perticularly vvhat vve are like to expect : *In* the mean time *I* moſt humbly beg your holy prayers for all our undertakings, and that you vvill pleaſe to honour me ſo far as to eſteem me, vvhich *I* am, entirely and vvithout any reſerve

Sir, Moſt *Reverend Father,*

Your Reverences *moſt humble*

and moſt obedient Servant

PART THREE

Public Hysteria and Its Fomenters

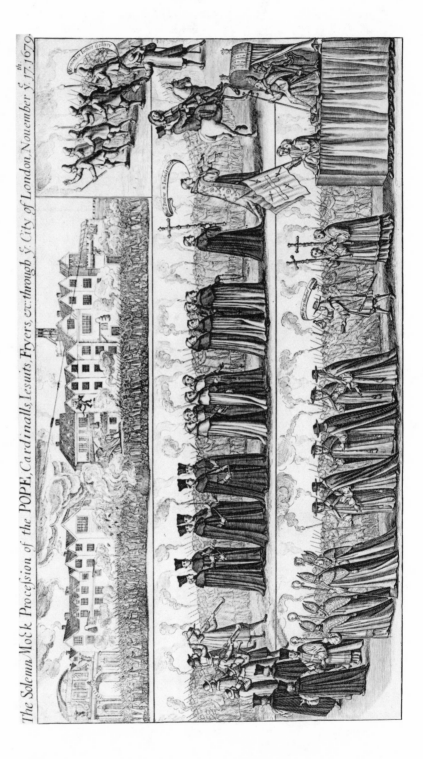

The Solemn Mock Procession of the POPE, Cardinalls, Iesuits, Fryers, &c: through ye City of London, November ye 17, 1679.

Illustration of "The Solemn Mock Procession of the Pope." This broadside shows the anti-Catholic pageant that was held in London on the anniversary of Queen Elizabeth's accession (November 17) in 1679. This one, like those of 1680 and 1681, was underwritten by the Green Ribbon Club and was reported to have been witnessed by 200,000 people. The cavalcade first wound its way through London's streets. In the front were the whistlers and links to clear the way, then a bell-man shouting "Remember Justice Godfrey" (who was believed to have been murdered by Jesuits), then came Godfrey's effigy, on horseback, carried by a Jesuit; after them came a Jesuit giving out pardons and indulgences, a group of friars, six Jesuits with bloody daggers, and "a consort of wind music called the Waits." More Jesuits followed, then four popish bishops in purple and lawn, six more berobed churchmen, the pope's physician, carrying "Jesuit's powder" (quinine) and a urinal, and finally—on a platform adorned with banners whose bloody daggers symbolized the supposed practice of murdering heretical kings—the pope; behind him there lurked "his counsellor the Devil" (quoted by Ogg, II, 595–96). When the procession reached the statue of Queen Elizabeth, the pope was burned in effigy. Narcissus Luttrell reported that for the 1681 event, a "store of fireworks concluded the solemnity" (Luttrell, I, 144). This broadside was printed in 1679; it originally contained a brief explanatory text not given here.

Roger North's *Examen*
on Godfrey's Funeral and Oates (1740)

Justice Godfrey's murder unleashed the great fear of popery in England. Rumors appeared of Jesuits landing on obscure stretches of the shore, or mysterious armed bands riding at night, or even of French or Spanish armies massing for invasion. In London, chains were put across the streets at night and citizens bought "Protestant Flails" (short clubs filled with lead and attached to the wrist with a strap) or daggers inscribed with Godfrey's name (Miller, pp. 160–61). If London suffered most severely from panic, it had two direct agencies to stimulate its fears. The debates in Parliament were filled with inflammatory speeches about the popish threats represented first by Danby and later by York, and the trials in 1678 and 1679 of those named by Oates and other "witnesses" captured public attention, with each conviction further confirming the plot.

The first of the items in this section is an account of Godfrey's extraordinary funeral by the Tory lawyer and biographer Roger North (1653–1734), whose book *Examen* (1740—published posthumously) is an angry critique of another history which he judged to be unfair to the memory of Charles II. North was consistently hostile to the exclusionists; he believed, for example, that Oates must have been responsible for Godfrey's murder, because he gained the most from it.

The Intent of the Plotters was, that the Papifts, or whoever was 1
to be charged with the Murder, fhould be cheated into a vain Defence,
which, being plainly confuted, they muft fuccumb in an utter defencelefs
State. For, when this Shew of Suicide had, in their Minds, filled the Place
of a Defence, there was a Sort of Acquiefcence in it, and the Parties
would be lefs induftrious to bufk about for any other, as might poffibly
blunder on fome Difcovery of the Cheat. Now, together with thefe Signs
of Suicide, Care was taken that the Evidence of the contrary fhould be de-
monftrable; for his Shoes were fo exquifitely clean, that it was impoffible
he could by any Means convey himfelf there, in that dirty Time and Place.
And his own Sword (for that was it) was run through him, and, being
drawn out from his Body, thofe, that had Skill, could difcern it was not
put into him while he was alive; and there were manifeft Marks of being
ftrangled about his Neck, to fhew it was not his own Sword, but other
external Violence, that killed him. And Care was alfo taken that it might
not be pretended Thieves killed him; for, upon Search of his Pockets, there
was found his ordinary Modicum of Guineas, and his Sword Hilt was of
Silver, as rich as any, which no Thieves would have left about him.   2

CXXIV. 11. There is an Oration, at the End of *Quintilian's* Works, The Effect of
that proves Circumftances may be too appofite to be true; and the very thofe Art
clinching in of all Points (as before, about *Wakeman's* Handwriting) is rather   3
a Teftimony of Invention than Reality. So here it is almoft impoffible
that all thefe Circumftances, of a murdered Corps, arguing *pro* and *con*, one
Way and other, fhould be collected without fome Contrivance for Purpofes
that do not obvioufly appear; and nothing but Trap can refolve them. For,
if there be an obvious falfe Defence, which is provided by the Symptoms of
felf Murder, and an abftrufe true one; it is moft likely the former (which
the Artifts have provided to be cleverly confuted) will be taken, and then
the true one is fafe. This had its Effect; for the Papifts faftened greedily
on the falfe Defence, and, thinking clearly to difculpate themfelves, gave it
out boldly that *Godfrey* killed himfelf; and a Pamphlet was printed to that   4
Effect, for which one *Tompfon*, a Printer, and one *Farewell*, were tried
for Mifdemeanor and punifhed. That was done for Example to others, and,
to confirm the Plot, as it was called. And, in the Trial, which is alfo in
Print, one may obferve with what fatisfactory Glee, and Fulnefs of Evidence, it was triumphantly demonftrated that the Knight did not kill himfelf. And then, O then it was plain he was killed by the Papifts, and thefe
Men were Stiflers of the Plot, which was now made as clear as the Sun.
Such Logic and Language was current then, and the Author accordingly
ferves himfelf of it now.   The Bottom of
CXXV. 12. The Sequel of this tragical Spectacle, which put the Peo- the Plot aimed
ple into a great Ferment and Diforder (not at all moderated by the Preten- at the King,
C c 2   ders the Duke, or
                                                                both.

---

1. *Intent:* This continues a section on Godfrey's murder in which North suggests
that the theory of his suicide was a trap set for the papists.

2. *Quintilian's Works:* his *Institutio Oratoria* (95 A.D.).

3. *handwriting:* an important issue in Oates's testimony at Wakeman's trial. See
the excerpts reprinted below (p. 107).

4. *Pamphlet:* a series of letters published in the *Loyal Protestant Ingelligencer* in
1681; the authors and publisher were convinced of libel on June 20, 1679.

ders to Moderation, but exaggerated with all their Art and Coffee-Houfe
Rhetoric) was a furious Expectation that now the Bottom of the Plot would
foon come up. The common Place was that this daring Fact (an odd Sort
of Daring, to kill a Man in a Corner, and hide him three Miles off in a
Ditch) was to hinder a farther Search into the Bottom of the Plot. After
this, every new Witnefs, that came in, made us ftart; now we fhall come
to the Bottom: And fo it continued from one Witnefs to another, Year after
Year, till at laft it had no Bottom, but in the Bottomlefs Pit. This Bot-
5 tomlefs Expectation went far and near; the Factories abroad had it in the
fame Manner, and to as little Purpofe, as we at home here. And I muft
note that this Word *Bottom,* which lafted in Vogue a huge While, carried
a devillifh Intention with it; and the Refult had made its Appearance, if
6 Time had been ripe, and the Faction had dared to have put their Defign
in Execution; which was to charge the Murder upon the Queen, Duke of
York, or the King himfelf, as Opportunity ferved. And why not at the
7 *Oxford* Parliament, by Means of *Fitzharris?* Of which whole Affair, fully
8 in it's Place. For, although the three Men were convict of the Fact and
hanged, the Matter in Queftion, who employed them, was ftill in Referve,
Res integra. And there is the Art. I touched what Profers were made at
the King. If the Accufation, againft the Queen, had gone on, fhe had had
it. And it is more than probable, if the *Oxford* Libels may be any Guide,
at that Congrefs, Matters againft the Crown going fairly on, the Duke of
York, and perhaps both Brothers, had enjoyed it. I make no Doubt, but,
if the Faction durft have imputed it by Way of Slander, it had gone fo;
but they were afraid of having the Matter brought to a public Examination, which had fupplanted all its Virtue. The Loyal Party would not
have endured it, and the Nation was not corrupted enough to encourage
fuch high Play. But yet, in Whifpers, blind Hints, and pointing Infinua-
tions, that ftrange Things would rife, if they could once come at the Bottom of the Plot, they did not a little towards it: And, in real Expectation
that the King, or the Duke, or both, would be charged with procuring that
9 Murder, Multitudes of factious People inceffantly figed about, hearkening
after this fame Bottom of the Plot.

The tremen-
dous Funeral
of *Godfrey,* and
portentous
Spectacle in
the Pulpit.

CXXVI. 13. The next, and laft, Act, of this Tragedy, was the Funeral of this poor Gentleman; and, if it had been poffible the Rout could
have been more formidable than at the Expofition of him, it muft have now
appeared: For, as about other Party Concerns, fo here, the Time and Place
of the Affemblation was generally notified, as alfo what learned Divine was
to preach the Funeral Sermon. The Crowd was prodigious, both at the
Proceffion, and in and about the Church, and fo heated that any Thing,
called Papift, were it Cat or Dog, had, probably, gone to Pieces in a Moment. The Catholics all kept clofe in their Houfes and Lodgings, thinking
it a good Compofition to be fafe there; fo far were they from acting violently at that Time. But there was, all this while, upheld among the
common

---

5. *Factories:* trading establishments in foreign countries.

6. *Faction:* the exclusionists.

7. *Fitzharris:* when arrested for treason, he claimed to have information on the plot, but the government refused to grant him a pardon in return for his disclosures or to allow the House of Commons to interrogate him. See Introduction (p. 11).

8. *three Men:* Green, Berry, and Hill: tried February 5, 1679, hanged in the same month.

9. *figed about:* moved briskly and restlessly.

common People, an artificial Fright, fo as almoft every one fancied a Popifh Knife juft at his Throat: And, at the Sermon, befides the Preacher, two other thumping Divines ftood upright in the Pulpit, one on each Side of him, to guard him from being killed, while he was Preaching, by the Papifts. I did not fee this Spectre, but was credibly told by fome that affirmed they did fee it; and, although I have often mentioned it, as now I do, with Precaution, yet I never met with any that ever contradicted it. A moft portentous Spectacle fure! Three Parfons in one Pulpit! Enough of itfelf, on a lefs Occafion, to excite Terror in the Audience. The like, I guefs, was never feen before, and, probably, will never be feen again; and it had not been fo now, as is moft evident, but for fome Stratagem derived upon the Impetuofity of the Mob. And, however clear of the black Purpofes of the Plotters, we cannot acquit their Reverences of fome lower Defigns, relating to the Royal Family, and the Succeffion, which fhould not have been found covered with their venerable Habits, who could thus pretend to do Evil, that Good, in their Senfe, might come of it.

CXXVII. Here I end thefe particular Obfervations about the Matter, which I have made to fhew that fomewhat elfe, than what was pretended and fworn, was the Caufe efficient of this devillifh Murder; which I fhall (and I think I need) not to take Pains to apply farther, but proceed now with our *Spanifh* pretended Doctor, and his Pefadumbres. He was now in his trine Exaltation, his Plot in full Force, Efficacy, and Virtue; he walked about with his Guards (affigned) for fear of the Papifts murdering him. He had Lodgings in *Whitehall*, and 1200 *l. per Annum* Penfion: And no Wonder, after he had the Impudence to fay to the Houfe of Lords, in plain Terms, that, if they would not help him to more Money, he muft be forced to help himfelf *. He put on an Epifcopal Garb (except the Lawn Sleeves) Silk Gown and Caffock, great Hat, Sattin Hatband and Rofe, long Scarf, and was called, or, moft blafphemoufly called himfelf, the Saviour of the Nation, Whoever he pointed at, was taken up and committed; fo that many People got out of his Way, as from a Blaft, and glad they could prove their two laft Years Converfation. The very Breath of him was peftilential, and, if it brought not Imprifonment, or Death, over fuch on whom it fell, it furely poifoned Reputation, and left good Proteftants arrant Papifts, and fomething worfe than that, in Danger of being put in the Plot as Traitors.

CXXVIII. Upon his Examination before the Commons, the Lord Chief Juftice *Scroggs* was fent for to the Houfe, and there figned Warrants for the Imprifonment of five *Roman* Catholic Peers, upon which they were laid up in the *Tower* †. The Votes of the Houfes feemed to confirm the whole.

The State of Oates in his Exaltation.

10
11
12

The extreme Rigors of the Plot.

---

* *Chron. Hift. of* England, Jan. 9, 1678.
† The Bill, to exclude the reft of them from being fitting Members of the Houfe of Peers, paft.

A folemn

---

10. *Doctor:* Titus Oates claimed a doctorate of divinity from the University of Salamanca (cf. *Absalom and Achitophel*, ll. 658–59).

11. *Pesadumbres:* mischief (Spanish).

12. *trine Exaltation:* a favorable aspect of the stars in which two heavenly bodies are a third part of the zodiac, i.e., 120 degrees, distant from each other.

A folemn Form of Prayer was defired upon the Subject of the Plot; and, when one was prepared, it was found faulty, becaufe the Papifts were not named, as Authors of it; God furely knew whether it were fo or not: However it was yielded to, that Omnifcience might not want Information. The Queen herfelf was accufed at the Commons Bar. The City, for Fear of the Papifts, put up their Pofts and Chains; and the Chamberlain, Sir *Thomas Player*, in the Court of Aldermen, gave his Reafon for the City's ufing that Caution, which was that *he did not know, but, the next Morning, they might all rife with their Throats cut.* The Trials, Convictions, and Executions of the Priefts, *Jefuits*, and others, were had, and attended with vaft Mob and Noife. Nothing ordinary or moderate was to be heard in People's Communication; but every Debate and Action was high flown and tumultuous. All Freedom of Speech was taken away, and

13 not to believe the Pot, was worfe than being, *Turk, Jew,* or Infidel.

The hard Cafe of three Men of *Somerfet-houfe*, tried for Godfrey's Murder. CXXIX. For this Fact of *Godfrey's* Murder, the three poor Men of *Somerfet-houfe*, were, as was faid, convicted. The moft pitiful Circumftance was that of their Trial, under the popular Prejudice againft them. The Lord Chief Juftice *Scroggs* took in with the Tide, and ranted for the Plot, hewing down Popery, as *Scanderbeg* hewed the *Turk*; which was

14 but little propitious to them. The other Judges were paffive, and meddled little, except fome that were Takers in alfo; and particularly the good Re-

15 corder *Treby*, who eafed the Attorney General; for he feldom afked a Que-
16 ftion, but one might guefs he forefaw the Anfwer. Some may blame the (at beft) paffive Behaviour of the Judges; but really, confidering it was impoffible to ftemm fuch a Current, the Appearing to do it, in vain, had been more unprofitable, becaufe it had inflamed the great and fmall Rout, drawn Scandal on themfelves, and difabled them from taking in when Opportunity fhould be more favourable. The Prifoners, under thefe Hardfhips, had enough to do to make any Defence; for where the Teftimony was pofitive, it was conclufive: For no Reafoning *ab improbabili* would ferve the Turn;

17 it muft be *ab impoffibili*, or not at all. Whoever doth not well obferve the Power of judging, may think many Things, in the Courfe of Juftice, very ftrange. If one Side is held to Demonftration, and the other allowed Prefumptions for Proofs, any Caufe may be carried. In a Word, Anger, Policy, Inhumanity, and Prejudice had, at this Time, a planetary Poffeffion of the Minds of moft Men, and deftroyed in them that golden Rule, of doing as they would be done unto.

The Evil of paid Witneffes. CXXX. Whoever it was that murdered *Godfrey*, it is certain enough that the Effect was as I have defcribed; juft as if it had been done exprefs, and on pure Purpofe to favour *Oates* and his Difcovery: For, after that, all Things went off Hand fmooth, without Hefitation or Scruple; and there-upon a Trade of Swearing was inftituted, fuch as never was heard of fince

18 the *Roman Delatores*. *Oates* had his Penfions and Lodgings, as I faid,
where

I

---

13. *Pot:* plot (a misprint).

14. *Scanderbeg:* celebrated Albanian warrior, George Kastriota (1404–1467), who led Christian forces against the Turks after the sultan, Amurath II, seized his ancestral lands.

15. *Treby:* Sir George Treby (1644?–1700), a prominent Whig lawyer, then recorder of London.

16. *Attorney General:* Sir William Jones (1631–1682), the prosecutor.

17. *ab improbabili/ab impossibili:* arguments from the improbable or impossible; rhetorical tropes.

18. *Delatores:* an accuser, informer (Latin).

where he had his Plate, kept his Table, and lived like an Epicure. Vaſt Rewards were publiſhed, by Proclamation, for farther Diſcoveries; which one would think muſt bring out Evidences enough: And the Generality of the People had not the leaſt Reflection on the Barbarity of ſuch a Proceeding, where Mens Lives are concerned. Paid Witneſſes ever were, and muſt be, odious and diſcreditable; but now few thought the Payments large enough, but rather that Swearing was ſlack for Want of more. I cannot reſolve the Spirit of indiſtinct Prejudice of the People, at that Time, into any Thing but the Artifice and Juggle of ſome devilliſh Cabal, that had the Government of a broad-ſpread confederated Party, who acted under Preſcriptions what to ſay and do, and thereby influenced others that underſtood them not, and thoſe yet others, wider and wider, ſome for Knavery, many out of Folly and meer Imitation and Credulity, and not a few for Malice and Humour, without any Reaſon at all. By which Means the Community ſwang, as it were, in a Body, wrapped up in the Imagination of ſomething they called *the Plot, killing the King, Prieſts and* Jeſuits, *&c.* All indiſtinct Images of they knew not what; and not without a good Share of Accident, as well as a ſingular Diſpoſition of the Times and Government: All which muſt be the Apologetic Account of the monſtrous Agitations of the Public at that Time. All which Matters, according to what I have before noted in this Relation, amount, as I think (to uſe a familiar Word of the Author's) to a *Demonſtration* of the Sort I may term *cui bono.* That the Generation, or rather Preſervation, of *the Plot* was the Deſtruction of poor *Godfrey.*　　19　20

CXXXI. I know it will be objected, that this is a heavy Charge of a foul Offence, that every one's Fancy will be apt to pitch upon ſome individual Perſon or Perſons, and perhaps wrongfully; which ought not to be left in that Latitude, without Evidence prefixed to accuſe ſome, and clear every one elſe; and, as may ſeem, the very Fault of the Author, who works ſo much by the Imagination of his Readers. But I muſt interpoſe this Difference; that he uſes Imagination to create the very Evil, where none, or rather the contrary, appears; and is free enough to name the Perſons, not ſparing Majeſty itſelf: As for Inſtance, ſtifling and ridiculing; horrid Sins indeed, in the Imagination of his prejudiced and ignorant Readers; and, at all Turns, charged flat and plain upon the King and his Loyal Subjects. But here I have the Evils broad, ſtaring with Saucer Eyes, and want no Imagination to create or augment them: But, ſince, for wicked Ends, they muſt be contrived and put forth by ſomebody, whom Subtilty, and perhaps Mortality have concealed, there is no Remedy but to aſſiſt the Imagination with Reaſons, if poſſible, to find them out; and every one is free to uſe his Faculties that Way, ſo long as no poſitive Charge is apertly made to the Prejudice of any one, by Name or Token, farther than real Evidence will carry it.　　21

Reaſonable to gueſs the Authors of bad Actions from the Nature of Things.

---

19. *Author's:* White Kennett's *Complete History of England,* vol. 3 (1706, rev. ed. 1719); the history which North's *Examen* is designed to impugn.
20. *cui bono:* for what good?
21. *apertly:* openly, publicly.

"The Proceedings Against William Staley" in Henry Care's
The History of the Damnable Popish Plot (1680)

The following is a narrative of the arrest and trial of William Staley, the first papist to die as a result of the plot, though his plotting consisted, at the most, of a few unwise words spoken in a tavern. The author, Henry Care, was an energetic propagandist for the exclusionist cause. This piece is a chapter from *The History of the Damnable Popish Plot* (1680), a work of 384 pages, plus an appendix listing the papists' plans for conquest. In its twenty-five chapters, Care describes the papists' eagerness to assassinate Protestant monarchs, beginning with the time of Queen Elizabeth.

CHAP. IX.

The Proceedings against William Staley, *Goldsmith, and his Execution for speaking Treasonable words.*

THE late Discovery had so *unexpectedly frustrated* the designs of the Papists, that being therewith *enraged*, they could hardly contain themselves within any bound of patience or moderation, but the Traiterous *Poison* which had long *rankled* in their *hearts*, began now to *blister* out at their *tongues*; and since they were prevented from *Acting*, they descended with a kind of Female malice, to vent their Resentments in talking and uttering lewd Expressions and *Menaces*. Of this kind of Traitors was *William Staley*, a *Goldsmith* in *Covent-Garden*, a Strict and Zealous Papist, bred beyond the Seas at one of the English *Seminaries*, intended for a Priest; in order to which, he took the degrees of a Deacon, as is related by those that well knew him, but afterwards altered his resolutions, and began to study Physick, in which Art he took his *Degree* in *Italy*; but coming home, and his other Brother being unhappily *Kill'd* by an Accident, he staid at home as an Assistant to his Father in the Shop, who had a great Trade, being much Entrusted with the Cash of the Roman Catholick Nobility and Gentry, who upon this notice taken of the Plot, *calling in* their money on a sudden, and he (as 'tis said) not being able readily
to

to make up his *Accounts* to his Father, and finding their *Trade* hereby like to be ruined, grew so far disturb'd, that on the 14th. of *Novemb.* in the Forenoon, being in the Company of one *Fromante*, a Foreigner, at a Cooks Shop in *Kings-Street*, by *Long-Acre*, discoursing together about the Plot, *&c.* in *French*, the said *Fromante* said that the King of *England* was a great *Tormenter of the People of God* (meaning the Papists) To which the said *Staley* Answered, *The King of* England, *the King of* England (repeating the words twice as in a great fury) *is a grand Heretick, and the greatest Rogue (Bouger* the word was in *French*) in the world: *There's the heart* (striking his hand on his Breast*) and here s the hand that will Kill him, my self:* And then he said further, *The King and Parliament think all is over, but the Rogues are deceived or mistaken.* When he spoke these words, he was in a Room with the door open, and just over against him in another Room on the same Floor, were three *Scotch Gentlemen*, of whom two understood *French*, who not only plainly heard, but as plainly saw him speak them; and being mightily concern'd to hear such desperate expressions, when he was going, enquired who he was, having never seen him before, and set one to watch him to his Fathers, where next day they apprehended him. And because there were a sort of men that endeavoured to cry down the Discovery as *fictitious*; alleadging, that although Roman Catholicks in *England* might endeavour to promote their Religion; yet it was nothing probable that they should have any design against the Kings *Person* : Therefore it was thought fit to bring this Man to Tryal first, before any of the

others in Cuſtody, thereby to convince thoſe people, that there was ſuch a deſign ; ſeeing the Priſoner even ſince the diſcovery of this Deviliſh Plot,
and after ſo many had been Impriſoned for it, did
perſiſt in a Treaſonable mind, and a Traiterous
attempt againſt the Kings Perſon ; a clear Evidence of which, was his ſpeaking ſuch words.

Accordingly for the ſame , on the 20th. of
Novemb. he was Arraigned at the *Kings-Bench Bar*,
and the 21th. brought to his Tryal, where a Jury
was Impannell'd ; and the Priſoner not making
any Challenge, they were Sworn, being all Perſons of good quality, *viz.*

Sir *Philip Matthews*,	*Simon Middleton*, Eſq;
Sir *Reginald Foſter*,	*Thomas Croſs* Eſq;
Sir *John Kirke*,	*Henry Johnſon*, Eſq;
Sir *John Cutler*,	*Charles Umfrevile*, Eſq;
Sir *Richard Blake*,	*Tho. Eaglesfield*, Eſq;
John Bifield, Eſq;	*William Bohee*, Eſq;

The Witneſſes, *William Corſtairs* and *Alexander
Sutherland*, did both poſitively Swear the words
before-cited, for they both underſtood *French* very
well, having been Officers abroad , and juſt then
returned into *England* : And the *third Witneſs*,
though he did not underſtand *French*, Swore he
heard the Priſoner ſpeak ſomething with great
earneſtneſs, and that Capt. *Corſtairs* at that inſtant
told him it was in Engliſh, *That he would Kill the
King* ; and was ſo fill'd with Indignation, that he
ſaid he would not endure to hear him uſe ſuch
Language , and therefore would have drawn his
Sword and run upon him preſently , but that
Mr. *Suthe-*

Mr. Satherland prevented him. They also proved that they writ down the words in *French*, as they were spoken and now sworn to, before they came out of the said Cooks. The Prisoner own'd that he was at that time with *Fromante* at that Cooks, but *denied* that he spoke the words, and said they only spoke of the *French* King, and that the words Sworn by the Witness in *French*, must signifie, *I will Kill my self*, rather than *I will Kill him my self*. But as to this the Court observ'd, First, that the Witnesses Swore directly that it was the King of *England* he spoke of, and nam'd him twice; nor did he sure count the *French* King an Heretick: And as for the Second, that evasion could not be allow'd; for what sense would it be to say, the King of *England* is a great Heretick, and the greatest Villain in the World, and therefore here's the hand, and here's the heart, *I will Kill my self*. The Prisoner had little more to say for himself, besides general Protestations of his Loyal Intentions. And therefore the Lord Chief Justice having repeated the proof to the Jury, they without going from the Bar, brought him in Guilty of Treason; and Sentence was pronounced on him to be Drawn, Hang'd, and Quartered.

On *Tuesday* the 26. of *Novemb.* he was Executed, behaving himself in his passage to *Tyburn* in a very sober penitent manner: His Quarters upon the humble Petition of his Relations, to his Majesty, were delivered to them privately to be Buried, and not to be set upon the Gates of the City: But to the great Indignity and Affront of such his Majesties

See an account of digging up his Quarters, Publish'd by Order of the Lord Chief Justice Scrogs.

K 3

mercy

ercy and favour, the Friends of the said *Staley* caused several *Masses to be said over his said Quarters*, and used other Ceremonies according to the manner of the Church of *Rome*, and Solemnly appointed a time for his Interment, from his Fathers House in *Covent-Garden*; at which time there was made a *Pompuous Funeral*, many People following the Corps to the Church of St. *Paul Covent-Garden*, where he was Buried; which his Majesty hearing of, was justly displeased, and Commanded the Coroner of *Westminster* to take up the Body of the said *Staley*, and deliver it to the Sheriff of *Middlesex* to be set upon the Gates. Accordingly it was taken up, and brought back to *Newgate*, and then the Quarters exposed on the Gates of the City, and the Head on *London-Bridge*, as the Limbs of Traitors usually are.

November the 27th. his Majesty emitted a Proclamation for the further discovery of the late horrid design against his Person and Government; whereby he declared, That if any person before the 25th. of *Decemb.* then next, should make any further Discovery to one of his Majesties Principal Secretaries of State, he or they should not only have and receive 200 *l.* immediately paid, but also his gracious *Pardon*, if a Principal or any way concern d in the Treason.

Gilbert Burnet's
History of My Own Time
on the Trials of Langhorn
and the Five Jesuits (June 13–14, 1679)

The following selection is a description of the plot trials of the five Jesuits—Whitebread, Fenwick, Harcourt, Gavan, and Turner—and of Richard Langhorn. The cases against them rested mainly upon the testimony of Oates; to refute him, witnesses were introduced from St. Omers to show that Oates had actually been in France during the previous summer when he claimed to be in London learning of the plot. But since these witnesses were all Catholics, their oaths were easily disregarded. However, even in the unsympathetic narrative by Bishop Gilbert Burnet, in his *History of My Own Time* (begun in 1683), one can sense the dignity of the defendants. Burnet's credulity was typical of the strong anti-Catholic prejudice shared even by intelligent Protestants.

The edition reproduced here is by Martin Joseph Routh, 6 vols. (Oxford, 1823), II, 215–19.

The king upon the prorogation of the parliament became sullen and thoughtful: he saw, he had to do with a strange sort of people, that could neither be managed nor frightened: and from that time his temper was observed to change very visibly. He saw the necessity of calling another parliament, and of preparing matters in order to it: therefore the prosecution of the plot was still carried on. So five of the Jesuits that had been accused of it were brought to their trial: they were Whitebread their provincial, Fenwick, Harcourt, Govan, and Turner. Oates repeated against them his former evidence: and they prepared a great defence against it: for sixteen persons came over from their house at St. Omers', who testified that Oates had staid among them all the while from December seventy-seven till June seventy-eight; so that he could not possibly be at London in the April between at those consultations, as he had sworn. They remembered this the more particularly, because he sat at the table by himself in the refectory, which made his being there to be the more observed; for as he was not mixed with the scholars, so neither was he admitted to the Jesuits' table. They said, he was among them every day, except one or two in which he was in the infirmary: they also testified, that some of those who he swore came over with him into England in April had staid all that summer in Flanders. In opposition to this, Oates had found out seven or eight persons who deposed that they saw him in England about the beginning of May; and that he being known formerly to them in a clergyman's habit, they had observed him so much the more by reason of that change of habit. With one of these he dined; and he had much discourse with him about his travels. An old Dominican friar, who was still of that church and order, swore also that he saw

him, and spoke frequently with him at that time:
by this the credit of the St. Omers' scholars was
quite blasted.   There was no reason to mistrust
those who had no interest in the matter, and swore
that they saw Oates about that time; whereas the
evidence given by scholars bred in the Jesuits' college, when it was to save some of their order, was
liable to a very just suspicion.   Bedlow now swore
against them all, not upon hearsay as before, but on 465
his own knowledge; and no regard was had to his
former oath mentioned in Ireland's trial.   Dugdale $\frac{1}{2}$
did likewise swear against some of them: one part
of his evidence seemed scarce credible.   He swore,
that Whitebread did in a letter that was directed to
himself, though intended for F. Evers, and that came
to him by the common post, and was signed by
Whitebread, desire him to find out men proper to
be made use of in killing the king, of what quality
soever they might be.   This did not look like the
cunning of Jesuits, in an age in which all people
made use either of ciphers or of some disguised
cant.   But the overthrowing the St. Omers' evidence
was now such an additional load on the Jesuits, that
the jury came quickly to a verdict; and they were
condemned.   At their execution they did with the
greatest solemnity, and the deepest imprecations possible, deny the whole evidence upon which they were
condemned: and protested, that they held no opinions either of the lawfulness of assassinating princes,
or of the pope's power of deposing them, and that
they counted all equivocation odious and sinful.   All
their speeches were very full of these heads.   Govan's was much laboured, and too rhetorical.   A very
zealous protestant, that went oft to see them in pri-

---

1. *former Oath:* Burnet gives an account earlier of Bedloe's perjury, as he offered
to change his testimony against the Jesuits; he adds: "the truth was he ought to have
been set aside from being a witness any more" (Burnet, II, 199).

2. *Dugdale:* Stephen Dugdale, one of the leading plot witnesses.

1679. son, told me, that they behaved themselves with great
decency, and with all the appearances both of innocence and devotion.

Langhorn, the lawyer, was tried next: he made
use of the St. Omers' scholars: but their evidence
seemed to be so baffled, that it served him in no
stead. He insisted next on some contradictions in
the several depositions that Oates had given at several trials: but he had no other evidence of that
besides the printed trials, which was no proof in
law. The judges said upon this, (that which is perhaps good in law, but yet does not satisfy a man's
mind,) that great difference was to be made between
a narrative upon oath, and an evidence given in
court. If a man was false in any one oath, there
seemed to be just reason to set him aside, as no
good witness. Langhorn likewise urged this, that it
was six weeks after Oates's first discovery before he
named him: whereas, if the commissions had been
lodged with him, he ought to have been seized on
and searched first of all. Bedlow swore, he saw him
enter some of Coleman's treasonable letters in a register, in which express mention was made of killing the king. He shewed the improbability of this,
3 that a man of his business could be set to register
letters. Yet all was of no use to him; for he was
cast. Great pains was taken to persuade him to
466 discover all he knew; and his execution was delayed for some weeks, in hopes that somewhat might
be drawn from him. He offered a discovery of the
estates and stock that the Jesuits had in England,
the secret of which was lodged with him: but he
protested, that he could make no other discovery;
and persisted in this to his death. He spent the

---

3. *be set to register:* go to work to record in a precise manner.

time, in which his execution was respited, in writ- 1679.
ing some very devout and well composed medita- And death.
tions. He was in all respects a very extraordinary 4
man : he was learned, and honest in his profession ;
but was out of measure bigoted in his religion. He
died with great constancy.

These executions, with the denials of all that suffered, made great impressions on many. Several
books were writ, to shew that lying for a good end
was not only thought lawful among them, but had
been often practised, particularly by some of those
who died for the gunpowder treason, denying those
very things which were afterwards not only fully
proved, but confessed by the persons concerned in
them : yet the behaviour and last words of those
who suffered made impressions which no books could
carry off.

Some months after this one Serjeant, a secular 5
priest, who had been always in ill terms with the
Jesuits, and was a zealous papist in his own way,
appeared before the council upon security given him;
and he averred, that Govan, the Jesuit, who died
protesting he had never thought it lawful to murder
kings, but had always detested it, had at his last
being in Flanders said to a very devout person, from
whom Serjeant had it, that he thought the queen
might lawfully take away the king's life for the in-
juries he had done her, but much more because he
was a heretic. Upon that Serjeant run out into
many particulars, to shew how little credit was due
to the protestations made by Jesuits even at their
death. This gave some credit to the tenderest part
of Oates's evidence with relation to the queen.

---

4. *meditations:* see Part Six (p. 171).
5. *Serjeant:* Father John Sergeant, a leading Catholic apologist and a Blackloist.
The Blackloists were a dissident group within the church.

Charles Blount's
An Appeal from the Country to the City (1679)

A violent example of anti-Catholic hysteria may be seen in Charles Blount's 29-page tract, *An Appeal from the Country to the City* (late 1679). It begins with a memorable vision of popish rapine, murder, and "another" burning of London. Blount's purpose is to refute the evidence that undermined the public's faith in the plot, to bolster the damaged reputations of the witnesses, and to support Monmouth's claim to the throne. In this latter purpose, his reasoning is suspiciously republican, for he admits that Monmouth is illegitimate and argues that "He who hath the worst Title, ever makes the best King" (p. 25). This is a more radical view than that taken in the following year by the supporters of the theory of the Black Box, which was rumored to contain evidence that the king had married Monmouth's mother. But the exclusionists never could agree on the issue of the Protestant succession.

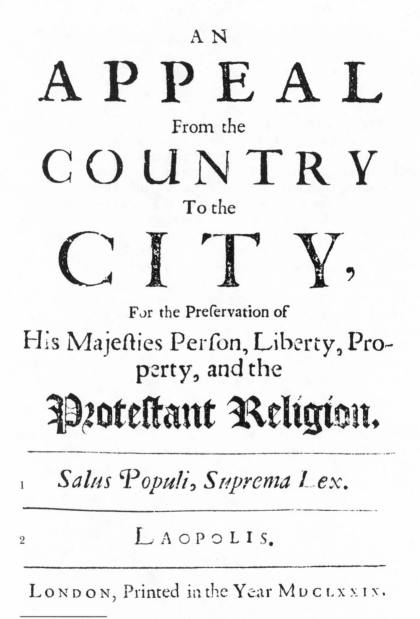

AN
APPEAL
From the
COUNTRY
To the
CITY,

For the Prefervation of

His Majefties Perfon, Liberty, Property, and the

𝕻𝖗𝖔𝖙𝖊𝖘𝖙𝖆𝖓𝖙 𝕽𝖊𝖑𝖎𝖌𝖎𝖔𝖓,

1 *Salus Populi, Suprema Lex.*

2 LAOPOLIS.

LONDON, Printed in the Year MDCLXXIX.

---

1. *Salus Populi, Suprema Lex:* the people's welfare is the highest law.
2. LAOPOLIS: perhaps an allusion to Laodicea, the ancient city described in Revelations 3:14–22 as a place where the people are lukewarm to religion; thus a city
(Greek: *polis*) of lukewarm Christians.

A N
A P P E A L

From the

COUNTRY to the CITY.

Moſt brave and noble Citizens,

AS the City of *London* is the great Metropolis and Soul of our once flouriſhing and glorious Kingdom, ſo is it no ſmall honour to you the Inhabitants thereof, to be Citizens of ſo brave a City. Wherefore 'tis the hopes of the whole Nation, that you have Spirits and Courage to act according to the Character you bear, that upon all neceſſary occaſions you may vindicate the juſt Concerns of your City: In them we are all involv'd; with you we ſtand, and with you we fall; your example directs our conduct; and they who deſire to lay you in aſhes, are the only perſons who would ſubvert our Religion and Property; for when you are once ruined, the next thing will be, *Up* Ahab, *and take poſſeſſion.*   3

Now Gentlemen, before we repreſent to you the eſtate of our miſery, and ground of our jealouſies and fears, 'tis our humble requeſt, that thoſe who have moſt Power amongſt you, would ſo far trouble themſelves, as to go to the top of your new rais'd Pyramid, and from thence take a Survey of that magnificent Pile of Building,

A 2   where-

---

3. *possession:* I Kings 21:15. The context is the story of Naboth's vineyard. See John Caryll's "Naboth's Vineyard" (p. 258).

whereof you are yet Master: In which posture, to ani-
mate you with true *English* Spirits, be pleas'd to fancy
to your selves these following Objects, which you will
infallibly see come to pass, when ever Popery prevails.

Firſt, Imagine you see the whole Town in a flame, occafioned this ſecond time, by the ſame Popiſh malice
4   which ſet it on fire before. At the ſame inſtant fancy,
that amongſt the diſtracted Crowd, you behold Troops
of Papiſts, raviſhing your Wives and your Daughters,
daſhing your little Childrens brains out againſt the walls,
plundering your Houſes, and cutting your own Throats,
by the name of Heretick Dogs. Then repreſent to your
ſelves the Tower playing off its Cannon, and battering
down your Houſes about your Ears. Alſo caſting your
5   eye towards *Smithfield,* imagine you ſee your Father, or
your Mother, or ſome of your neareſt and deareſt Rela
tions, tyed to a Stake in the midſt of flames, when with
hands and eyes lifted up to Heaven, they ſcream and cry
out to that God for whoſe Cauſe they die; which was a
6   frequent ſpectacle the laſt time Popery reign'd amongſt
us. Fancy you behold thoſe beautiful Churches erected
for the true Worſhip of God, abuſed and turn'd into
Idolatrous Temples, to the diſhonour of Chriſt, and ſcan-
dal of Religion; the Miniſters of God's holy Word torn
in pieces before your eyes, and their very beſt Friends
not daring even to ſpeak in their behalf: Your Trading's
bad, and in a manner loſt already; but then the only
Commodity will be Fire and Sword; the only object,
Women running with their hair about their ears, Men
cover'd with bloud, Children ſprawling under Horſes
feet, and only the walls of Houſes left ſtanding : When
thoſe that ſurvive this fatal day, may ſigh and cry, Here
once

---

4. *before:* the Great Fire of 1666.
  5. *Smithfield:* an area just northwest of London's medieval walls where, during
the sixteenth century, heretics were burned.
  6. *Popery reigned:* during the time of Queen Mary ("Bloody Mary"), 1554–1558.

once ftood my Houfe, there my Friend's, and here my
Kinfman's ; But alas that time is paft! The only noife
will then be, O my Wife, O my Husband, O my dear-
eft Children! In fine, what the Devil himfelf would do,
were he here upon Earth, will in his abfence infallibly be
acted by his Agents the Papifts ; thofe who had fo much
ingratitude and bafenefs to attempt the Life of a Prince
fo indulgent to them, will hardly be lefs cruel to any of
his Proteftant Subjects.

Wake drowfie Subjects, and prevent your doom,
Let England *not be twice enflav'd by* Rome.

If the approaching ruine of the Father could open the
dumb Son's mouth, then all that are either true Proteftants, good *Englifh*-men, or well-wifhers to the Intereft
of this Nation, have now the fame reafon to fpeak and
complain, when without a miracle our apparent ruine is
at hand, the Sword already hangs over our heads, and
feems to be fupported by no ftronger force than that of
one fingle hair, his Majefties Life. We in the Country
have done our parts, in choofing for the generality good
Members to ferve in Parliament ; but if (as our two laft
Parliaments were) they muft be diffolv'd or prorogu'd,
when ever they come to redrefs the Grievances of the
Subject, we may be pitied, but not blam'd. If the Plot
takes effect, (as in all probability it will) our Parliaments are not then to be condemn'd, for that their not
being fuffer'd to fit occafion'd it. The Plot is now got
fo far out of our Enemies reach, that no fubtil evafion or
trick can ever hope to extinguifh it ; wherefore they
muft either fuffer all to come out, or begin by force to
justifie

7

---

7. *dumb Son's mouth:* an Irish folktale.

juftifie it, which we fee they are going to do, by their
endeavouring to get thofe worthy and brave Comman-
8   ders banifh'd, who (as they think) are the moft likely
perfons to conduct and lead us up againft any Popifh Army ; the Wolf hath nothing more to do, but to deftroy
the Shepherd; and then fall upon the naked Sheep.   But
Gentlemen, be not difmaid, the Lord of Hofts will be
of your fides ; for fo long as you fight his Caufe, he will
fight your Battels ; and if God be for you, who dares
be againft you ? Fear nothing, but as your Interefts are
united, fo let your Refolutions be the fame ; and the
firft hour wherein you hear of the King's untimely end,
let no other noife be heard among you but that of Arm,
Arm, to revenge your Soveraign's Death, both upon
his Murtherers, and their whole Party, for that there is
no fuch thing as an *Englifh* Papift who is not in the Plot,
at leaft in his good wifhes.   Let not fear of lofing part
by your action, make you lofe the whole by your patience : Think not to fare better than the reft, by medling
lefs, for that Conquerours promifes are never kept, efpecially coming from that fort of people, whofe Maxim it
is, never to keep their words with Hereticks.   Wherefore if ever a Popifh Succeffor comes amongft you, let
his promifes of keeping your Religion and Laws, or of
his Converfion, be never fo plaufible, credit 'em not ;
for if you do, you will infallibly be deceiv'd, and in time
find them to be but like the Bait to a Moufe-trap.   Or
9   if you think to bind and fetter him by Laws, that will
10 be no better than the wife men of *Gotham*'s hedging in
the Cuckow ; for when he (as all other Popifh Kings
do) governs by an Army, what will all your Laws fignifie ? You will not then have Parliaments to appeal to ;
                                                    He

---

8. *banish'd:* the army was being disbanded in 1679.

9. *Laws:* the compromise, supported by Lord Halifax, to allow York to succeed
to the throne but to limit his powers by statute.

10. *Gotham:* the men of Gotham were proverbially foolish—one example of their
folly was an effort to hedge in a cuckoo which was perched on an old bush.

He and his Council will levy his arbitrary Taxes, and his
Army fhall gather them for him : Therefore you may
much eafier prevent the Diftemper at firft, than remedy
it when it has once got a head.   Now Gentlemen, left
any amongft you fhould be ignorant either of your Enemies, or their Defigns both againft the King and Kingdom, be pleas'd to confider what follows, and then think
how to prevent it.

I.

Firft then, That you may know who are your Enemies at this time : They are young beggarly Officers,
Courtiers, over-hot Church-men, and Papifts.   The
young Officer or Souldier his Intereft makes him wifh
for a ftanding Army, not confidering any further than
his own Pay and Plunder, and fo helps to ruine you that
way.   The Courtier endeavours to advance Taxes, op-
prefs the people by vaft and illegal Impofitions, when
looking upon his Prince but as his Ox, he fattens him
upon his Neighbours Pafture, only for his own eating.
Over-hot Church-men are bribed to wifh well to Popery, by the hopes (if not of a Cardinal's Cap) yet at leaft
of a Command over fome Abbey, Priory, or other Ec-
clefiaftick preferment, whereof the *Roman* Church hath
fo great plenty.   Thefe are the men who exclaim againft
our Parliaments Proceedings, in relation to the Plot, as
too violent, calling thefe Times by no other Name but
that of 40 or 41. when to amufe as well his Sacred Ma- 11
jefty as his good People, they again threaten us with
another 48. and all this is done to vindicate under-hand 12
the Catholick Party, by throwing a fufpicion on the Fanaticks.   Thefe are the Gentlemen, who fo magnifie the 13
Principles of Bifhop *Laud*, and fo much extol the Wri- 14
tings

---

11. *40 or 41:* the years in which the rebellion against Charles I began.
12. *48:* the execution of Charles I, January 30, 1648 (Old Style—with the new
year beginning March 25).
13. *Fanaticks:* dissenting Protestant sects; cf. L'Estrange's *A Further Discovery of
the Plot* (p. 186).
14. *Laud:* William Laud, archbishop of Canterbury from 1633 to 1645; known
for his attempts to suppress dissenting sects.

15 tings of the late fame fpirited Prelate Dr. *Heylin*, who
hath made more Papifts by his Books, than Chriftians
16 by his Sermons. Thefe are thofe Epifcopal Tantivies,
who make even the very Scriptures Pimp for the Court,
17 who out of *Urim* and *Thummim* can extort a Sermon,
to prove the not paying of Tithes and Taxes to be the
Sin againft the holy Ghoft, and had rather fee the Kingdom run down with blood, than part with the leaft hem
of a confecrated Frock, which they themfelves made
holy. Thefe are the perfons who commend *Oates* and
Bedlow, but yet find fault with their Evidence, when
by crediting fome part of the Plot, and fufpecting the
reft, by fpeaking three words for it, and two againft
it, they cunningly endeavour to invalidate the whole.
Laftly, The chief and moft dangerous of your Enemies
are Papifts, who to make fure of their own Game, allure
all the three fore-mention'd Parties to their fide, by the
Arguments aforefaid. Their defign is to bring in Popery, which they can no ways effect, but either by a Popifh Succeffor, or by the *French* Arms : The firft of thefe
we may our felves prevent ; and for the latter, if they
conquer, they will undoubtedly conquer for themfelves,
and not for him that brought them in. And if we ever
fhould be reduced to that extremity, either to fubmit
to the *French*, or to our own Popifh Succeffor, every
man that hath any brains or generofity, will foon find
it his intereft of the two, rather to fubmit to a foreign
Power, who hath not violated the Laws of Nature, in
fighting againft his own Subjects, and who will alfo be
lefs revengeful, and more likely to let us enjoy our own
Religion and Liberties, than any Popifh Succeffor will :
Befides , 'tis natural for every noble Spirit, to bear a
Cud.

---

15. *Dr. Heylin:* Peter Heylyn (1600–1662), an anti-Puritan prelate, controversialist, and supporter of Laud.
16. *Tantivies:* a nickname for high churchmen and Tories, based on a cartoon
of such men riding "tantivy" (at full gallop) behind the duke of York.
17. *Urim and Thummin:* mysterious objects adorning the breastplate of the Jewish
high priest, by which means Jehovah's will was held to be declared.

Cudgelling from another man's Servant with lefs regret, than from his own ; however, God deliver us from
both.

I I.

In the next place, to difcover to you how long this
Plot hath been on foot ; I muft acknowledge, that there
is fome coherence between the beginning of the late
Civil Wars, and this our prefent Age ; for as well then,
as now, the ambitious *Popiſh* and *French* Faction were
the chief, nay the only Incendiaries which fet us all in a
Flame ; the *Catholick Caufe*, like the Chefnut in the Fable, hath ever fince Queen *Maries* Reign been in the   18
Fire : wherefore as the Fox made ufe of the Ape's, fo
both then and now the *Papiſts* make ufe of the *Epiſcopal*
and *Court*-Parties claw, to take it out ; the firft of thefe
they allure to their affiftance, by the fright of *Presbytery* ; 19
the latter, by the apprehenfion of a *Republick* : although
nothing is lefs defign'd, or more improbable. Secretary
Windebank's many Orders (which ftand recorded at this   20
day) to fecure the *Roman Catholicks* from the execution
of all Penal Laws againft them, in the late King's time,
are a fufficient evidence, that they then received no lefs
countenance, than now : and for that vain pretence of
their Loyalty to the late King, nothing will appear more
ridiculous, if we confider, 1. That they had no other
Party to expect any advantage from, for that no Government but Monarchy, can in *England* ever fupport
or favour that Religion ; neither (notwithftanding their
many offers) could they ever be entertain'd or received
by the Parliament-Party, unlefs 'twas under a difguife,
which many for that purpofe made ufe of : So as their
Loyalty and good Service paid to the King, was merely
B   in

---

18. *Fable:* a fox uses an ape's paw to scrape hot chestnuts out of a fire; other
animals were often substituted; e.g., an ape uses a cat's claw, etc.

19. *Presbytery:* the anti-episcopal views of Presbyterians threatened the Anglican
Church's hierarchy.

20. *Windebank:* Sir Francis Windebank (1582–1646), an Anglo-Catholic secretary of state from 1632 to 1640.

in their own defence, well knowing, that the foundation of thofe Commotions, was only in oppofition to their Party : who as well then, as now, had a defire to run the hazard of a War. 2ly. and laftly, Their Fidelity to their Soveraign appear'd in its true colours, when
21 they were fo earneft with *Oliver* to accept of the Crown ; which fhew'd, that fince nothing but a Crown'd Head could do good to the *Popifh Religion*, they did not care who wore it, fo long as it was but worn. Now in acquainting you herewith, I do in effect fhew you what is at this time acting amongft them, for 'tis the fame Play, though an old one newly revived: and as that which the *Papifts* then acted, was laid upon the *Fanaticks*, fo was the like to have been done in this prefent Plot ; in order whereunto, juft before the difcovery of the fame, they had feiz'd upon, and imprifon'd one
22 Mr. *Claypole*, for having (as they pretended) a defign to murder His Sacred Majefty ; thinking, when it was once reported abroad, that he and the Old *Oliverian* Party had a Confpiracy to take away the King's Life, then in the mean while the *Papifts* themfelves might fafely do it, (as we fee they had at that time, *viz.*
23 *Auguft* 1678. refolv'd upon) and that then it would all have gone upon the *Non-Conformifts* fcore ; for however there was never any perfon living more generous and obliging to the King's whole Party, than this very man the Lord *Claypole* was, when he bore that Honour ; yet he having married *Oliver Cromwell's* Daughter, rendred him a fit fubject to put this trick upon : which by Dr. *Oates's* difcovery of the Plot, came to light, the Evidence againft him vanifh'd, and the poor Gentleman releas'd. Much fuch another defign was that of the
Papifts

---

21. *Oliver:* Cromwell was offered the crown in 1657 but refused.

22. *Claypole:* John Claypole, Cromwell's son-in-law, was arrested on July 19, 1678, for speaking of assassinating the king and York at Newmarket.

23. *August 1678:* the time of the Jesuit Consult according to Oates's *Narrative.*

Papists in *Scotland,* who firſt by their Counſels procured 24
the poor Inhabitants to be oppreſſed, and then ſending
their diſguis'd Prieſts and Emiſſaries amongſt them, encouraged the poor ſilly Natives to Mutiny againſt thoſe
oppreſſions, hoping yet by this ſecond Stratagem to caſt
the Plot upon the *Presbyterians :* for no only Dr. *Oates*
mentions this in his Evidence, but we all know the
Papists themſelves were ſo well aſſur'd of this Riſing,
before it happen'd, that at the disbanding of this late
Popiſh Army, many of the Officers and Souldiers had
ſecret orders not to ſell their Horſes, but to be in a readineſs, for that they ſhould have occaſion to uſe them
again within a fortnight ; and ſo it happen'd, for within leſs than a fortnight after the disbanding, the Rebellion broke out in *Scotland :* So well acquainted were
the Authors of this miſchief, with the time when it
would happen. Now this Inſurrection was in two re-
ſpects advantageous to the *Catholick Party* ; for firſt,
among Foreigners and Strangers who were not acquainted with the depth of their Intrigues, it ſeem'd to caſt
the Plot upon the *Non-Conformiſts* ; and 2ly. being
beaten by the King's Forces, (whereof no other was 25
to be expected) it might make both them and us
leſs apt to riſe upon any account whatſoever. But
here give me leave to preſent you with one obſervation, which is, that if this had been a Fanatical Plot,
the ſame Party would certainly have riſen in *England,* at the ſame time when their Brethren of *Sco-
land* were in Arms, the encouraging of one another
being of more conſequence to both, than the expectation of the others ſucceſs.

B 2　　　　　　　　III.

---

24. *Scotland:* the Covenanters' (Presbyterians) Rebellion began in May 1679.
25. *King's Forces:* the royal army under Monmouth defeated the rebels at Bothwell Bridge on June 22, 1679.

PART FOUR

The Plot Trial: The Case of
Sir George Wakeman

The Trial of Sir George Wakeman
(July 18, 1679)

The summer of 1679 was the plot's worst period of judicial bloodletting. Between the beginning of June and the end of August, fourteen Roman Catholics were executed as traitors. This meant that they were taken from the noose and disemboweled and quartered while still alive. Each conviction contributed to the atmosphere that made the next possible, and other events contributed as well. A rebellion broke out in Scotland among the Covenanters, and the duke of Monmouth had to be sent with an army to suppress it. In August, the king became seriously ill, making the succession a matter of such immediate concern that both York and Monmouth returned from exile in foreign lands to protect their interests. Though Parliament had been prorogued to prevent its passing the Exclusion Bill, the situation, especially in London, remained tense.

In many ways, the trial of Sir George Wakeman, the queen's physician, on July 18, 1679, was typical of the trials for treason during this difficult summer. Its format was, of course, representative: the accused was allowed no defense counsel, the judges acted as advocates for the government's case and spoke out freely to the prejudice of the defendant, and the entire trial was compressed into one day, even if that meant that meals had to be delayed well into the night. Witnesses not available on that day were not considered. The evidence in this instance was typical as well; the charges were based mainly upon the testimony of the two central plot witnesses, Titus Oates and William Bedloe. They accused Wakeman of taking a large bribe to poison the king. Three Benedictine monks, William Marshall, William Rumley, and James Corker, were tried with him as fellow conspirators. The trial was held at the Sessions House of the Old Bailey in London. Sir Robert Sawyer acted as chief prosecution counsel, and Sir William Scroggs, the lord chief justice of the King's Bench (the highest criminal court) presided, along with Justices Sir Francis Pemberton, Sir Edward Atkins, and the lord chief justice of Common Pleas, Sir Francis North.

Yet fundamentally this trial was unusual. It was, as Burnet wrote, "the Queen's trial," for Wakeman's close connection to the queen meant that a guilty verdict would implicate her. Eight months earlier, Oates had accused her before the House of Commons, but the result had been a setback for him. Even in those passionate times, no one believed that Queen Catherine could be guilty. She had established her reputation securely, and the king, though he was unfaithful to her, refused to see her injured. As the trial of Wakeman approached, Charles summoned the chief witnesses to the Privy Council to ask if they had any new information against the queen. They prudently replied that they did not. These preparations help to account for the most remarkable feature of this trial—the defendants were acquitted.

This outcome was a signal defeat for the exclusionists, and their anger at Scroggs was intense; it soon found expression in angry satires and in an effort to have him removed from the bench. After that failed, the House of Commons voted to impeach him, in January 1681, but he never came to trial owing to Parliament's dissolution soon afterward. Wakeman fled the country after the trial, allowing the exclusionist press to picture him as acknowledging his guilt. Two other defendants, Corker and Marshall, were arrested again and tried with five other priests on January 17, 1680 for the crime of being priests (high treason by law); this time they were found guilty and sentenced to death, though none was actually executed. In spite of all the exclusionists could do, the point remained that their witnesses had been badly tarnished by Wakeman's trial, for their words had not been believed.

The excerpts given here, taken from fifty well-filled pages in *State Trials* (1816, vol. 7) are based upon one of the contemporary reports taken privately during most such trials and published soon afterwards. The first selection shows Oates's charges, the trial's only reference to the queen, and Wakeman's strong, confident cross-examination.

1 Sir *R. Sawyer.* But now, gentlemen, it will behove you to take notes, for we shall come home to you, and we begin with Dr. Oates. [Who stood up.]

2 Mr. *Ward.* Pray, Sir, will you tell your whole knowledge of this matter, and apply yourself as near as you can to every one of the prisoners at the bar?

Oates. My lord, in the month of July Mr.
3 Ashby came to town sick, and being sick, and one of the society, the prisoner at the bar, sir George Wakeman, was his physician, and being his physician he did write him some instructions how he should order himself before he went, and at the Bath; That he should, in the first place, take a pint of milk in the morning, and a pint of milk at night, and should drink no morning's draughts but milk, and that he should have one hundred strokes at the bath, at the pump; I do not so well understand what that means, but I suppose the court doth; but these were the words of the instructions: In this letter sir George Wakeman did write, that the queen would assist him to poison the king, and this letter was brought by a messenger to Mr. Ashby. Within a day or two after I saw Mr. Ashby and sir George Wakeman, the prisoner at the bar (he was so called, but I had no acquaintance with him, but just the sight of him) I saw him sit in a writing posture, I saw him lay by his pen, rise up and go away, and the same hand that he left behind him in a paper where the ink was not dry, was the same hand that writ the letter to Mr. Ashby. And, my lord, in that time of converse, while he was writing this, Mr. Ashby did give him some instructions concerning the commission he had received of being physician to the army. Now, my lord, in some few days after there came a gentleman for some of the Fathers from Wild-House, that had the title either of sir Richard or sir Robert, but he was a middle statured man, and a brisk man, about the age of four or five and forty, and he came with commands from the queen for the Fathers to wait upon her at Somerset-House, and I did wait upon these Fathers, there was Father Harcourt, Father Kaines, Father Langworth, and Father Fenwick, and another Father, I cannot remember his name. And, may it ple se your lordship, we did attend at Somerset-House, and the Fathers went in to the queen, into a chamber where she was, and I waited in an anti-chamber, and I did hear a woman's voice

which did say, that she would assist them in the propagation of the Catholic religion with her estate, and that she would not endure these violations of her bed any longer, and that she would assist sir George Wakeman in the poisoning of the king. Now, my lord, when they came out I desired that I might see the queen, and so when I came in I had, as I believe, from her a gracious smile. Now, if it pleases your lordship, while that I was within I heard the same voice speak thus to Father Harcourt, and asked him, whether he had received the last 1,000*l.* and it was the same tongue, as I can possibly guess, the same voice which I heard when I was without; and I saw no other woman there but the queen, and there were these Fathers. My lord, in that very month of July, sir G. Wakeman was proposed 10,000*l.* in the presence of Father Harcourt, and Father Fenwick, I think was there, and Father Ireland.

L. C. J. Were you there? 4

Oates. I was there. 5

L. C. J. Was this proposal made to sir G. Wakeman after this discourse you heard at Somerset-House?

Oates. My lord, I will not be positive whether it was before or after, but it was near that time this 10,000*l.* he did refuse.

L. C. J. But you say you heard the 10,000*l.* was proffered him; pray, who did propose it to him?—*Oates.* Ashby was to do it.

L. C. J. But who did it?

Oates. It was Ashby in the name of the provincial, from whom he had received instructions so to do.

L. C. J. But you say, in your hearing 10,000*l.* was offered him by Ashby.

Oates. Yes, my lord.

L. C. J. What said he?

Oates. He refused it.

L. C. J. What words did he use?

Oates. He said it was too little.

L. C. J. What was the 10,000*l.* to be given for?—*Oates.* To poison the king.

L. C. J. Were those the words?

Oates. Yes, they were.

L. C. J. How did the discourse begin?

Oates. I will tell your lordship how: There was a meeting of the Fathers for this very purpose to treat with sir G. Wakeman before Ashby went to the Bath, and there being a meeting they did break this business to him; but what preamble they made to it I cannot remember. My lord, as for the other prisoners at the bar, Mr. Corker——

L. C. J. But before you go from this matter, you say you know not how they brought it in, but they brought it in some way, he was to meet them to that purpose, and there Ashby did tell him he should have 10,000*l.*; what answer made he to it?

Oates. He said it was too little for so great a work.

L. C. J. Is that all?

Oates. That is all that I remember.

L. C. J. Did he say what he would have?

---

1. *Sir R. Sawyer*: Sir Robert Sawyer, chief prosecution counsel.

2. *Mr. Ward:* Edward Ward, a prosecution counsel.

3. *Mr. Ashby:* Father Richard Ashby, a Jesuit. Also called Thimbleby—see p. 107 of the trial.

4. *Harcourt, Fenwick, Ireland:* by this time all three had been convicted for the plot and executed.

5. *L. C. J.:* Lord Chief Justice Sir William Scroggs.

Oates. I can't remember that, but he said that was too little.

L. C. J. Did he say he would have five more, or any other sum?

Oates. No, that was not then mentioned; but there were letters presently dispatched to Whitebread to tell him, that sir G. Wakeman had refused 10,000*l.* and then this same Whitebread did order the Fathers in London to propose five more, which proposal was made to sir G. Wakeman. This I speak but by hearsay, and it was accepted, and 5,000*l.* of it received in part, and sir G. Wakeman's name was subscribed to the Entry-book.

L. C. J. Did you see his name subscribed?

Oates. Yes, my lord. I did.

L. C. J. Where?—*Oates.* To the Entry-book.

L. C. J. Where was that book kept?

Oates. It was the book that the Jesuits kept: it was then in our custody.

L. C. J. Whose custody?

Oates. The Fathers custody.

L. C. J. Whose particularly? and at whose chamber was it kept?

Oates. At Wild-house.

Sir *Rob. Sawyer.* Do you know who was the keeper of it?

Oates. I cannot positively say that, I suppose the secretary and the Fathers.

Sir *Rob. Sawyer.* And what did you see writ in that book?

Oates. That such a day, (which day I cannot remember) but such a day in August so much was proposed to sir G. Wakeman, and he accepted it, and received it: those were the words, or to that purpose.

L. C. J. Were those the words writ in the book?

Oates. Yes, or to that purpose.

L. C. J. Do you know whose hand writ that?

Oates. Yes, my lord, I can tell whose hand, it was Father Harcourt writ those words.

L. C. J. Sir G. Wakeman's hand was not to it, was it?

Oates. Yes, it was just underneath: Received so much money of Father Harcourt by the order of Edward Coleman: now there was the goldsmith's name to it, I cannot undertake to say who it was, but in my conscience I think it was Staley.*

L. C. J. How much was the money?

Oates. Five thousand pounds.

L. C. J. Was sir G. Wakeman's hand subscribed to that receipt?

Oates. Yes, it was.

L. C. J. Once more, what were the words in the book?

Oates. Memorandum. Such a day 15,000*l.* was proposed to sir G. Wakeman which he accepted. I tell you the purport, and the words as near as I can.

L. C. J. Was it said for what the money was proposed.

* See his Case, *ante,* vol. 6. p. 1502.

Oates. I will not be positive in that, I suppose it was.

L. C. J. But you say it was written such a day 15,000*l.* was proposed to sir G. Wakeman, and by him accepted?

Oates. Yes, my lord, and then underneath it the receipt was written, and this receipt was written thus, " Received in part of this " 15,000*l.* 5,000*l.* of Father Harcourt by order " of Edward Coleman.   Geo. Wakeman."

L. C. J. Was the receipt, which is said such a day, the same day with the other?

Oates. There was no other date to it.

L. C. J. Had the first a date to it?

Oates. Yes, my lord, it had.

L. C. J. What day was it?

Oates. It was in August?

Corker. What day in August?

Oates. I cannot tell.

Corker. About what time in August?

Oates. It might be betwixt the beginning and the middle.

L. C. J. But we will suppose for the present question a day: Suppose it was written the 10th of August, " There was proposed 15,000*l.* " to Sir G. Wakeman and by him accepted," and then comes afterwards this note, " Received " then 5,000*l.* in part of this 15,000*l.*" with his name to it. Was there any other date to that?

Oates. No, that was set down at the same day, " Received 5,000*l.* in part by the order of " Edward Coleman."

L. C. J. And then sir G. Wakeman's name was set to it at length, was it?

Oates. Yes, it was.

Sir *G. Wakeman.* Where was that received? In whose chamber?

Oates. I cannot say that.

L. C. J. Was there any place mentioned in the note where it should be received?

Oates. No, my lord. I was then sick of the stone, and was not at the payment of the money.

L. C. J. But did the note mention any name? Received of any body?

Oates. It was by order of Mr. Edward Coleman 5,000*l.* in part of this 15,000*l.*

Sir *Geo. Wakeman.* Does he say this was in the entry-book?

Oates. Yes, it was.

Sir *Geo. Wakeman.* Where was that kept?

Oates. Sometimes at Wild-House, sometimes Mr. Langhorn had the custody of it.

Sir *Geo. Wakeman.* I humbly beg of the Court that Mr. Staley may be sent for.

L. C. J. He only says he believes Mr. Staley paid it.

Sir *Geo. Wakeman.* Does he mention no place where it was received?

L. C. J. No.

Sir *Geo. Wakeman.* Nor no person it was paid to?

L. C. J. No, he says, All I saw is this, that in the entry-book sometimes kept at Wild-House, sometimes by Mr. Langhorn, there was written, ' This Day' (which was some day in

6. *Whitebread:* the Jesuit provincial, executed June 20, 1679; see Oates's *Narrative.*

7. *Staley:* the father of William Staley, the young man who was executed for treasonable words (and whose case is recorded in volume 6 of *State Trials*). See the Introduction, p. 2 of this volume.

8. *Langhorn:* Richard Langhorn, the Catholic lawyer executed four days earlier.

August) ' was proposed to sir G. W. 15,000*l.* ' and by him accepted,' and under that a line or two more, which contained, ' Then received ' 5,000*l.* by order of Edward Coleman, being ' part of this 15,000*l.*   Geo. Wakeman.'

Sir *Geo. Wakeman.* Will your lordship please to give me leave to speak something now, I may forget it hereafter.

Mr. *Ward.* We have not done yet.

Just. *Pemberton.* Sir George, they have not yet done with this witness for the king.

L. C. J. *North.* Take a Memorandum of it in your paper.

Sir *R. Sawyer.* Pray, what do you know more of the prisoner at the bar, sir George Wakeman?

Oates. This is all I can recollect at present.

Sir *R. Sawyer.* Do you know any thing of any commission that he had?

Oates. I did urge that he received a commission to be physician-general of the army.

L. C. J. Did you see that commission?

Oates. Yes, I saw it in sir George Wakeman's hands.

L. C. J. Had you seen it before?

Oates. Yes, I had.

L. C. J. Where did you see it in his hand?

Oates. When he was writing at Mr. Ashby's.

L. C. J. What note was that he left behind him there?

Oates. It was an apothecary's bill, as I suppose.

L. C. J. What month was it that you saw the commission?

Oates. It was in July.

Mr. *Ward.* What do you know of his being privy to the consult in April?

Oates. I cannot speak any thing to that.

L. C. J. Did he write his name to that bill?

Oates. I cannot say that, my lord, it was finished, but I cannot be positive about the name.

L. C. J. But you say, that you believe that the name of George Wakeman was the same hand with that you saw when he writ the apothecary's bill?

Oates. It was, as near as I can guess, the same with that letter that was writ to Ashby, wherein he does direct him to take a pint of milk in the morning, and a pint of milk in the evening, and that he should have an hundred strokes at the Bath: And this hand was the same with that of the apothecary's bill.

L. C. J. You never saw sir George Wakeman write in your life, did you?

Oates. I saw him in a writing posture, and I saw him lay by the pen.

L. C. J. But you did not see him write?

Oates. No, my lord; but the gentleman that sat by him was lame of both his hands and could not write: And I saw him lay by the pen, and when he was gone away the ink was not dry.

L. C. J. You speak of that only to shew the likeness of the hand.

Sir *Geo. Wakeman.* Have you not said that you do not know my hand?

Oates. I have told the Court before how far

I have known your hand. I saw a letter, that I say was signed and subscribed George Wakeman, and that was the same hand that was to the receipt, and to the apothecary's bill.

Sir *Geo. Wakeman.* Have you not said positively that you do not know it, and is not that matter on record?

Oates. I did see a letter subscribed George Wakeman, it is a fine genteel hand, and after I saw him in a writing posture, I saw him lay by the pen, the ink and paper was wet; I did not indeed see him write, but there was nobody in the room that could write, or in a writing posture but he, for the other gentleman was lame of both hands.

Sir *Geo. Wakeman.* But I pray give a positive answer to what I ask you; have you not said you do not know my hand?

Oates. I do not remember I have said so.

Just. *Pemberton.* But he says now he believes that hand that writ the letter to Ashby, and the bill that he saw green, when nobody was by that could write but you, were the same.

Sir *G. Wakeman.* Have not you said, before the king and council, that you never saw me in all your life, and that you did not know me?

Oates. My lord, you may be pleased to know, when I saw sir George Wakeman at the council I had been up two nights together, and the king was willing once to excuse me from staying any further examination, and being so ill and indisposed for want of rest, in respect both of my intellectuals, and every thing else, I might not charge him so home; but now I have a proper light whereby I may see a man's face, I can say more to him.

Sir *Geo. Wakeman.* This is just Coleman's Case, the light was in your eyes.

Oates. This is the same gentleman: I desire he may propose his questions to the Court.

L. C. J. This is his question, whether you did say before the king and council, you did not know sir George Wakeman?

Oates. I do not remember whether I did or did not. I saw one called sir G. Wakeman, and this is that man; but I will not say, this was the man that was before the council when I was there.

Just. *Pemberton.* Did you see the commission in this man's hand?

Oates. Yes, I did.

L. C. J. Did you know this gentleman before he was at the council?

Oates. I saw this gentleman with Mr. Ashby, and he cannot deny it.

Sir *G. Wakeman.* Cannot deny it! Yes. I hope you will be able to prove it. You said you never saw me in your life, before you saw me at the Council.

L. C. J. Did you ever see him more than once?

Oates. Yes, twice in Mr. Ashby's chamber.

L. C. J. What, two several days.

Oates. Yes, two several days.

Just. *Pemberton.* Where was it that you saw him when the writing you say was green that he left behind him?

4

Oates. It was at Mr. Ashby's chamber.

L. C. J. You never saw him before that, did you?

Oates. No.

L. C. J. How often after?

Oates. But once after that.

L. C. J. Was that at the council?

Oates. No.

L. C. J. Look you what he says, he never saw you but twice before he saw you at the Council.

Oates. I saw you when the 10,000*l.* was proposed to you.

Sir G. Wakeman. Where was that?

Oates. At Wild-House.

Sir G. Wakeman. Did Mr. Ashby lie there?

Oates. He did lie there, because the provincial was beyond sea, and he came up to London in order to go to the bath.

Sir G. Wakeman. What day was that proposal made to me?

Oates. It was before Mr. Ashby went to the Bath.

Sir G. Wakeman. In what month?

Oates. In the month of July.

Sir G. Wakeman. By whom? By Mr. Ashby?

Oates. Yes.

Sir G. Wakeman. In the presence of whom?

Oates. Father Harcourt, Father Ireland, and Father Fenwick.

Sir G. Wakeman. You will be sure to name those that can be neither witnesses for me nor against me.

L. C. J. Who can help that?

Oates. I reckon up such as you did keep company with.

L. C. J. Do you know when Mr. Ashby went to the bath?

Oates. The latter end of July, or the beginning of August, as I remember. And this was before he went: he stayed but fourteen or sixteen days, as I remember, in town.

L. C. J. He says he saw you but twice, once when you writ that note, and the second time when the proposal was made to you.

Sir G. Wakeman. And you know all these things, at that time when I was examined before the king and council? Turn this way and answer me.

Oates. I am not bound to answer that question.

L. C. J. But you must answer his questions, if they be lawful.

Sir G. Wakeman. I say, I ask him, whether he knew all these things before that time I was examined before the king and council?

L. C. J. That must needs be, for all these things were done before.

Sir G. Wakeman. Then I ask him this question, why did you say before the king and council, that you knew nothing of me, but concerning one letter that was writ from Mr. Ashby to Mr. Fenwick? I shall prove this upon you; but, my lord, let me observe this, can any one believe, that if such evidence had been given in to the king and council, against me, as he now speaks of, that I should not have

VOL. VII.

been immediately taken into custody, but that I should have my liberty so long as I had?

L. C. J. I will tell you, Sir George, you will do very well and properly to call up your witnesses by and by, when you come to make your defence, and to prove what he said at the council-table. Pray, Dr. Oates, what was the reason you did not give the same evidence then you do now?

Oates. I can, by and by, give an answer to it, when it is proved by him what I did say. As to Mr. Corker, I say this, he had a patent from the See of Rome, to be bishop of London, and Mr. Corker was privy and consented to a proposal that was made by Langhorn to the Benedictine monks, whereof he is one. And these Benedictine monks did contribute 6,000*l.* to the society of the Jesuits, in order to be carrying on of this design. And Mr. Corker, though he did deny before some justices of the peace, that he did go out of the kingdom, yet he did go over to Lampspring in Germany, and staid there some short time, and he did write a letter, but whether it was dated from Lampspring in Germany, or no, I cannot tell, because there was only the date of the month, but not of the place from whence it came, but the latter end of August, it was, and therein he wrote, that he did consent to the proposal, for the raising of the said 6,000*l.* for he is president of the Benedictine monks, and therefore it was necessary that he should give the suffrage, and he had been with Father Le Chaise and the   9
English monks in Paris, and had given an account what prospect of affairs he had in England, and how the design went on.

L. C. J. Was this in a letter?

Oates. Yes, it was.

L. C. J. To whom was that letter directed?

Oates. It was directed either to Father Hitchcot, or to Father Howard, then in London.

L. C. J. You saw the letter?

Oates. Yes, I saw the letter.

L. C. J. Were you acquainted with his hand writing?

Oates. I will shew you how far I might be acquainted with his hand. My Lord, this gentleman, as I think, went away in July, as near as I can remember, I will not be positive in the time he went over; but in the month of June I saw this gentleman with Mr. Fenwick, and he had given him an account either of some friend or kinsman of his at St. Omers, that had not had his pension paid, and Mr. Corker did give a note under his hand, to Mr. Fenwick, where to take up so much money, and the money was to be received of Mr. Langhorn.

L. C. J. How much was that money?

Oates. It was about 20 or 25*l.* and he subscribed his name to it, James Corker; for that is his name, though he is indicted, I know not how, by the name of Anthony: And I have a summons to give evidence against Anthony Corker.

L. C. J. He is indicted by the name of James.

---

9. *Le Chaise:* Louis XIV's confessor; see note above (p. 34) and Coleman's letter to him printed in this collection.

This passage concerns the testimony of Bedloe, who—when prompted—provided accusations that disconcerted Wakeman, and the evidence of the Bath apothecary Chapman.

no more than what is true upon any man whatever. I would be loth to keep out Pop' ry by that way they would bring it in, that is by blood or violence : I would have all things go very fair; Pray what, upon your oath, was the first part of sir G. Wakeman's discourse with Harcourt when they met?

L. C. J. North. Relate again your whole knowledge concerning sir G. Wakeman, and the Bill of Exchange, and the discourse after it, because we are now upon the consideration of it, what effect it will have upon him.

Bedlow. My lord, I was with Harcourt in the chamber, and sir George Wakeman came in, and walked a turn or two about the room, and seemed to be discontented. How do you, sir George? said Harcourt. Says sir George, For what am I drilled on thus in a concern of this importance? What is the matter with you sir George? said Harcourt. Why, is this a business to be slighted, said sir George, as I am? For I have no performance of your promises. Why, said Harcourt, what would you have? we are ready for you. Then said he, I am ready for you. And then Harcourt spoke merrily to him, Why are you so angry, sir George? And upon that he goes to his cabinet, and searching among his bags he found a little note among them, and gave it to sir George; saith he, There is a bill for you : I have been to-day at Whitehall, and received it by the queen's order, from such a gentleman : [whose name I cannot now remember ;] and it is upon such a man for 2,000*l.* [but I cannot remember the goldsmith's name neither.] Well, said sir George, it is well somebody gives me encouragement; I have more encouragement from my good lady and mistress, than from any of you. Nay, said Harcourt, for encouragement, that you shall not want ; for the rest shall be paid in due time.

Sir G. Wakeman. If the queen had given me 2,000*l.* for the service I had done her, was that any harm? I have deserved it, I am sure, for 9 years service.

Sir R. Sawyer. What other discourse had they then?

Bedlow. Said Harcourt, But sir George, this must be well followed, and closely observed, because so much depends upon it ; for if we should miss to kill him at Windsor, or you miss in your way, we will do it at New-market.

L. C. J. Who said so?

Bedlow. Harcourt.

L. C. J. Did Harcourt say, before sir George's face, If we miss killing him at Windsor, and you miss your way, we will do it at New-Market?

Bedlow. Yes, he did say, If we miss killing him at Windsor, and you miss in your way (which we hope you will not) we will do it at New-market.

L. C. J. He says now quite another thing than he said before.

L. C. J. North. }
Mr. Recorder. } No, he said the same before.   10
Sir R. Sawyer. }

2 T

L. C. J. Well, call your witnesses, sir George.

Sir G. Wakeman. Call Mr. Chapman.

L. C. J. But before they begin, sir Robert Sawyer, we must do all the right to every one we can. I do not find, by the strictest observation that I have made, that Mr. Bedlow, who is the second witness, does say any great thing, any material thing against any one of them ; but as for Rumley he says nothing at all. He says, in effect, against sir George Wakeman, no more than this, That he saw Harcourt give him a note for 2,000*l.* which he said was from the queen ; upon which sir George said he was more beholden to his good lady and mistress, than to any of them all. The note he does not know who drew it, nor upon whom it was drawn ; nor does he say what it was for, more than what Harcourt told him, which was in doubtful words, That it was about the old business ; but Harcourt did not tell him this in the presence of sir George Wakeman, but he spoke to Harcourt about it. It is no more, than sir George Wakeman received from Harcourt the bill of exchange, he does not know upon whom, nor for what.

Sir Robert Sawyer. My lord, he says more, with submission ; for he says this further, That there was a discourse about the business ; and he did tell you, That sir George Wakeman should complain, that they had done well with him, and asked why he was drilled on ; but when the note was produced, he said, My matters are already prepared, but you are not so ready to perform your promises. Then said Harcourt, ' If you are ready for us, we are ready for you : And told him, If he did not do it, they would do it at New-market.'

L. C. J. What is all this? Pray Mr. Bedlow stand up again : We are now in the case of men's lives, and pray have a care that you say

VOL. VII.

<hr>

10. *Mr. Recorder:* Sir George Jeffreys (1645–1689) was later the infamous lord chief justice at the "Bloody Assizes" after Monmouth's rebellion in 1685.

L. C. J. What answer made sir George Wakeman?

Bedlow. Sir G. Wakeman said, If I find you ready, I will be ready in all things.

L. C. J. Was the word spoke of poisoning?

Bedlow. I have spoken that already. ' If ' we miss at Windsor, and you miss in your ' way;' I do not remember whether the word Poison was used ; but I knew by what Mr. Harcourt and others had told me that Poison was meant by it.

L. C. J. Was all this one intire discourse?

Bedlow. Yes, my lord.

Then Sir *George* said privately to his fellow-prisoners, ' There is my business done.'

Sir *R. Sawyer.* Here is a positive proof of the receipt of money, which coupled with what Oates says, and the discourse that Mr. Bedlow tells you of, makes it out what it was for. This was paid in part, was it not, Sir?

Bedlow. The answer that Mr. Harcourt gave to sir George, was, That he should have the rest in due time.

L. C. J. But what say you to Marshal, but that he carried letters?

Sir *G. Wakeman.* Was there nobody present but you?

Bedlow. There was only Harcourt, you, and I.

L. C. J. But what say you to Corker?

Bedlow. Corker hath been in the company
11 with Le Faire, talking of news, what encouragement they had by letters from beyond sea, as those they had from France; such and such letters speak that they are in readiness of money, men and arms; and if we are ready here, they are ready for us. This was usually the discourse, and all upon the same design. Now when we talked of this business, we did not say the word Plot, but we all know what was intended by it, that is the Plot.

L. C. J. And what said Corker?

Bedlow. He said it was well. He did know what readiness such and such persons were in, when the design was likely to take effect. I know not their names; we were talking of several persons several times, some in England, and some beyond sea.

L. C. J. What can you say to Marshal?

Bedlow. I do say, that he hath been to consult of the return of letters which were the answers to those I brought from beyond sea.

L. C. J. Did he know the contents of those letters?

Bedlow. Yes, my lord, he hath been in consultation what answer to make again.

L. C. J. And was all this about the Plot?

Bedlow. Yes, for the subverting the Protestant religion, and bringing in Popery, and raising of an army.

Marshal. Can you prove I knew any of those gentlemen the letters were carried to?

Bedlow. I name one, that was to sir Francis
12 Radcliff.

Marshal. How does he know that I know sir Francis Radcliff?

L. C. J. Well, sir George, will you call your witnesses?

Sir *G. Wakeman.* Call Mr. Chapman. 13
[Which was done.] My Lord, there was a letter or note of directions from me to Mr. Ashby, and it is affirmed by Mr. Oates, that in that letter I should let Mr. Ashby know I did approve well of the proposals that were made to me to poison the king, and that the queen would assist me in it; and that in the same letter there were directions given what he should take, and how many strokes of the pump he should make use of, and several other things fit for a physician to direct his patient in. Now, my lord, I will prove by this gentleman Mr. Chapman, who is Mayor of Bath, that he received this very note from Mr. Ashby, that he read it from the beginning to the end of it; that there was no word in it, or mention of the king or queen in the whole letter, unless it be of the king or queen's bath. And, my lord, I think he hath a piece of this letter still, that part that was the physical part he tore off, and kept himself. Now it is none of my hand, I never writ a letter to Ashby upon any occasion whatsoever; and I will tell your lordship how it came to pass I did not write that letter; I hope by a providence, for I never but used to write my physical directions with my own hand. It happened that I came home late, and I was very ill; Ashby sent to me for his note, because he was to go out of town the next morning; being weary and indisposed, I laid me down on the couch, and sent for my man, who is an apothecary now, and is better able to write such a letter; I dictated the letter to him, all my family, and all that were by, can testify the same: he knows very well my hand, and hath part of it to produce; for when the queen was there, I made use of him for my apothecary, and those physical directions I sent down for the bath, I sent always to him. He is a very good witness as to my hand.

L. C. J. But you may speak of one letter, and Mr. Oates of another.

Sir *G. Wakeman.* Why, did I write two letters of directions? what need that? He says he saw a letter with my name subscribed to it.

L. C. J. Yes, it was so, and that you should be assisted by the queen to poison the king; and being asked how he did know that was your hand? he said, I did not see him write, but I saw him in the posture of writing; and when he went away, there was left on the table, and the ink was not dry, a physical bill, which was the same hand with that the letter was.

Sir *G. Wakeman.* Ay, my lord, but he does not call that a letter, but it was a physical bill, and not a letter; so that there was but one letter.

L. C. J. But there was a note of physical directions in the letter.

Oates. That letter was at least half a sheet of a side, close written, wherein were those passages that I mentioned ; but I cannot give an account of all contained in it; but this, my lord, I

---

11. *Le Faire:* a Jesuit priest invented by Bedloe and accused by him of plotting Godfrey's murder.

12. *sir Francis Radcliff:* Ratcliffe was a wealthy Catholic landowner accused by Oates of taking part in the plot.

13. *Mr. Chapman:* an apothecary from Bath.

remember, that he should take a pint of milk in the morning, and a pint of milk in the evening, and should have so many strokes at the bath; but this was several days before Ashby went to the bath, I believe at least ten. Presently after he came to town. And I say, that this letter that the court asks me how I prove it to be his hand, I prove it thus: I saw him write a bill to an apothecary for Mr. Ashby to take something when he was in town.

L. C. J. But was that business of being assisted to kill the king in the same letter that the physical directions were in?

Oates. Yes, my lord.

Sir G. Wakeman. Then it is the same letter.

L. C. J. How does that follow? might there not be two?

Sir G. Wakeman. There is only that part of it which is the physical prescriptions, he hath torn off the other part.

Then Mr. *Chapman* was examined.

Chapman. My Lord, the 17th of July last, Mr. Thimbleby came to the bath.

L. C. J. Who?

Chapman. Mr. Thimbleby; a man of about fourscore years of age, a very feeble and infirm man. As soon as he came to me, he told me that sir G. Wakeman recommended me to him, and desired me that I would provide a lodging for him as near the king and queen's bath as I could: I did so; and then he shewed me a letter from sir George, whereof this was the lower part of half a sheet of paper; there was full directions how to take the physic, and after the taking the bolus, to drink the waters so many days, and then to use the bath, and after that the pump, and after that he was to take a dose of pills after his bathing. I took off this latin bill that concerns me, my lord, and gave him the English part.

L. C. J. Did you read the English part?

Chapman. My Lord, my son read it as well as I, who should have come up, and testified the same, but that it is impossible for both my son and me to leave the shop and come together, because of my employment.

L. C. J. But in that letter there was nothing mentioned of killing the king, was there? nor of the queen?

Chapman. No, my Lord, not upon the word of a christian, except it were the king and queen's bath.

Then the Paper was shewn him.

L. C. J. Whose hand is that? do you believe it is sir George's hand?

Chapman. No, my lord: I have brought some of sir G. Wakeman's bills here.

L. C. J. Do you know whose hand it is?

Chapman. No, my Lord.

Just. Atkins. What name was subscribed to that letter?

Chapman. There is none subscribed to this paper.

L. C. J. Was there no name to it?

Chapman. I did not take notice of that.

L. C. J. But look, you, this cannot be that letter, because that letter Mr. Oates speaks of was of sir George's own hand, as he thinks by comparison, and his name subscribed to it.

Sir G. Wakeman. I never writ any other letter, but what was dictated to my man, and sent by Ashby to the bath. My Lord, he hath owned it himself before the House of Lords, that I writ but one letter, and I had my liberty before. Now it was told him there, that if he had mentioned that letter when I was examined before the council, I had been certainly taken into custody then, and should never have had my liberty so long. I had my liberty from the last of September, and could have gone to Constantinople in the time I had my liberty; and certainly I should have provided for myself if I had known myself guilty, seeing so many cast into prison upon that account.

Recorder. It is not probable that Mr. Ashby would communicate such a letter to this gentleman, that had such a design in it.

Sir G. Wakeman. But if any one can, let him prove that I had any other business with him than merely the business of a physician with his patient. My Lord, I have a physician in town, that will testify, that I was to meet him in consultations about Ashby.

L. C. J. The answer is no more than this, That you did write a letter, or there was a letter writ by your directions, to Ashby, which hath not any such matter in it as Oates speaks of; but this answers not Mr. Oates's testimony; it is true, the question will be upon Mr. Oates's credit, how far the jury will believe him: if Mr. Oates swears true, then you did write another letter, and this is not the letter, and there is no contradiction in your answer, to what he says, but Mr. Oates stands with the jury how far they will believe him.

Sir G. Wakeman. Gentlemen of the jury take notice, I never writ any letter but that.

L. C. J. How does that appear? if Mr. Oates swears true, you did write another letter.

Justice Atkins. Mr. Chapman, was there any mention of milk in that letter?

Chapman. No, my Lord. It is ridiculous to drink milk with the waters, it will make it curdle.

Oates. That is not the hand the letter I saw was in.

L. C. J. He says it is not the same hand.

Oates. It was another, a genteel hand.

Justice Pemberton. And there was no mention made of milk in it, the contents are not the same.

Sir G. Wakeman. The contents were the same but as for the milk, it is so ridiculous a thing, that never a physician in England, but will say it is perfect poison. I appeal to Mr. Chapman, who hath so long known the way there used, if any one prescribed milk to any one that took the waters.

L. C. J. Mr. Oates, was there, in the letter you saw, where mention is made of the strokes that were to be received from the pump, any mention of the milk to be taken?

---

14. *Mr. Thimbleby:* also called Ashley; see p. 101 above.

15. *the bolus:* a medicine of round shape adapted for swallowing—larger than an ordinary pill.

16. *ridiculous:* the mineral water at Bath would curdle the milk.

17. *pump:* newly installed, the pump was used to bathe the afflicted parts of the body directly with hot water.

The following section contains the crucial evidence of Sir Philip Lloyd, who confirmed that during the previous September Oates had denied having any information against Wakeman. Thereafter Corker and Marshall presented their cases, the latter's so oratorical that it brought from Scroggs a fiery tirade on popish iniquities and the Gunpowder Plot.

18

I told him, Mr. Ashby had sent for some directions for the bath; and being weary and indisposed, (for it was late, and he was not well said he, 'I cannot write myself, do you take my pen and ink, and write.' I did take the pen and ink, and write; and when I had written, something was false in it; 'Pray,' said he, 'correct that:' I did so, and interlined it, and when my master was in bed I writ it over again, and the next morning, before he was awake, I carried it to Mr. Ashby myself, and there were only directions in it what to do at the bath.

L. C. J. When was Mr. Ashby to go to the bath? How soon after?

Hunt. He was to go the next morning.

L. C. J. If what Mr. Oates swears, be true, this letter that he saw was ten days before, so what he speaks is another thing.

Sir *G. Wakeman.* I never writ any such letter in my life, and I hope the jury will take notice of it.

Justice *Atkins.* Do you know any thing of Mr. Ashby's drinking milk while he was here?

Hunt. No, but he was saying he was advised by a friend of his to drink milk.

L. C. J. When, at the bath?

Hunt. No, when he was in town.

L. C. J. When he was in town? that is consistent with Mr. Oates's testimony.

Sir *G. Wakeman.* My lord, there is a physician that was in consultation with me about Mr. Ashby, I think it of great consequence to shew that I came to him about no treasonable affair, I vow to Almighty God I did not.

L. C. J. If you have any more witnesses, call them.

Sir *G. Wakeman.* Call Elizabeth Henningham [Who stood up.]

L. C. J. Sir George, What do you ask her?

Henningham. I was present, my lord, at the writing of the letter. His servant writ, and he dictated to him, every word of the letter I saw, but there was no such thing in it.

L. C. J. I am very confident that this is true that you say, but it is not to the thing that Mr. Oates speaks of, and charges you withal: that you did write such a letter as these people mention, and there was nothing in it but like a physician's directions to his patient, I do believe, and this was just when he was going to the bath? but Mr. Oates tells you (if he says true) that this letter he speaks of, to which sir G. Wakeman was subscribed, was ten days before he went to the bath; and that there was no mention of any bolus in that, but the direction was in the first part how he was to use himself, while he staid in town to drink milk, and when he came to the bath, to use the pump, so that this your witnesses say, and you urge, is true, but not pertinent.

Sir *Geo. Wakeman.* I say, my lord, it is not probable that I should write directions so long before he went.

Henningham. My lord, he said himself he wanted directions to go to the Bath, in my own hearing.

Justice *Pemberton.* Yes, he might, and indeed he did so, for the first contained none, but how he should behave himself while he was here.

L. C. J. Have you any more witnesses? Pray call them.

Sir *Geo. Wakeman.* My lord, I have this to say, as I told you before, that I had my liberty for twenty-four days after my examination before the council. Mr. Oates called at the bar of the House of Commons, and there gave an account of this very Letter that he mentions now, I say it was at the bar of the House of Commons. And thereupon the Commons sent an Address to the House of Lords, with astonishment that I was not under confinement; and thereupon Mr. Oates was called to the bar of the House of Lords, and was commanded to give an account what it was he knew concerning me, that should create such an astonishment in the House of Commons: He told them of this Letter, and my Lord Chancellor said to him, Do you know it was sir G. Wakeman's hand? No, said he: How do you know it was his Letter then? I know it only by this, said he, it was subscribed, 'George Wakeman.' If he had such proof as he says he hath now, if he had seen me writing, and came into the room where the paper I writ was yet wet, whether he would not have mentioned it there when he was examined about the knowledge of my hand.

L. C. J. Call your witnesses: But what say you, Mr. Oates, yourself to it?

Oates. My lord, sir G. Wakeman had his liberty because I was so weak, by reason of being up two nights together, one whereof was so very wet, and being hot, wet, and cold, all in a few hours time, so that I thought it would have cost me my life; not being used to such hard services, I did not charge sir George so fully: Though it may be objected to this court, that I was bound to speak the whole truth; and so I did, as opportunity and health would give me leave. And as to the Letter, and what I said about it in the Lords' House, sir George is mistaken. He says here that I said I knew his hand no otherwise, but by seeing sir George Wakeman subscribed to it.

Sir *G. Wakeman.* I will prove it by the Record.

Oates. Now, my lord, I humbly desire that he may propose his questions to the court: and I desire to know, whether I did say, I did not know it any other ways but by its being signed G. Wakeman.

Sir *G. Wakeman.* Pray, my lord, be pleased to give me leave——

L. C. J. Mr. Oates, did you mention in the House of Lords, whether you knew his hand or no?

Oates. My lord, I cannot call to mind what I then said, I did say, I saw such a letter, signed George Wakeman; but if he will bring the record, and one that shall swear those were the words, I will leave it to the jury. But this, my lord, I would add, if you will give me leave; the words I did say as near as I can remember, were these, when they asked me, how I knew sir G. Wakeman's hand? I said, I saw such a letter signed George Wakeman. Now, my lord, upon this information, they did think fit to take sir G. Wakeman up and secure him; and now I come face to face, and am not only to satisfy judges, but a jury, I shew you what reasons I have to believe it, and what they may have, that it was his hand: For I say, I saw him in a writing posture, I saw him lay by the pen, I saw him withdraw from the paper, I saw none but another gentleman there, that was lame of both his hands, and the ink was not dry, and it was the same hand with the letter.

Sir G. Wakeman. Was my name to that note?

Oates. No, I will not swear that; but the character of the hand was the same, if I may judge of writing.

L. C. J. North. Look you, sir George, you spoke of witnesses you would call to prove what he swore in the House of Lords; if you can call any witnesses for that, do.

Sir G. Wakeman. Call sir Philip Lloyd: I hope your lordship will please to allow me, at least, this advantage (I know not whether it be an advantage) that the record of the House of Lords may be made use of as a record here. If I prove it by the record, it will be a good evidence.

L. C. J. Have you that record here?

Sir G. Wakeman. I have a copy of that record, and a witness that will swear it.

19   Then Sir *Philip Lloyd* appeared, and stood up.

L. C. J. What do you ask sir Philip Lloyd?

Sir G. Wakeman. I desire to know of sir Philip Lloyd, what Mr. Oates said of me before his majesty and the council, the last day of September; Sir, you were there present, and sent by the king to me, and commanded to bring me in to the council.

Sir Philip Lloyd. I will, my lord, as well as I can, recollect and tell you, as near as I can, what Mr. Oates did then accuse him of. It was upon the 31st of September, Mr. Oates did then say he had seen a letter, to the best of his remembrance, from Mr. White to Mr. Fenwick at St. Omers, in which letter he writ word, that sir G. Wakeman had undertaken the poisoning of the king, and was to have 15,000*l.* for it; of which 5,000*l.* had been paid him by the hands of Coleman. Sir G. Wakeman, upon this, was called in, and told of this accusation; he utterly denied all, and did indeed carry himself as if he were not concerned at the accusation, but did tell the king and council, he hoped he should have reparation and satisfaction for the injury done to his honour. His carriage was not well liked of by the king and council, and being a matter of such consequence as this was, they were willing to know further of it; and because they thought this evidence was not proof enough to give them occasion to commit him, being only out

of the letter of a third person, thereupon they called in Mr. Oates again, and my Lord Chancellor desired Mr. Oates to tell him, if he knew nothing personally of sir G. Wakeman, because they were in a matter of moment, and desired sufficient proof, whereupon to ground a commitment; Mr. Oates, when he did come in again, and was asked the question, did lift up his hands (for I must tell the truth, let it be what it will) and said, No, God forbid that I should say any thing against sir G. Wakeman, for I know nothing more against him. And I refer myself to the whole council, whether it was not so.

Oates. I remember not one word of all this.

Sir G. Wakeman. My lord, this is a Protestant witness too.

Oates. My lord, give me leave to make an answer: when I did report this letter, the council did ask me whether or no sir George was any ways concerned in this letter? I replied, I had it by report, that sir George had received 5,000*l.* of this money. My lord, the council did not press me, to my knowledge; I will not be positive; but if the council did press me, and I did make that answer, I do appeal to the whole board, whether or no I was in a condition to make any answer at all, when, by reason of my being hurried up and down, and sitting up, I was scarce *compos mentis.*   20

L. C. J. What, must we be amused with I know not what, for being up but two nights? You were not able to give an answer; that when they call and send for Mr. Oates again to give a positive charge, and then you tell us a story so remote: what, was Mr. Oates just so spent, that he could not say, I have seen a letter under sir George Wakeman's own hand?

Oates. My lord, I did, to the best of my remembrance, make mention of that letter that sir George Wakeman writ, before the board. I say, to the best of my skill and knowledge; but I will not be positive in it.

L. C. J. You have heard what sir Philip Lloyd says.

Just. Dolben. What say you, did Mr. Oates make any mention of this letter?

Sir P. Lloyd. Truly, my lord, I can't remember that there was any such letter mentioned. I tell you what I do remember; and afterwards because he came and gave this deposition before the Lords and Commons, that he found such a letter upon the table from sir George to Ashby, indeed I did very much wonder at it, and it made me reflect upon that other passage at the council, of his denying to accuse sir George further, and it hath been in my mind ever since.

L. C. J. And you do declare, that when the lords of the council asked him, whether he knew any thing more particularly against sir G. Wakeman, he did lift up his hands and said, 'No, God forbid I should charge him any further, I know no more against him.'

Sir P. Lloyd. Yes, my lord, so it was.

Oates. My lord, I believe sir Philip Lloyd is mistaken; but however I was so weak, and the

---

18. *I told him:* this section continues the testimony of Hunt, Wakeman's manservant, concerning the letter to Ashby.

19. *Lloyd:* one of the clerks of the Council.

20. *compos mentis:* sane and responsible.

king and council were so sensible of it, that the king himself had like to have sent me away once or twice before, because he found I was so weak.

L. C. J. It did not require such a deal of strength to say, 'I saw a letter under sir George's own hand.'

L. C. J. North. Well, it must be left to the jury: If you have any more witnesses call them.

L. C. J. Mr. Oates, sir G. Wakeman urged it right that he should not have been permitted to have his liberty so long, if you had charged him home then.

Sir G. Wakeman. Call Mr. Lydcot.

Oates. To speak the truth, they were such a council as would commit nobody.

Recorder. That was not well said.

Sir G. Wakeman. He reflects on the king and all the council.

L. C. J. You have taken a great confidence, I know not by what authority, to say any thing of any body. But this is naturally true, that when the council were offended at the carriage of sir G. Wakeman at the board, and therefore sent for Mr. Oates again, doubting in themselves, whether what they had would be sufficient to commit him; for indeed it was only a wild thing, of what was mentioned in a letter of a third person's, that sir George had accepted of 15,000*l.* and received the five; therefore, said they, we will know of Mr. Oates some more particulars, and sent for him in again, and asked him, ' Do you know any thing of your own knowledge ? If he had come in then and said, ' Yes, I have seen a letter subscribed under sir G. Wakeman's hand,' would not they have committed him ? surely they would. And now the council's not committing him, is an argument that they had not sufficient evidence, and Oates did omit at that time to charge him with this letter.

Then Mr. *Lydcot* stood up.

Sir G. Wakeman. Mr. Lydcot, have you a copy of the Lords records ?

Lydcot. Yes, it is.

Sir G. Wakeman. Pray, what did Mr. Oates say to my lord chancellor in the House of Lords ?

L. C. J. You must have that which is proper evidence : You shall have all the fair dealing that can be, and all that can be admitted for your defence shall be.

Sir G. Wakeman. My lord I humbly thank you I find it.

L. C. J. Ay, but this is now what the clerk writes down as minutes. It is an hard construction to make this evidence. Were you present when Mr. Oates was there and said this?

Lydcot. No, my lord, all I say, is this, this is a copy of the record in the Lords House.

L. C. J. Did Mr. Oates set his hand to that record.

Lydcot. Yes, in some places. It is Titus Oates set in diverse places as his hand to examinations.

L. C. J. But is Mr. Oates's own hand set to the record ?

Lydcot. I know nothing of that.

L. C. J. This is the objection. It will be hard that if a clerk takes the depositions of Oates or any one else, and takes them as near as he can, but he never subscribes it, and you prove only it is a copy of what the clerk wrote, that cannot be allowed as evidence.

Lydcot. It is a copy in most places of what is under Mr. Relf's own hand.

L. C. J. But you can't swear the clerk writ true ?

Lydcot. No, that I can't.

L. C. J. It may be an entry of what the House of Lords did upon the examination : That is not evidence here.

Just. Pemberton. If you can produce any one that heard Mr. Oates give in his information, you say well.

Sir G. W. I believe there is a difference between the entry-book and the book of records; and I hope you will look upon the book of the House of Lords as the highest evidence, beyond any verbal averment. My life is in your hands, I ask you whether it be not so, or no ?

L. C. J. North. If there be a record in any court of record, that such a man appeared in court, it is an evidence that he was in court, and a record for it; but when there is an examination in a court of record, these not passing the examination of that court, but being taken by the clerks, we always in evidence expect there should be somebody to prove, that such an examination was sworn and subscribed to.

L. C. J. Have you any witnesses here, that were by, and heard what Mr. Oates did then depose, and can testify what Mr. Oates said when he was called in, and particularly what answer he made to that single question of my Lord Chancellor's how he came to know it was your hand?

Sir G. W. I can bring none but these records or the lords themselves, and I can't expect it from them. And that which they call a record, I am not able to judge whether it be a record or no.

L. C. J. Were there not others called with him into the Lords House?

Sir G. W. No, there was none but the lords themselves.

L. C. J. You should have had the clerks here that made the entry, or saw him set his hand to the examination.

L. C. J. North. This is nothing, but, as he says, a transcript out of the Journal.

Lydcot. I believe it is written most under Mr. Relf's own hand. There is a great deal of it that contains the whole narrative that Oates gave in.

L. C. J. North. You desire to give in evidence what Mr. Oates said at the bar of the House of Lords to what my lord chancellor asked him; if you have any witnesses that can prove it, they shall be heard.

Sir G. W. My lord, I have no witnesses, only the record.

2

---

21. *Relf:* John Relf, usher of the House of Lords.

22. *Peter Pence:* see p. 22n.

23. *Jennison:* Robert Jennison, a lapsed Catholic, had testified earlier that the alibi given by Ireland in his previous trial was false. By this time Ireland had already been convicted and hanged.

In this final excerpt, we see Scrogg's summation of the evidence (rather remarkable since he, like all judges then, took no notes during the trial) which was so favorable to the defendants that Bedloe objected—only to be firmly rebuked. The jury took only an hour to reach its verdict.

L. C. J. Well, have you done? Look you, gentlemen of the jury.

Marshal. I desire but one word : These things I have insisted upon as far as I can for myself; but the main matter I relied upon was, that Mr. Oates did not know me, neither as to my calling, conversation, words nor actions. He can bring no person, man nor woman, that ever saw him in my company, nor took notice of our meeting together, nor Bedlow neither; he can name no place where he saw me, none but the Savoy, against which no proof can be found. And then at the searching of the house, I desire the jury to take notice, that at that time he disowned us, and said he did not know us. A sufficient rational cause cannot be given why, he should say now he knows me, and did not then take me.

Justice Pemberton. You have said all this before.

Marshal. Then, my lord, for a conclusion, I have been told, and I will only desire the jury to take notice of it, that every jury that finds a man guilty of death, upon the testimony of witnesses that come in against him, do take it solemnly upon their consciences, that what such witnesses swear is true.

L. C. J. That they believe they swear true: For we have no infallibility with us : It is one thing to say it is true, and another thing to say we believe it is true. Look you, the jury may give a verdict that is false, and yet go according to their consciences. Do you understand that, priest ?

Justice Pemberton. You need not teach the jury what they are to do.

Marshal. But considering in case an oath be false, and the jury have reason to doubt what the prisoners say in their own defence, upon what they hear or have learned of their own knowledge, if they find such doubt grounded upon that double matter, then they are in great danger to bring the fault to their own doors, and make the crime of perjury their own.

Justice Pemberton. What, do you go over things again and again ?

L. C. J. All this signifies but little ; if you had Popery here, you would get but little by it. We should hardly part with our Peter Pence for all your speeches. We all know what things are, it is not a parcel of words patched thus together, will do your business.

Marshal. I wish all thoughts were as open-faced as ours are.

L. C. J. Look you, gentlemen of the jury, here are four prisoners ; as to one of them, that is Rumley, the truth of it is, there is but one witness against him, and by the law there ought to be two ; so I cannot say, but you ought to discharge him : we do not find that there is testimony sufficient, according to the law, to condemn him, and therefore you ought to acquit him. As to the rest, here is sir George Wakeman, Mr. Corker, and Mr. Marshal; there hath been two sorts of evidences given, I will repeat them as well as I can, and as short as I can. There hath been a general evidence, and a particular evidence : there was a general evidence given by Mr. Dugdale, of the Plot in general, and by Mr. Praunce, and something of intimation by Mr. Jennison. These of Dugdale, Praunce, and Jennison, do not mention so much as the names of the three gentlemen that are upon their lives; but I will tell you why it was necessary, and answers a great objection that they seem to make: for you are to believe men, say they, and to believe men upon probable circumstances, something to guide you besides the positiveness of an oath ; and that is well enough said: Now here is something besides, and that is the Plot ; that there was a conspiracy to introduce popery, by the likeliest means, which was to kill the king ; and that such people as these men were to do it. Now that there was such a general design to do it, is a circumstantial evidence, (as to these men I call it so.) And these are circumstances which may answer the objection they make, when they say, You are not to give credit to positive oaths without any thing to govern you by; for you have this to govern you by, besides the oath, that there was a Plot.

The testimony of Mr. Jennison does go more particularly to the business of Ireland, which I would observe, by the way, for the sake of that gentleman that stands so much upon the innocency of those men, and would have them to be believed upon their own assertions, because he says they dare not die with a lye in their mouths. I believe it is notorious enough, Mr. Jennison that comes here is a man of quality, and one against whom there is no objection, and he is justified by one or two more. He says, he saw Mr. Ireland the 19th of August, when he, to his death, took upon him to aver he was then in Staffordshire, and brought several of his own religion, who would outface it to the court, that he kept them company so many days, and was in the country all the while. There was a maid, before this, that came and testified that she saw Ireland, and saw him at his own door, in August, but this gentleman comes and proves it upon him more particularly, and tells you when, the day of the week, and of the month, that he was with him at his own lodging, that night he came from Windsor, that he was pulling off his boots, and pretended to come post from Staffordshire, and so that he was in Staffordshire is true, because he came thence post, but he hath always constantly denied that he was here, and that may serve for the integrity even of their dying oaths. And you are not going, according to your own doctrine, so immediately to Hell, I hope you suppose

22

23

purgatory, where you may be purged from such peccadillos as this of dying with a lye in your mouths.

As for the testimony of the particular evidence, first, against sir George Wakeman, Mr. Oates says he saw a letter subscribed George Wakeman; and it was writ to Mr. Ashby, and therein, among other expressions, was this particular, That the queen would assist him to kill the king. He was asked, How he knew it was his hand? He said, He had never seen his hand before, but afterwards he saw him writing, (as he thinks, writing,) in a writing posture, and there he looked upon that paper when he was gone from it, while it was wet, and that character, to his thinking, was just the character of the letter. Now I must observe this to you. First, Supposing it to be true, yet it is somewhat hard, for a man that had never known a man's hand in his life, to see a hand to-day, and some time after to come and see his hand to a bill of physic, and to recollect the character so much backward, as to know, this is that, or that man's hand that I saw before. It is one thing to know hands we are used to, but it is another thing, if we see a hand we never saw before in our lives, and then by reflection at another time, and by comparison of hands to say this is the same, that is hard; but that is supposing it to be true. Sir George Wakeman, as all people will that are accused, does deny the fact, and says there was no such thing. Against him besides, he says he saw, in a book that the Jesuit priests kept among them of their transactions and affairs, he saw, in Harcourt's chamber, a book, wherein was written, this day, (and there was a certain day in August named, but he cannot tell what day,) this day agreed with sir G. W. for 15,000l. to which he consented. And under was written, Received 5,000l. part of 15,000l. by order of Mr. Coleman. George Wakeman. This he says he saw, and he believes that to be the very same hand he saw before, so it is by a comparison of hands. He does not charge sir George Wakeman, to the best of my memory, with any positive things of his own knowledge, more than as I tell you of this matter.

Sir R. Sawyer. Yes, my lord, he says he saw his commission.

L. C. J. Indeed he does say, he saw a commission in his hands, to be physician-general of the army that was to be raised. And that he denied 10,000l. and would have 15. The truth I leave with you, gentlemen. Look you, gentlemen, we will show ourselves what we ought to do, let them be as they will; we would not, to prevent all their Plots, (let them be as big as they can make them) shed one drop of innocent blood, therefore I would have you, in all these gentlemens cases, consider seriously, and weigh truly the circumstances, and the probability of things charged upon them. There is an additional evidence against sir George Wakeman, by Bedlow: he says he saw him have a note for 2,000l. which was

said came from the queen, there were discourses of doubtful words, but whether they be plain enough to satisfy your consciences, when men are upon their lives, I leave to you. That sir George Wakeman should say, Are you ready for me? Why am I drilled on thus, in a matter of this concern? This he would have to imply the poisoning of the king; but there is but one thing that sounds any thing plain to the matter, and that was this, said he, If they miss (speaking of killing the king) if they miss at Windsor, and you miss your way, then it shall be done at New-Market. This he did swear directly, and then sir George Wakeman replied, He would be ready. Now if you believe this, then there are two witnesses against sir George Wakeman, for the matter of the bill alone would do nothing, but when he says he saw such a bill, it must be for something; and if he did say so, If they miss killing him at Windsor, and you miss your way, we will do it at New-Market; and he replied, I will be ready, the thing is made plain; I leave it to you; and this is all the evidence against sir George Wakeman, as I remember: I hope my brothers, if they remember more, will repeat it to you. I cannot undertake to repeat every word; I remember so much as is material, and my brothers I hope will help me out, in what they have better observed.

As to Mr. Corker, Oates says, that he saw a letter under his hand, that is, his name, I suppose was to it, wherein he consented to the raising the 6,000l. which was to be raised out of the Benedictine estates, and was in order to the carrying on of this Plot. I do not find that he does prove that he did know Mr. Corker's hand. And he says of him further, he was their president, and so it was necessary to have his consent for the raising the 6,000l. and particularly he says, that he did except against Pickering's being designed for the murdering of the king; for, said he, He is a man that waits at the altar, and methinks you should choose some fitter person. For that, says Mr. Corker, which he says, that I was president; I was not president; and he makes it necessary for me to set my hand, because I being president, it was supposed it could not be done without me: and Dr. Oates does intend such a thing by his enforcing of it too: but he does produce to you two or three witnesses, that do say, Mr. Stapleton hath been president for four or five years; and said he, If I were not president, what needs all this ado about my consent? So he contradicts him in that particular, that he was not president, and it is not only a bare immaterial thing, because his being president made his hand more necessary to the raising the 6,000l. And for that matter of his saying, that he did except against Pickering, and they might have chose another, he does not charge him to be actually at the consultation, but he says he knew of it, because he said Pickering was not a fit man to do it. And he said, they had better choose a layman. He proves no fact, but only these words. And Mr. Bedlow

24

---

24. *Pickering:* Thomas Pickering, a Benedictine accused by Oates of plotting to kill the king; see p. 29.

he speaks against him, and what he says is rather less than what Oates says. For it is, that he talked with La Fevre the priest about the Plot in general words. It may be, he was talking with some body else, and yet he could hear that they talked together in general about it. That is all against him.

Against Mr. Marshal, it is rather less than against Corker, that is, that he did consent to the 6,000*l.* that should be raised among the Benedictines, he being a Benedictine too, and that he took exceptions against Pickering, as Corker did, that it was not convenient to employ him in killing the king. And this is that Oates says, and that he was a carrier of letters up and down, and a factor that way. And Bedlow says, that he knew that he carried letters, and was at the consult where they were read and answered, and when they asked him, Where? He said, At the Benedictine convent in the Savoy. And names in particular, a letter to sir Francis Radcliff, and that there was a discourse concerning the plot, in his hearing.

They say for themselves, they cannot answer any more than by circumstances, it is a very strange thing, if Dr. Oates knew this of us, why did not he take us before? And says sir George Wakeman, Why did not he accuse me of this letter that he talks of, before the king and council? He makes an answer (which to me indeed is a very faint one) at if he were so weak and tired, that he could not speak any word farther. When the council asked sir George Wakeman what he had to say for himself, and he behaved himself ruggedly, they call for Oates again, What, said they, ' do you know any thing of ' your own knowledge?' No, said he, God forbid; I know nothing more; as sir Philip Lloyd says, and as the matter speaks: For if he had charged him that he had seen that letter, the lords would infallibly have committed him. If he had but said, I saw a letter with his name to it, which by the character I believe was his, because I saw his writing elsewhere: And it is wonderful to me; I do not know, if a man be never so faint, could not he say, I saw a letter under his hand, as well as, I knew nothing more of him? There are as few words in one, as in the other. If he had said, I beg your lordships or his majesty's pardon, I am so weak I cannot recollect myself, it had been something; but to make a great protestation that he knew nothing of him. This is that that is said by sir Philip Lloyd, on his behalf.

These other gentlemen say, that Oates did not know them, and the woman does say, that she did tell them, when they came to search, that Corker and Marshal were there, and Dr. Oates and they said, they had nothing to do with any but Pickering. They make answer now and say, that they had no commission to take any but him. But it is strange indeed, if they were there, and they did see them, that they did not apprehend them. For what defence they make about what talk was had at the Gate-house, it is all contradicted by sir William Waller. And indeed, if it were possi-

ble, they have almost undone themselves in their own defences, by making weak observations, and insisting upon trivial things; improper for the Court to hear, and impertinent for them to urge. But I deal faithfully with you, I will discharge my own conscience to you. It lies upon the oaths of these two men. Though there was a Plot in general proved, yet that does not affect these men in particular, but was only used to answer that objection, that it should not be believed upon positive swearing, hand over head, without something else. Here was something else, the Plot in general, and their being priests, is another circumstance to me, who are mad to bring in popery, and would do any thing to get their tyranny again established amongst us. And there is more than probable evidence of that I assure you.

Sir Tho. Doleman did indeed say Mr. Oates was very weak, so that he was in great confusion, and scarce able to stand; weigh it with you how it will, but to me it is no answer. I tell you plainly, I think a man could not be so weak but he could have said, he saw a letter under his hand. It was as short as he could make an answer, and it is strange that he should go and make protestation that he knew nothing. And so I pray you weigh it well. Let us not be so amazed and frighted with the noise of Plots, as to take away any man's life without any reasonable evidence. If you are satisfied with the oaths of these two men; so, I have observed to you what objections they make for themselves, and those objections are material: What sir George Wakeman says about his not accusing him before the council, and what these men say that he did not apprehend them. And it is very strange, they should have so little knowledge, and so little acquaintance with Oates and Bedlow, and so great a matter as they speak should be true. And it is well enough observed, that he was a begging there; it is very much that such a man should know of such a great design on foot, and they should use him in that manner. These are the things that I remember, worthy of your consideration. These men's bloods are at stake, and your souls and mine, and' our oaths and consciences are at stake; and therefore never care what the world says, follow your consciences; if you are satisfied these men swear true, you will do well to find them guilty, and they deserve to die for it: If you are unsatisfied, upon these things put together, and they do weigh with you, that they have not said true, you will do well to acquit them.

Bedlow. My lord, my evidence is not right summed up.

L. C. J. I know not by what authority this man speaks.

Cl. of Cr. Make way for the jury there; who keeps the jury?

[Then an officer was sworn to keep the jury: The judges went off the bench, leaving Mr. Recorder and some justices to take the Verdict. And after about an hour's space the jury re-

25. *Gatehouse:* Oates had claimed to recognize Marshall when he saw him at Gatehouse Prison; Marshall denied it; Sir William Waller, a justice of the peace for Westminster who was known for arresting many priests, supported Oates.

26. *Doleman:* Thomas Doleman, a clerk of the Council.

turned, and the foreman coming up to the table, spoke thus to Mr. Recorder.]

Foreman. Sir, the gentlemen of the jury desire to know, whether they may not find the prisoners guilty of misprision of treason?

Recorder. No, you must either convict them of high-treason, or acquit them.

Foreman. Then take a Verdict.

Cl. of Cr. Gentlemen, answer to your names, Ralph Hawtrey.

Hawtrey. Here, &c.

Cl. of Cr. Gentlemen, are you all agreed of your Verdict?

Omnes. Yes.

Cl. of Cr. Who shall say for you?

Omnes. Our foreman.

Cl. of Cr. Sir George Wakeman, hold up thy hand. [Which he did.] Look upon the prisoner. How say you, is he guilty of the high-treason whereof he stands indicted, or Not Guilty?

Foreman. Not Guilty.

Capt. Richardson. Down on your knees.

Sir G. Wakeman. God bless the king and the honourable bench.

And in like manner were the other three acquitted. After the Verdict was recorded, the Court adjourned 'till 5 in the afternoon.

John Evelyn's
Diary (July 18, 1679)

The following selection is the entry for July 18, 1679, from the *Diary* of John Evelyn, the Tory courtier and man of letters. Though he has doubts of his own about Oates and Bedloe, he finds this trial rather disturbing because the acquittals reflect upon the "King's evidence." The edition reproduced here is that of E. S. deBeer, 6 vols. (Oxford: Clarendon Press, 1955), IV, 173–76.

18 I went early to the *old-Baily* Sessions-house to the famous Trial of Sir *Geo: Wakeman*[5] (one of the *Queenes*

[5] George Wakeman, of Beckford, Glos.; created a baronet 1661; except in connexion with his trial very little is known about him: *D.N.B*. One of the three monks tried with him was James (Maurus) Corker: *D.N.B.*; below, p. 175 n.   1

---

1. *p. 175n.:* the notes for Evelyn are by his editor, E. S. deBeer.

Physitians) & 3 *Benedictine Monkes*; The first (whom I was well acquainted with, & take to be a worthy gent: abhorring such a fact) for intending to poyson the King: The other as complices to carry on the Plott, to subvert the Government, & introduce *Poperie*: The Bench was crowded with the Judges, Lo: Major, Justices, & innumerable spectators. The chiefe Accusers Dr. *Oates* (as he called himselfe) ⟨and⟩ one *Bedlow*,[1] a man of inferior note; but their testimony were not so pregnant, & I feare much of it from *heare-say*, but sworne positively to some particulars, which drew suspicion upon their truth; nor did Circumstances so agree, as to give either the bench or Jurie so intire satisfaction as was expected: After therefore a long & tedious tryal of 9 houres, the Jury brought them in not guilty to the extraordinary triumph of the *Papists*, & not without sufficient disadvantage & reflections on the Witnesses, especialy *Oates* & *Bedlow*: And this was an happy day for the *Lords* in the *Tower*, who expecting 2 their Triall (had this[a] gon against the Prisoners at the barr) would all of them ⟨have⟩ ben in uttmost hazard: For my part, I do looke on *Oates* as a vaine, insolent man, puff'd up, with[b] the favour of the Commons, for having discovered something realy true; as more especialy[c] detecting the dangerous intrigue of Coleman, proved out of his owne letters: & of a generall designe, which the *Jesuited* party of the Papists, ever had, & still have to ruine the Church of England; but that he was trusted with those greate seacrets he pretended, or had any solid ground for what he accused divers noble men of, I have many reasons to induce my contrary beliefe; That amongst so many Commissions as he affirm'd he delivered to them from *P: Oliva*[2] & the *Pope*, he who made no scruple of opening all other Papers, letters & seacrets, should not onely, not open any of those pretended Commissions, but not so much as take any Copy, or Witnesse, of any one

---

[a] Followed by *pro-* deleted.　　[b] Followed by *wh-* deleted.
[c] Followed by *the* deleted.

---

[1] William Bedloe, 1650 (or 1651)–
80: *D.N.B.*; I.H.R., *Bull.*, viii. 188.
[2] Giovanni Paolo Oliva, 1600–
81; general of the Society of Jesus
1664–81: *Encic. univ. ilustrada*;
Catholic encyc.

---

2. *Lords in the Tower:* the five Catholic lords arrested in October 1678: the earl of Powis, Viscount Stafford, Lord Petre, Lord Bellasis, Lord Arundel of Wardour.

of them, is^a ⟨almost⟩^b miraculous: But the Commons (some leading persons I meane of them) had so exalted him, that they tooke for Gospell all^c he said, & without more ado, ruin'd all whom he nam'd to be Conspirators, nor did he spare whomsoever came in his way; But indeede the Murder of Sir *Ed: Godferie* (suspected to have ben compassed by the *Jesuite* party, for his intimacy with *Coleman* (a buisy person whom I also knew) & the feare they had he was able to have discovered some thing to their prejudice)^d did so exasperate, not onely the *Commons*, but all the nation; That much of these sharpnesses against^e even the more honest *Ro: Catholicks* who lived peaceably, is to be imputed to that horrid fact:¹ The *Sessions* ended I dined, or rather indeede supped, (so late it was) with the Judges, in the large ⟨roome⟩^f annexed to the^g Place,² & so returned to my house: And though it was not my ⟨Custome⟩^h or delight, to beⁱ often present at any *Capital Trials*, we having them commonly, so exactly published, by those who take them in short hand;³ Yet I was inclined to be

---

^a Followed by *also* deleted.   ^b MS. *almast*.   ^c Altered from *as*.
^d Closing bracket supplied; MS. has colon.   ^e Followed by *th* deleted.
^f MS. *raame* or *raome*.   ^g Followed by *S-* deleted.   ^h MS. *Castome*.
ⁱ Followed by *much* deleted.

---

¹ The general reflections in this passage date probably from about 1684, when the trials for the plot were well past; it was certainly written before the trials of Oates for perjury in 1685.

² 'Over the Court Room is a stately Dining Room, sustained by ten Stone Pillars': Strype's Stow, iii. 281. The sessions house had been rebuilt after the Great Fire and was destroyed in the Gordon Riots in 1780.

³ The accuracy of the published reports of the Popish Plot trials has been questioned by various writers, and notably by J. G. Muddiman, in *State Trials: the need for a new and revised edition of "State Trials"*, 1930, principally following [Father J. M. Corker], *Some of the most*

material Errors and Omissions in the late Printed Tryals of the Romish Priests . . . Jan. 17. 1679, 1680. The reports vary considerably in character. Some are ostensibly verbatim reports, while others are clearly not more than summary reports set out in a form similar to that of the verbatim reports. No critical investigation of the whole group has as yet been published. So far, however, no adequate evidence has been produced to prove serious and deliberate falsification in the better reports; statements made in the course of the trials suggest that they were accepted as reliable by Sir William Scroggs and Sir George Jeffreys, although for technical reasons they could not be used in court.

at this signal one, that by the occular view of the carriages, & other Circumstances of the Manegers & parties concerned I might informe my selfe, and regulate my opinion of a Cause that had so alarm'd the whole Nation, & filled it with such expectations:

Henry Care's
The Weekly Pacquet of Advice from Rome—
The Popish Courant (July 25, 1679)

A more violent, partisan reaction to the trial may be seen in the final piece in this section, Henry Care's *The Popish Courant* for July 25, 1679. *The Popish Courant* appeared regularly at this time with Care's newspaper, *The Weekly Pacquet of Advice from Rome*. In this number, the papist *persona* expresses astonishment that anyone could be surprised at Wakeman's acquittal; lest the irony be missed, Care has his speaker turn rapidly to more overt menaces. For Care, only a fool with a death wish could believe that Wakeman was actually not guilty; his religion condemns him *a priori*.

[23]
THE
Popiſh Courant.
July 25. 1 6 7 9.

1   *Quod Dies negavit, Dabit Dies.*

IN the name of Folly, What ail the Folks ? Is it ſuch a ſtrange wonderful miraculous thing that a few *Monks and Papiſts* ſhould be found *Innocent ?* Alas! we are all ſo, every Mothers Son of us as *clear as the Child unborn.* Upon my word, Gentlemen, *Harry* the third and *Harry* the fourth of *France*, were not *Murthered*, onely *tickled* a little under-the *ſhort Ribbs*, and decently run through the Lungs with a *ſacred Dagger.* The *Powder-Plot* was nothing in the verſal world but a ſmall Device of *Cecils.* The little Buſi-neſs in *Ireland*, all damn'd *Fanatical Lyes*, onely the Prieſts, 'tis true, had a mind to make a few Conſecrated *Tapers* of the Hereticks *Sewet*, and rid the world of an hundred thouſand curſed *Hugenots*, or ſo forth. We well hop'd to have done ſome ſuch petty Exploit too in *London* long before this day : But as for a *Plot* we *defie* it, and all its *Diſcoverers.* 'Sdeath, can you ima-gine the *Loyal*Catholicks would be guilty of a Rebellion againſt their *King ?* We truſt you will never believe any ſuch thing, till you feel it. And if any body can give Evidence after his *Throat's cut*, let us ſuffer for it. But what need we thus expoſtulate ? we are confident ſome of you believe us already, and then we have gain'd the *Point* ; let our Friends alone to revive the *Plot.*
                                         There

1. *Quod Dies negavit, Dabit Dies:* What one day denies, another day will give.
2. *Harry the third and Harry the fourth:* Henry III of France was murdered in 1589 by a fanatical friar, Jacques Clément; Henry IV, his successor, was assassinated in 1610 by François Ravaillac, a madman influenced by Jesuit doctrines.
3. *Powder-Plot:* the Gunpowder Plot of 1605, a scheme of fanatical Catholics to blow up the king and Parliament.
4. *Cecils:* Robert Cecil, earl of Salisbury, chief counselor to James I.
5. *Ireland:* the Irish rebellion of October and November 1641 involved the massacre of Protestants.
6. *Sewet:* suet (animal fat chopped up and used in cooking or—as here—candle making).
7. *Hugenots:* French Protestants, persecuted by Louis XIV.

There is a foolifh Story, I learn'd at School, in *Æfop* or   8
fomewhere elfe ; I am fure there is neither Treafon nor
Popery in't : therefore I'il tell it you.

A certain *crafty Pufs* having a long time prey'd upon
the *Mice*,the poor Creatures at laft, for their fafety,kept
themfelves within their holes. The Cat finding her
Game decay, as being known to the Mice to be their
mortal enemy, refolves on a Stratagem, changeth his
hue, puts on a Religious habit, wipes his mouth, fhaves
his crown, and walks about with a moft innocent look ;
yet perceiving the Mice ftill kept in, or if they lookt
out at any time, it was very warily, as fufpecting the
worft. He formally and Father-like, calls to them, and
tells them, *Quod fueram non fum, Frater, Caput afpice
tonfum : Oh, Brother, I am not what you take me for, I
am no more a Cat, fee my Habit and fhaven Crown.* Hereupon fome of the more credulous and bold amongft
them (fuch as were fit to believe *Whitebread's* Protefta-
tions, and *Marfhal's* Rhetorick) venturing forth, were   9 10
by this deceit fnatcht up and *devour'd* at a mouthful.
Whereupon, when afterwards he came to wheadle them
out with the fame pretenfions, they would not budge,
but anfwer'd, *Cor tibi reftat idem, vix tibi præfto fidem :
Talk as finely as you can, we will never believe you ; you
have ftill a* Cats heart within you ; *you do not watch
and* pray, *but you watch to* prey. And fo (under the
Rofe be it fpoken) do our Jefuits and Priefts too. But   11
Qui vult decipi, Decipiatur : Thofe that have a mind to
be trepan'd out of their Lives, let them : For we have
been told by Prophetique *Hudibras,*   12

--------*The Pleafure is as great*
In being Cheated as to Cheat.

Printed for *L. C.* 1 6 7 9.

---

8. *Aesop:* while his *Fables* do contain tales of dissembling cats, this one is Care's.

9. *Whitebread's Protestations:* one of Oates's main villains in the *Narrative,* Thomas Whitebread, the Jesuit provincial, proclaimed his innocence of the plot at his execution (June 20, 1679).

10. *Marshall's Rhetorick:* William Marshall was one of the Benedictine monks tried and acquitted with Wakeman; during the trial he delivered several long speeches which irritated the judges.

11. *under the Rose:* in strict confidence (*sub rosa*).

12. *Hudibras:* Samuel Butler's satire of the Puritans, first published in 1663. These lines are from Part II, Canto iii, ll. 1–2. They actually read: DOUBTLESS, The pleasure is as great, / Of being *cheated,* as to *cheat.*

PART FIVE

The Exclusion Crisis

Anchitell Grey's
Debates in the House of Commons
(November 4, 9, 11, 1680)

If the London summer of 1679 was dominated by the trials and executions of papists, the following fourteen months were given over to an anxious parliamentary struggle. Charles, in delaying the sessions of his new Parliament from October 1679, until October of the new year, hoped to see a diminishing of exclusionist zeal. And indeed the plot did appear to be subsiding. After Wakeman's acquittal there were no other convictions related to the plot during this period. Yet the Whig efforts remained confident and powerful. Petitioners assailed the king with demands for the new session of Parliament. During the summer of 1680, Monmouth, gathering support for himself, went on his "progress" through the western counties, and in London a number of pamphlets appeared supporting the "Black Box" theory that Charles had secretly married Monmouth's mother. Shaftesbury and his following sought in June to indict the duke of York as a popish recusant and to charge the duchess of Portsmouth, the king's French, and Catholic, mistress as a public nuisance. The judges thwarted these legal efforts, but they retained their value as propaganda.

By the time Parliament met, passions were running high on both sides, as we can see in the excerpts given in this section from the debates on the second Exclusion Bill. Shaftesbury had formulated a sophisticated set of tactics to gain his point, including the introduction at the last minute of a new plot witness, Thomas Dangerfield, who implicated the duke of York in plots to murder the king. However, as Dangerfield was a convicted felon, he proved to be an unconvincing witness. Further, the bill at first did not specify who would succeed to the throne after James was excluded. The first Exclusion Bill had provided for the succession to go on as if James had died. This expedient finally had to be introduced again to meet the objections of those Whigs who favored James's children over Monmouth.

These excerpts are from Anchitell Grey, *Debates in the House of Commons, 1667–94*, 10 vols. (London, 1763), VII, 418–21, 433, 445–59.

The first debate on the Second Exclusion Bill began on November 4, 1680.

Lord Ruffel *reads the Order* " for bringing in the Bill to 1
difable *James* Duke of *York* from inheriting the Imperial
Crown of *England,* &c."]   According to this Order, the
Committee have drawn a Bill, and have commanded me
to prefent it.
[The Bill was read the firft time.]

Sir *Leoline Jenkins**.] I crave leave to fpeak againft a
fecond reading of this Bill, till I am fatisfied that it is for
the fervice of the Crown, and the fafety of the Nation ;
till I am fatisfied of the Juftice of it, whether it be na-

> * *Jenkins,* now made Secretary of State in *Coventry*'s place, was the chief manager for the Court. He was fufpected of leaning to Popery, though very unjuftly : But he was fet on every punctilio of the Church of *England* to fuperftition, and was a great affertor of the Divine Right of Monarchy, and was for carrying the Prerogative high. All his Speeches and Arguments againft the Exclufion were heard with indignation. *Burnet.* 2

tural

---

1. *Russel:* Lord William Russell (1639–1683) was one of Shaftesbury's closest associates and an exclusionist leader.

2. *Burnet:* Gilbert Burnet in his *History of My Own Times*; see the selection included in this collection (p. 79). The notes printed with the text are by the anonymous editor of this 1763 edition of Grey's *Debates*.

tural to exclude the Duke, &c. before you hear him. I
would do in this, as one man would do by another.   In
Reafon we ought to do, as we would be done by.   Popery is a crime, and punifhed by a Law already made ;
but here is now a Law for this Prince alone to be excluded, &c. Confider whether it be juft to make a new Law
for one perfon.   Confider from what principle this Bill
does flow; whether it be not rank Popery.   It hath been
difputable among fome of the Schools, whether Dominion be founded in Grace, or no.   None but Papifts and   3
Anabaptifts preach that notion.   As to the principle of the
Duke's being a Papift, and therefore not fit to fucceed to
the Crown, it is maintained by the Schools, Councils, and
Common Law, that a King may be depofed for Religion's fake.   Confider the practice of the Papifts by this
principle.   *Germany* had fix Emperors depofed for Religion—But to come nearer to our own times, *Hen.* IV. of
France was firft King of *Navarre*, and then was declared by the Bull of *Sixtus* V. not only incapable of the
Kingdom of *Navarre*, but of fucceeding to the Crown
of *France*.   The Pope proceeded againft Queen *Eliza-*   4
beth upon the account of Religion only.   That I defire to
be confidered, whether this Bill is not founded upon the
fame principle and practice of the Papifts.   Farther, this
Bill, as it is drawn, does change the very effence and
being of the Monarchy.   Confider whether you do not
reduce it to an Elective Monarchy.   In the effence of the
Monarchy, the Duke is Heir to the Crown, and this Bill
is oppofite to Primogeniture.   We know the inconveni-   5
ence of an Elective Monarchy by the diforders of *Po-*   6
land.   Confider whether this Bill is confiftent with the
Oath of Allegiance we have all taken—By the bleffing of   7
God, the King has not his Crown by defignation ; he is
not an Elective Monarch.   Not that I have fworn Allegiance to the Duke during the King's life : I have taken
that Oath in the fenfe of him that impofed it.   I took it
ten, twenty years ago, and if I am afked what is meant
in that Oath by " Heirs and Succeffors ? " I anfwer, the
next Heir to the Crown is the Duke, in cafe the King
E e 2   have

---

3. *Dominion:* the argument is that only the papists regard Grace (a prince's
religious attitude) as a requirement for Dominion (political power); thus the Exclusion Bill is "rank Popery."

4. *Elizabeth:* she was excommunicated in 1570.

5. *Primogeniture:* the right of inheritance or succession of the firstborn.

6. *Poland:* since 1572, Poland chose its own sovereign by election. Party strife
and foreign intervention caused difficulties in 1664.

7. *Oath of Allegiance:* imposed in 1606, it demanded that Catholics renounce the
doctrine that the Pope may depose heretical princes.

have no children. If I am fworn to this Allegiance, whether can any intervenient Act annull it, and whether, under this obligation, any power on earth can abfolve me from it? I will not take upon me to difpute this Law when it is made; but before it be made, I may difpute its convenience. I believe it is not in the power of man to abfolve me from that Oath. When God gives us a King in his wrath, it is not in our power to change him; we cannot require any qualifications; we muft take him as he is. An infant, that knows not his right hand from his left, by our Law is not to be fet afide from the Throne, but is as much King, as if a man at full years. This Allegiance binds my faith nothing at all fo long as the King is alive, but my Oath binds me to his Succeffor. Lately, in *France,* when *Hen.* IV. came to the Crown, a Proteftant, the far greater and moft powerful part of both the Court and Army did make it a queftion whether they fhould fubmit to a heretic Prince : Some would not at all oppofe him; others would fet up his old uncle, the Cardinal of *Bourbon,* for King; another Party, a *fquadron volante,* would not acknowlege him till he turn-   8 ed Papift; but the greater Party thought it their indifpenfible duty to obey him, and did fo, becaufe they fhould be in lefs danger with a heretic Prince, than by a Civil War if the thing was contended. It is a fundamental maxim not to enter into an uncertain for a certain mifchief, and upon thefe confiderations, pray lay this Bill afide.

Mr *Montagu.*] The other day, this worthy Member   9 told you of the Laws abroad in relation to Succeffion, and now he fays, " This is a Popifh Bill." I obferve, that his knowlege of the Laws and Divinity abroad is more than at home. If any man thinks that the Duke, &c. is not in the Plot, nor a Papift, let him give his Vote againft the Bill : I am fatisfied in both, and therefore do defire the Bill may have a fecond reading. Till this Bill be paffed, the King is expofed to the malice of the Papifts, and importunities of follicitations from the Duke's friends; and I hope this Parliament will give as good teftimony of
                                        their

---

8. *squadron volante:* a body of cardinals hovering between the main factions; literally a flying regiment.

9. *Montagu:* Ralph Montagu (1638–1709) was famous for revealing Danby's secret letters to Louis XIV in 1678 and causing his fall from power.

their duty for preservation of the King's Person, and the Protestant Religion, as the last did. Saving the King from the malice of *Rome* is as great service as bringing him from *Bruſſels*. This Bill saves the King's Prerogative and Religion, and two good things it saves besides, the King's Life and his Authority ; and I am for a second reading.

Mr *Hampden.*] I apprehend, *Jenkins*'s Reasons have not that weight as he lays upon them. He tells us, " We should do as we would be done by." But this Rule is to be rightly underſtood ; it muſt be by a regulated will. No man but would be saved from death. A Malefactor would. Surely in that caſe it cannot hold, " To do as we would be done by." I am not of opinion that the Bill should singly exclude the Duke, becaufe he is a Papiſt, but that with the conſequences : Not so much as a Papiſt, but becaufe of the inſeparable principles of that Religion, in which it is impoſſible the Nation should be safe. It has always been said by the Papiſts, " That this is a bloody Law, to put men to death for Religion as we do." But that is Popiſh, to say " It is for Religion." You have always diſowned it ; it is for their conſequential principles. I do not think (as *Jenkins* said) that this Bill makes the Kingdom Elective. I know not but in an Hereditary Monarchy, if a Succeſſor will deſtroy the Kingdom, he may not be put by the Succeſſion, but the Pope is your King if you have a Popiſh Succeſſor, and it is not far remote when a King is a Papiſt. What will become of you when you have broken prison ? Shall you fare any better when the Inquiſition is ſet up, that nothing but the blood of ſo many Martyrs and Confeſſors at *Newgate* can elſe be expiated ? Do you think that will be forgotten then ? When Popery comes into *England*, it will come with advantage enough without all theſe provocations. Their Religion is none but the pride of avaritious Churchmen. Upon theſe conſiderations, I move for a second reading of the Bill.

The Bill was ordered to be read a second time [on *Saturday* next.]

10. *Brussels:* that is, his restoration in 1660.
11. *Mr. Hampden:* Richard Hampden (1631–1695), M.P. from Buckinghamshire.

Here the king lets the Commons know that he will not accept exclusion.

Tuesday, November 9.

[Mr Secretary *Jenkins* delivered the following Meſſage from his Majeſty :

"CHARLES *R.*

" His Majeſty deſires this Houſe, as well for the ſatisfaction of his people as of himſelf, to expedite ſuch matters as are depending before them, relating to Popery and the Plot ; and would have them reſt aſſured, that all remedies they can tender to his Majeſty, conducing to thoſe ends, ſhall be very acceptable to him, provided they be ſuch as may conſiſt with preſerving the Succeſſion of the Crown in its due and legal courſe of deſcent."]

The Exclusion Bill having passed its second reading on November 9, it now came up for its third and final reading in the House of Commons. As this excerpt shows, there was an impassioned debate in which James was personally attacked.

Houſe, and then your proceeding to Lord *Stafford's* Tryal.

Which was accordingly ordered.

Reſolved, Nemine contradicente, That this Houſe will proceed in the Proſecution of the Lords in the *Tower,* and will forthwith begin with *William* Viſcount *Stafford.*

Thurſday, November 11.

[Sir *William Jones* * reports, from the Committee, the follow-   12
ing Addreſs to his Majeſty, in Anſwer to his Meſſage, which was read, and agreed to by the Houſe :

" We your Majeſty's moſt loyal and obedient Subjects, the Commons in this preſent Parliament aſſembled, having taken into our moſt ſerious conſideration your Majeſty's gracious Meſſage, brought unto us the ninth day of this inſtant *November* by Mr Secretary *Jenkins,* do, with all thankfulneſs, acknowlege your Majeſty's care and goodneſs in inviting us to expedite ſuch matters as are depending before us, relating to Popery and the Plot ; and we do, in all humility, repreſent it to your Majeſty, that we are fully convinced that it is highly incumbent upon us, in diſcharge both of our duty to your Majeſty, as of that great truſt repoſed in us by thoſe whom we repreſent, to endeavour, by the moſt ſpeedy and effectual ways, the ſuppreſſion of Popery within this your Kingdom, and the bringing to public Juſtice all ſuch as ſhall be found guilty of the horrid and damnable Popiſh Plot : And though the time of our ſitting (abating what muſt neceſſarily be ſpent in the chuſing and preſenting a Speaker, appointing Grand Committees, and in taking the Oaths and Teſts enjoined by Act of Parliament) hath not much exceeded a fortnight, yet we have, in this time, not only made a conſiderable progreſs in ſome things, which to us ſeem, and, when preſented to your Majeſty in a Parliamentary way, will, we truſt, appear to your Majeſty to be abſolutely neceſſary for the ſafety of your Majeſty's Perſon, the effectual ſuppreſſion of Popery, and the ſecurity of the Religion, Lives, and Eſtates of your Majeſty's Proteſtant Subjects, but even in relation to the Tryals of the five Lords, impeached in Parliament, for the execrable Popiſh Plot, we have ſo far proceeded, as, we doubt not, but in a ſhort time, we ſhall be ready for the ſame : But we cannot, without being unfaithful to your Majeſty, and to our Countries, by whom we

---

* This Addreſs was drawn up under the ſanction of Sir *William Jones,* who was that very day introduced into the Houſe, as alſo appointed of the Committee, and by them placed in the Chair, out of a peculiar compliment. *Rapi.*

are

---

12. *Sir William Jones:* the former attorney general; see Grey's note below.

are intrusted, omit, upon this occasion, humbly to inform your Majesty, that our difficulties, even as to these Tryals, are much increased by the evil and destructive Counsels of those persons who advised your Majesty, first to the Prorogation, and then to the Dissolution of the last Parliament, at a time when the Commons had taken great pains about, and were prepared for those Tryals ; and by the like pernicious Counsels of those who advised the many and long Prorogations of the present Parliament, before the same was permitted to sit ; whereby some of the Evidence, which was prepared in the last Parliament, may possibly, during so long an interval, be forgotten, or lost ; and some persons, who might probably have come in as Witnesses, are either dead, have been taken off, or may have been discouraged from giving their Evidence : But of one mischievous consequence of those dangerous and unhappy Counsels we are certainly and sadly sensible ; namely, that the Testimony of a material Witness against every one of those five Lords, and who could probably have discovered and brought in much other Evidence about the Plot in general, and those Lords in particular, cannot now be given *vivâ voce*, forasmuch as that Witness is unfortunately dead, between the calling and the sitting of this Parliament.

" To prevent the like or greater inconveniences for the future, we make it our most humble request to your excellent Majesty, that, as you tender the Safety of your Royal Person, the Security of your loyal Subjects, and the Preservation of the true Protestant Religion, you will not suffer yourself to be prevailed upon by the like Counsels, to do any thing which may occasion, in consequence (though we are assured, never with your Majesty's intention) either the deferring of a full and perfect Discovery and Examination of this most wicked and detestable Plot ; or the preventing the Conspirators therein from being brought to speedy and exemplary justice and punishment : And we humbly beseech your Majesty to rest assured, notwithstanding any suggestions which may be made by persons, who, for their own wicked purposes, contrive to create a distrust in your Majesty of your People, that nothing is more in the desires, and shall be more the endeavours, of us your faithful and loyal Commons, than the promoting and advancing of your Majesty's true Happiness and Greatness."]

The Bill to disable the Duke of *York*, &c. was read the third time.

Sir *Leoline Jenkins*.] This Bill is of the greatest consequence that can come into Parliament, and withall, you
are

are about to do an act of injuftice, great and fevere, upon the offender. But by the way I will offer fomething of the prudential confideration of it, but crave leave to enter my diffent to the juftice of it, and the Oath of Allegiance I have taken to his Majefty. I will not offer to your confideration, that this Prince you are about to difable to fucceed, &c. is the fon of a King, a glorious Martyr, a Prince that has fought your battles, and no crime againft him in your eye, but his being perverted to Popery from the Proteftant Religion. But the difficulty I ftruggle againft is, fo great a defire in the Houfe to pafs this Bill. But I cannot fatisfy myfelf in the Juftice of this way of proceeding. What is effential Juftice to a man in his Place? It is always effential Juftice to hear a perfon before you condemn him. God, though he knew the heart and crimes of *Adam*, did not condemn him before he had 13 heard him. It feems hard to me, that this Law againft the Duke fhould come *ex poft facto*, which is not only 14 Banifhment, but Difinherifon; a thing ftrange in our Books of Law, that there fhould be two punifhments for one crime. I obferve next, that, by the fundamentals of the Government, how can you make a King by Parliaments? I have always taken it, that the Government had it's original, not from the People, but from God. Religion vefts that veneration in us for the Government, that it will be much lefs, when we fee it from the people, and not from God immediately. Several fettlements have been made by Act of Parliament, of entail of the Crown, which ftill do affert the Succeffor; but no Precedent can be found, where a Prince in proximity of Blood to the Crown has been fet afide. I do not know how to reconcile this to the Oath of Allegiance I have taken to the King, and fo often repeated, which is always taken in the fenfe of the Lawgiver and Impofer. The Perfon is next in Blood to fucceed to the Crown, and when I fwear Allegiance, it is not only to the King, but " his Heirs and Succeffors," and there can be no *Interregnum* in our Government. When 15 one King is dead, the other next in Blood muft fucceed;

and

---

13. *Adam:* Genesis 3:8–24.

14. *ex post facto:* after the fact.

15. *Interregnum:* the period between the reigns of monarchs; in England the period between 1649 and 1660.

and who can difpenfe with my Oath of Allegiance? All the Members of the Houfe make profeffion of being of the Church of *England*. I am afraid the Church of *England* will receive a great blow by this Bill. The reafon of one of the great beauties of the Church of *England* is, that it is fafe and fecure in the matter of Allegiance to all—Government muft be either active or paffive. If we are to defend a King made by Act of Parliament, as this Bill imports, that Law will receive a blemifh, for we are not to do evil that good may come of it, if there be any good in the Bill! But I know of none, and therefore I move to throw it out.

Sir *Robert Markham*.] If I could anfwer my own objections, I would not ftand up. Suppofe the Duke of *York* fhould furvive the King, and have a fon, is it reafon that the Duke's daughter fhould have the Crown? And fuppofe the Duke fhould come back again to the Church of *England*—This gives me the boldnefs to ftand up and make my objections.

Mr *Goodwin Wharton* *.] I have not yet troubled you fince I had the honour to be here, and fhould not at all upon any other matter. I know my own inabilities, in comparifon of many abler and wifer men than myfelf, but I cannot be filent when I hear the Juftice of the Houfe queftioned. If thofe things be true which are fuggefted in the Bill, the Duke has forfeited his life upon it. Paffing this Bill is in order to our fecurity only, and therefore it is juft. The Duke has done his utmoft endeavour to ruin this Nation, and to deftroy us all. It is faid, " that the Duke has fought our battles;" but I think he did not when he fell afleep †. It was not fair in the Duke to let 16 our fhips fight with the *Dutch*, and to fuffer the *French* to ftand ftill. At the great fire, when *London* was burnt, certain men were taken, actually firing houfes, and delivered to the Guards, who let them efcape, and the Officer that fet them at liberty was afterwards one of his

* A younger fon of Lord *Wharton*, and uncle to the late Duke.
† See Vol. I. p. 139.

greateft

16. *he fell asleep:* after the naval battle at Lowestoft in the Second Dutch War (1664), York fell asleep; while he remained so, a subordinate ordered in the duke's name that the ship be slowed. When York awoke, his ship was seriously out of position.

greateft favourites.   It was a fign of a very ill principle in
the Duke, that, when the Duke of *Monmouth* was fent into *Scotland* to fupprefs that Rebellion, it was thought
amifs by the Duke, that they were not all deftroyed.   I do   17
not think that you will chufe a Prince that will not fpeak
truth, to inherit the Crown.   When *Bedlow* gave in his
Information of the murder of Sir *Edmundbury Godfrey,*
and accufed one *Le Phaire* to have been one of the mur-   18
derers, and one of the Queen's fervants, I heard the Duke
fay to thofe about him, " There was no fuch man in the
World, nor about the Queen."   And within three or
four days after, there was a Bond found, under his hand.
A Prince not to fpeak truth!   I cannot exprefs what to
call it.   This is plain, that the Duke did hinder the Difcovery of the Plot.   I do not pretend, upon my memory,
to fay more particulars; but is fuch a Prince fit to fucceed?   Never were worfe things done, nor a worfe man
in betraying the *French* Proteftants, by placing the *French*
Ambaffador behind the hanging when he made fome over-
tures—

Here Lord Caftleton *interrupted him, to the Orders of the*   19
Houfe.] To hear a Prince thus fpoken of, I am not able
to endure it!

Mr Wharton *went on.*] It is not my bufinefs to make
a Speech, but what I know, and think to be real truth,
ought to be taken notice of.   But fince thefe things are
fo odious, I will not touch any more upon them now.
As for the prudential part of the Bill, an Honourable Perfon near me *(Jenkins)* told you, " he would not fpeak to
it," and he has kept his word very exactly.   And whereas
another Member before him objected, " That it was
poffible the Duke might turn Proteftant," I will only
anfwer, that I do not think it poffible, that any Perfon
that has been bred up in the Proteftant Religion, and
hath been weak enough (for fo I muft call it) to turn
Papift, fhould ever after (in that refpect) be wife enough
to turn Proteftant.   And therefore, upon the whole
matter, my Motion is, " That the Bill may pafs."

Vol. VII.   G g   Mr

---

17. *all destroyed:* Monmouth was merciful after his victory at Bothwell Bridge
(June 22, 1679); York criticized him for it.

18. *La Phaire:* in fact he did not exist.

19. *Lord Castleton:* George Saunderson, Viscount Castleton (1631–1714), an M.P.
from Lincoln.

Mr *Hyde*.] I am charmed very much by the Gentle-   20
man's reasons that moved first for reading this Bill (*Ver-*
non) as if he were not Proteftant, nor loyal, that was
against it. I take myself to be both, but am against it.
I offered formerly Expedients inftead of the Bill, which
I thought might be more conducible to your end. It is
not proper to offer any now, but to the whole Bill, why it
fhould not pafs. But I fhall take notice of a Provifo
offered, " That this Bill fhould extend only to the Duke,
&c." I appeal to you, whether that Provifo be clear?
If it be not clear, why is it not made clear? If the Duke
outlive the King, and the King have Heirs of his Body,
whether fhould it not be expreffed, " The Heirs of his
Body, lawfully begotten?" If you think it well enough
expreffed fo, or if it be better as I fay, I fubmit it to you.
Another thing offered you was the words " Prefumptive
Heir of the Crown." (*In the other Bill the laft Parlia-*
ment.) I would know whether the Duke be fo, or not?
I would be glad to be anfwered, If the Duke is not, who
is? Sure never fuch a Bill paffed before. There were feveral quarrels betwixt the Houfes of *York* and *Lancafter*;   21
but where there was an unqueftionable Title, as this of
the Duke's is, there cannot be found a Precedent of fuch a
Bill. I take this Bill to be extremely unjuft, let the fact
the Duke is charged with be what it will. When the
King was reftored, it was notorioufly known, who were
the murderers of the late King his Father; they had all
their Tryals for it, and were heard. This is faid to be a
merciful Bill, but it is not a juft Bill; but for the fatisfaction of my confcience, I had rather go the juft, than
the merciful way. You may take his head off, upon
Tryal, if he be guilty of what he is accufed of. I will
not difpute the power of King, Lords, and Commons.
The Act was made for the Perpetuity of the Parliament   22
—Yet they were diffolved, and gave not their confents to
it. Notwithftanding this Bill, Perfons of Loyalty will
adhere to the Duke if he outlive the King. If this Bill
pafs, it will be fuch an Act as the perpetual Parliament,
and many a loyal Perfon, out of that principle of
Loyalty

---

20. *Mr. Hyde:* Laurence Hyde (1641–1711)—Dryden's Husai in *Absalom and Achitophel*.

21. *York and Lancaster:* in the Wars of the Roses, 1450–1461.

22. *Perpetuity of Parliament:* see 16 Car I. c. 1 and 7 (*Statutes of the Realm*, 1819, rpt. London: 1963, vol. 5).

Loyalty and Honefty, will ftick to the Duke. Thefe are
my Reafons. (I am, I muft confefs, a little out.) The   23
Bill in itfelf is unjuft, and may yet be of fo much the
worfe confequence than without the Bill. Therefore I am
againft it.

Sir *William Jones* *.] I am unfit to fpeak upon this
great matter. I am a Member but of yefterday, and
know nothing ; but I cannot forbear, upon this occafion,
to fay fomething. As the Bill is opened, it is of great
importance. I have as much refpeé for the Duke as any
Perfon, but I muft have refpeé to Religion above all
things. This, of refpeé to the Duke, I will pafs over now.
But the Queftion is, Whether a Popifh Prince can inherit
the Crown of *England* without the lofs of all our Laws ?
It is happy for the Duke, that we go no farther than this
Bill. It may be, we might take notice of our infecurity
under him, and fome other accidents that belong to him,
fince you proceeded in this Bill. It is abfolutely neceffary that you pafs this Bill ; it is far from my nature to in-
fliét any fevere punifhment ; but this Bill is not a punifhment without hearing the Duke (as has been alleged.)
We do not punifh the Duke as a Criminal, but we
are preventing the Evil that is likely to befall us from
that Religion he profeffes. *Jenkins* made an Argument againft this Bill from the Oath of Allegiance,
as if we were perjured in maintaining this Bill. It is
the firft time I ever heard that thofe Oaths were to bring
in Popery, but to fecure us from Popery ; and he urges
much the point of " lawful Succeffor to the Crown."
But is any man the King's lawful Succeffor till the
King is dead ? *Nemo eft Hæres viventis* is a maxim   24
in *Jenkins*'s own Law (the Civil.) But when I take the

---

* The firft time he fpoke in Parliament.
    Sir *William Jones*, the late Attor-
ney General, at his firft entrance
into the Houfe, efpoufed the Bill
with a warmth and vehemence
which were not natural to him.
And this perfon having the fame
of being the greateft Lawyer in *Eng-*
land, and a very wife man ; being
alfo known to be very rich, and of
a wary or rather timorous nature,
made people generally conclude,
that the thing was fafe and certain,
and would at laft be agreed on all
hands, whatever countenance was
made at Court. *Temple's Memoirs.*

G g 2   Oath

---

23. *a little out:* at a loss, nonplussed.
24. *Nemo est Haeres viventis:* No one is an heir to a living person.

Oath of Allegiance, that Oath did never bind to above one Perſon at a time. I am not obliged to any Allegiance till that Succeſſor comes to act. Therefore I am not at all afraid that this Bill is againſt the Oath of Allegiance. As to *Hyde*'s objection to the form of the Bill, " That it is ſtrange," and that after " the King and Heirs of his Body," there want the words " lawfully begotten," he muſt know, that, in Law, " the Heirs of his Body," and " the lawful Heirs," are the ſame thing. But there might be an objection againſt the words, if they were in. It might be objected, " That the King might have Heirs of his Body, and not lawful;" nothing more plain. As to that of " Preſumptive Heir, &c." I never in all my life, in Books, met with ſuch an expreſſion. Sometimes there is mention made of " Heir Apparent," and I wonder any man ſhould call the Duke ſo, when it may be but a name; but the word " Preſumptive" as Heir, it is the firſt time I ever found it. And as to the other objection, " That this Bill may fall to the ground, becauſe it is like the Act of Perpetuity of the late Long Parliament," there is no reaſon for that conſequence. There is no need of executing this Bill in the King's life-time. Then only this Law is in force, after the King's deceaſe. One thing farther is objected, " That if this Bill paſs the Parliament, there will be a ſort of " loyal men," who will not obey this Law:" I have a wrong no-tion of this word " loyal," if that be ſo. He is loyal to the King that obeys his Laws; and he is otherwiſe that does not. This is a thing that may terrify a man that underſtands not the nature of it. The other objection is not to be anſwered, becauſe not weighty. It is for the benefit of the King and Proteſtant Religion that this Bill paſs, and I am for it.

Sir *Francis Winnington.*] I find here is an imputation   25
of Injuſtice upon us, if this Bill paſs. This Argument ſhould not come from an *Engliſhman,* unleſs from one bred in foreign Countries, where Popery and arbitrary Government are exerciſed. I would aſk any man that does pretend to know Hiſtory, or the Law of *England,*
whether,

---

25. *Sir Francis Winnington:* a lawyer from Worcester (1634–1700); he had lost his parliamentary seat from Windsor, which had been given by the king's command, and his position as solicitor general in 1679 after he supported exclusion.

whether, from the Conqueft, the beft fecurity for any Prince's Title has not been by Act of Parliament? You are told, " That the King's Title to the Crown is *Jure divino*." It is not Law, nor Reafon. When there was but one King in the World, what became of the King of *England?* From the time of the Conqueror, *William Rufus*, King *Stephen*, and before the queftions about the Title of *York* and *Lancafter*, we have feveral inftances of fettling the Succeffion of the Crown by Act of Parliament; and, in *Cotton's* Records, that the Crown has ⟨26⟩ paffed, not by Defcent, according to lineal Defcent, but has been fettled as emergencies have required. It has been argued, " That this Act will want Power to be executed:" But will any man affert, that the Parliament has not Power to order, or difpofe of the Government? Sometimes they have pared the Prerogative; but the Government is ftill the fame; and I hope our children after us will enjoy it, notwithftanding this unhappy occafion of Exclufion of the Duke. The Marriage of Queen *Mary* with King *Philip* was fettled thus by Par- ⟨27⟩ liament, That the eldeft fon of them fhould be King of *Spain*, the fecond fon fuch, and the third fon fuch; and in that Statute it was ordered, that King *Philip* fhould not be King of *England* for life, but during the Queen's life only: And why fo? Becaufe this Nation would not be governed by an arbitrary Prince, by *merum Imperium*, ⟨28⟩ which was fervitude and flavery; and this Act was ftill to keep our Liberties, and enacted, that the eldeft fon was to inherit. That was a great and a wife Parliament, that made it Treafon, during Queen *Elizabeth's* life, for ⟨29⟩ any one to fay, " That the Parliament cannot fet up the Succeffion, and alter it," and *Præmunire* for ever after. ⟨30⟩ But as to the Injuftice of this Bill, fhould that objection pafs filently, it would found ill abroad if that was not cleared. We are not punifhing the Duke for an offence committed. This Bill is not to do a prefent wrong to the Duke, but to prevent future mifchief. If an ancient family might poffibly be ruined by the eldeft fon, it is not unjuft to difinherit him. The Parliament does

G g 3 fee,

---

26. *Cotton's Records: An Exact Abridgement of the Records in the Tower of London* (1657) is a record of the Parliaments from the time of Edward II to that of Richard III. The author is the famous antiquary Sir Robert Bruce Cotton (1571–1631).

27. *Marriage of Queen Mary:* see *Statues of the Realm* I M. St. 3. c. 2 (1554).

28. *merum Imperium:* raw autocratic power.

29. *Queen Elizabeth's life:* 13 Eliz. c. 1 (1571).

30. *Praemunire:* to be put out of the king's protection and to forfeit all goods to the crown.

fee, that, if a Popifh Prince comes to the Crown, the
Kingdom will be ruined; and if the Parliament have
not Power to prevent it, it is ftrange.   This is but preventing a mifchief. The Duke is but a Subject, though
in proximity of Blood to the Crown. If you proceed by
way of Impeachment againft the Duke, it is not juft,
unlefs all things againft him are proved.   But I would
know, whether, as a Grand Jury, we may not pafs this
Bill, in our own confcience believing, that, elfe, Religion
and the Government will be deftroyed.   As to what has
been faid of " the Act of Perpetuity of the Long Parliament," thofe Acts which are not practicable come to
nothing. The King and Parliament is a Civil Marriage,
and there cannot be a fon without a father.   I remember that great cafe of Sir *Henry Vane*, where he alleged,   31
" That the King could not diffolve the Parliament without their confent."   But if the King demife, it is diffolved of itfelf. As to that point objected, of " the Heirs
of the King's Body only lawfully begotten, &c." in
Law it is as plain as can be expreffed.   No man is Heir
but the lawful Heir.   " Heir Prefumptive" is not to be
found in Law-Books. The King's eldeft fon is Prince of
Wales and Duke of *Cornwall*.   " Prefumptive" may be
Heir, or not Heir; it is not near the Crown. As for the
Juftice of the Bill; we fhould not do our duty to our
Country, nor Pofterity, nor Religion, if we take not
care of all thefe by this Bill, which is much more than
the remote Right of any Perfon to the Crown.   Gentlemen that have no children, may not poffibly have that
warmth in thefe confiderations.   It is terrible to me to
think they fhall be made Slaves and Papifts.   Let every
man lay his hand on his heart, and confider it.   If Popery come in, all will be loft. I have refpect for the
Duke, but there are degrees in things.   I hope this Bill
will pafs as unanimoufly without doors as here.

Colonel *Legge*.] I humbly crave the liberty that other   32
Members have had, to be heard. Though I am talked
of abroad to be a Papift, yet, I thank God, I am none.
And for an inftance that I am not any, I will not pay
that

---

31. *Sir Henry Vane:* Puritan statesman (1613–1662); at his trial for treason in
1662 he made such arguments for the sovereignty of Parliament (see *State Trials*,
vol. II [London, 1703], pp. 440–41).

32. *Colonel Legge:* George Legge (1648–1691), a distinguished officer and friend
of the duke of York; see also Grey's note on p. 141.

that refpect to *Peter's* Chair, as to *deny my Mafter* †. I am forry to hear the unmannerly Speeches of the Duke from a Gentleman *(Wharton.)* Many Laws have been made about the Succeffion of the Crown, but none without blood and mifery. My father was twice condemned to die for afferting the Right of the Crown, and I hope I fhall never forfake it. There has been a talk in the world of another Succeffor than the Duke, in a black Box ‡; but if *Pandora's* Box muft be opened, I would have it in my time, not in my childrens, that I may draw my fword to defend the right Heir. Has any happinefs ever come to Princes, who came to the Crown, and the lawful Heir thus put by? After *Edward* VI, *Jane Grey* was proclaimed, but it proved unfortunate to her. If my Mafter the Duke be Popifh, God's curfe be on him that was the caufe of it! I hope you will take a courfe, that mifery may not fall on pofterity. I have Church-Lands, and reafon to apprehend Popery coming in as other men—I cannot recollect what I had farther to fay; but this Bill will fet us all together by the ears.

Sir *Henry Capel.*] No objection to this Bill has yet been made, but what has been fully anfwered formerly: But this is a new Parliament, and fo the matter ought to be fully opened. Two objections, now ftarted, remain. The one, " That the Duke has fought the Battles of the Nation." Let the Duke be what he will, he is under misfortunes, to be the Son of a King that hath maintained the Proteftant Religion. There has been an acknowlegement for fighting our Battles. The Parliament at *Oxford* did an extraordinary thing; there was Money

† He was Mafter of the Horfe, and Gentleman of the Bed-chamber, to the Duke of *York*; and afterwards Lord *Dartmouth*.

‡ A report was induftrioufly propagated, that a Marriage had been folemnized, or at leaft a Contract had paffed, between his Majefty, while abroad, and Mrs. *Walters,* otherwife *Barlow,* his Grace of *Monmouth's* Mother; that the late Bifhop of *Durham* had configned a writing in a black Box, relating thereto, into the cuftody of Sir *Gilbert Gerrard,* and that the faid writing had been communicated to feveral perfons of diftinction, and had fully fatisfied them that the fact was fo. *Ralph.*

G g 4   given

---

33. *Pandora's Box:* containing in Greek mythology all the multitude of human ills.

34. *Jane Grey:* put forward as the Protestant heir when Edward VI died in 1553, she was overthrown by the Catholic Mary Tudor ("Bloody Mary") and was executed in 1554.

35. *Sir Henry Capel:* (d. 1696), one of the strongest supporters of the Exclusion Bill; in 1692 made Lord Capel of Tewkesbury.

given to the King, but it was for the Duke, in acknowlegement of his fervice at fea. *Legge* tells you of " Blood   36
and Confufion that may follow this Bill ;" but I conceive
that this Bill is intended to prevent Blood. What has
been may be again. There has been no occafion, fince
the Proteftant Reformation, of this kind. But in *France*
Hen. III. did but declare the King of *Navarre* rightful
Heir to the Crown ; yet, becaufe a Proteftant King
might be in a Popifh Country, that Kingdom was not
able to bear it, and there was, in the life of the King, a
Rebellion, though the King of *Navarre* was able to raife
a great Army. You fee we have been patient. The
Law of the Teft againft Popery was directed to the
Duke, and he laid afide all his Commiffions upon it,
and, in 1678, you put all the Popifh Lords out of that
Houfe, for refufing that Teft, when it was enjoined
them, and this was directed to the Duke. But what are
twenty one Lords to be removed out of their Houfe?
There is ftill a majority to pafs the Provifo to exempt the
Duke from the Teft in that Houfe. This fhows you,
that the Duke is a Papift, and all this is done with peace
and quietnefs ; not as in *France*, when the Nation fell into a Civil War upon *Hen.* IV. being declared Succeffor.
At a Court of Juftice out of Parliament, the Grand Jury   37
was difmiffed, when Evidence was proffered as to the
Duke's being a Papift *, when great matters were prefented
them, when all our fafeties were at ftake. If Judges
may do thefe things, neither the Laws we make, nor can
make, will protect us. If the Duke, now a Subject,
have fo great an influence in the Courts of Juftice, what
will he do when he comes to be King! And yet all is
quiet ; but in *France* it was not fo ; there was a Rebellion,
and *Hen.* III. was killed ; and *Hen.* IV, as he was a Proteftant, had no quiet ; yet his Character was great as to
War, great as King of *Navarre*, had great intereft in
Germany, and with Queen *Elizabeth* in *England*, yet made
no fhock with that Nation to keep him out. No Proteftant can be King in a Popifh Country. The *Englifh*

* See p. 364.

are

36. *service at sea:* in 1665, Parliament had granted York £120,000 "in token of
the great sense they had of his conduct and bravery" (quoted in John Kenyon's
James II [London: J. M. Dent & Sons, 1977], p. 85).

37. *Grand Jury:* Shaftesbury and others attempted to have York indicted as a
popish recusant on June 26, 1680 before the Middlesex Grand Jury, but the judges
dismissed the jury before it could return a bill.

are of a quiet nature; but fhould we be fo unfortunate as to have a Popifh King, it would bring us all into Confufion and Blood. If this Bill pafs not, all the Nation will be in Blood. Therefore pray pafs the Bill.

Mr *Finch.*] I am againft the Bill, and much more 38 fince I heard the explanation of a difficulty. When it was objected, " That this Bill was a punifhment to the Duke without hearing him," it was anfwered, " Not fo, becaufe it was in order to the prevention of it." I would know, whether any Gentleman that had an Eftate fettled upon him would not call this a punifhment? To a Prince, this is to him as a Civil Death, and to a man of Honour, and of the Duke's fpirit, it is worfe than Death. That Act of *Henry* VIII. was as obligatory as any other, and 39 with limitation to another—And yet to affirm, " That a Parliament can be bound up in declaring the Succeffion," is on the borders of High Treafon. When *Edw.* IV. came to the Crown, the feveral Acts of *Hen.* IV, *Hen.* V, and *Hen.* VI, were made void. That Parliament of *Edw.* IV. 40 looked upon what the other Kings had done in Parliament as invalid; fo little Right had thofe Kings. *Henry* VII, who had no Right to the Crown, and was of the Houfe of *Lancafter*, was attainted, yet he perfectly refufed an Act to reverfe his Attainder, fo little did he 41 think that fit, who had no Act for his Title. The main thing that I object to, is the laft Claufe in the Bill. I will not difpute the words of " Prefumptive Heir," but there might be other words in the Bill to make it clear, that nothing fhould prejudice the Heirs of the Duke—It is not faid, after " Iffue begotten," " Such a day," then it is clear for the Duke's children. This does not neceffarily fuppofe pretenfions, but if there be any fuch fetting up a new Title, not to make matters clear, is not becoming the wifdom of Parliament. The Princefs of *Orange* is next Heir, if the Duke have no fons. Sup- 42 pofe the Duke furvive the King, and this Bill difables the Duke to inherit the Crown, and the Duke have a fon, and the Princefs of *Orange* be in poffeffion of the Crown five or fix years; this fon ought to inherit the Crown.

Will

---

38. *Mr. Finch:* Daniel Finch (1647–1730), a strong Tory; in 1682 he became earl of Nottingham upon the death of his father Henage Finch.

39. *Act of Henry VIII: Statues of the Realm*—25 Hen. c. 22 (1533–1534).

40. *Parliament of Edw. IV:* this occurred in the Parliament of November 1461.

41. *Attainder:* judgment of death or outlawry without trial; the extinction of all legal rights.

42. *Princess of Orange:* Mary, York's Protestant daughter who had married William of Orange in 1677.

Will you give the Princefs of *Orange* fuch an actual poffeffion of the Crown, and yet a defeifible one too ? So   43
that between the Right Line, it may be the caufe of infinite confufion. I was in Parliament (though not of the
laft) when firft it was moved to remove the Duke from
the King, and then there was no thought to prejudice his
Right to the Succeffion. In the laft Parliament, the
Duke was called " Prefumptive Heir to the Crown" in the
Bill of Exclufion, which did denominate him the King's
immediate Succeffor. But in this you do not only exclude the Duke the Succeffion, but you leave it doubtful
to his children. Lay your hands upon your hearts, and
I am afraid, that, inftead of fecuring ourfelves, we fhall
gratify our enemies. All Acts mention our King, " King
of *France*," in Ceremony ; and I am afraid we fhall gratify him more yet by our confufion, and putting the Nation into diforder by this Bill. It is the intereft of the
Papifts to divide Proteftants, that always fome of the
Proteftants may be in their intereft, as the Declaration
for Liberty of Confcience proved to do; and the Papift   44
and Proteftant were punifhed by the fame Law ; and we
are going about, by this Bill, to divide Proteftants, which
will gratify the Papifts : Now that we have a Bill depending to unite them, I would not raife fcruples, nor mag-
nify them, but from what I have faid, I would throw
out the Bill.

Mr *Trenchard.*] I am unwilling to trouble you, after   45
fo many learned Gentlemen. I fhall fpeak a few words
to the Injuftice objected, of " laying the Duke afide in the
Succeffion before he be cited to be heard." There is a
great difference betwixt putting a man barely out of his
Right, and where there is danger that he will involve the
Nation in mifery. There is no more Injuftice in excluding the Duke from the Crown, than in excluding
the Popifh Lords from the Parliament, and in for-
feiting two thirds of their Eftates to the King. But
when a thing is *pro bono publico*, we ever ftep over private   46
Rights. The King's Right to the Crown is by Com-
mon and Statute Law, and the Houfe of *Lancafter* had
                                    * three

---

43. *defeifible:* liable to be made void.

44. *Conscience:* the Declaration of Indulgence (1672) suspended the penal laws
against nonconformists and recusants.

45. *Mr. Trenchard:* John Trenchard (1649–1695), an outspoken Whig; knighted
in 1689.

46. *pro bono publico:* for the public good.

three Defcents by Act of Parliament; and as for *Henry*
VII, notwithstanding he married the Heir of the House
of *York*, yet he had an Act of Parliament for a special
Entail of the Crown.   *Henry* VIII. had an Act of Parliament to impower him to dispofe of the Crown by his
last Will and Teftament; which he did, with several re-
ftrictions and limitations; and there was an objection to
void the Will, becaufe he figned it not with his hand.
This Bill will be a fecurity to the King's Perfon, and a
terror to his enemies.   There is one inftance of a colla-
teral Heir, (39 *Hen.*VI,) who was made Heir Apparent
by Act of Parliament, for pacifying the Wars.   *Edw.* IV.   47
was declared as Heir Apparent, and the Great Lords
fwore to him fix [times] after *Henry* VI. was depofed.
It is neither fafe for the King nor Kingdom to do otherwife than this Bill; and if you do not nominate a Succeffor, he may come to the Crown without Blood.   And
fo may the Bill have an eafy paffage.

[The Bill paffed, and Lord *Ruffel* was fent up with it to the
Lords*.]

Friday, November 12.

[Sir *William Jones* was fent up with a Meffage to the Lords,
to acquaint them with the Refolution of this Houfe to proceed to
the Tryal of the Lords in the *Tower*, and forthwith begin with
William Vifcount *Stafford*; and to defire their Lordfhips to ap-
point a convenient day for the Tryal of the faid *William* Vifcount *Stafford*, &c.   And their Lordfhips accordingly appointed
Tuefday fortnight for the faid Tryal.]

Saturday, November 13.

Mr *Peter Norris* [being called in,] gave an Information in
writing, relating to the Popifh Plot; which was read at the
Clerk's Table †.

---

* It is worthy remark, that tho'
the Exclufion Bill was paffed by the
Commons, and ordered to the
Lords, on *Tuefday Nov.* 11, it was
not carried up till *Monday* the 15th
following; and there is no other
way to account for that demur, after it had been hurried through all
the forms of the Houfe with fuch
rapidity before, than by fuppofing
that this interval was employed by
the Party-leaders on both fides in
endeavouring to bring the matter
to a compromife.   Bifhop *Burnet* is
exprefs as to the fact, but not as to
the time.   *Ralph.*

† Even Mr Secretary *Jenkins*, for
the fins of his Office, became ob-
noxious

---

47. *Act of Parliament:* in October 1460, Parliament made Richard Plantaginet,
duke of York, the heir of King Henry VI.

The Right Honble Antho:^{ny} E: of Shaftsbury

Natus est July 1621.

Mortuus est 21.º Jan: 168$\frac{2}{3}$

LOVE SERVE

Portrait of the Earl of Shaftesbury. Published as the frontispiece of *Philanax Miso-pappas* (1683), an anonymous biography of Shaftesbury that appeared shortly after his death.

Shaftesbury's
"Speech upon the Bill of Exclusion and the Popish Plot"
(December 23, 1680)

The Commons concluded its intense debate on November 11 with passage of the bill. After a short delay, the House of Lords began its deliberations. The Whig maneuvers had been based on the hope that the king would yield to their pressure, but he surprised them by resisting all coercion. Indeed, he remained in the House to make sure of his supporters. The sessions he observed produced a famous debate between Shaftesbury and Halifax, in which the latter was widely believed to have won the day. Unfortunately no transcription of their parliamentary duel has survived, but Shaftesbury's speech, published the following year, gives a good indication of his views, which oppose the royal prerogative in the name of the people's rights. The royalists, it would seem, might well fear him more than the papists.

It was soon published as "A Speech by a Noble Peer of the Realm." Yet despite Shaftesbury's defeat and the popular outcry that resulted, the royalists' fears of another revolution were not realized. The annual pope burning, a huge procession organized by the City Whigs' Green Ribbon Club, took place in London, as usual, on November 17 (see p. 64). Yet there was no violence. These displays were riotous symbols of the Londoners' hatred and dread of popery, but they were not political insurrections.

The version reproduced here is from the duke of Buckingham's *Miscellaneous Works* (London, 1707), part 2, pp. 76–83.

A Speech by the R. H. the Earl of Shaftf-bury *concerning the* Popifh Flot, *the Bill of Exclufion, &c. in the year* 1680.

My Lords,

IN this great Debate concerning the *King's* Speech, the fad State and Condition we are in, and the Remedies thereof, I have offered you my Opinion, and many *Lords* have fpoken admirably well to it with great Freedom and Plainnefs, as the Cafe requires Give me Leave to offer you fome few Words in Anfwer to two or three of my *Lords* of the *Earl's Bench*, that have maintain'd the contrary Opinion. My *Lord* near me hath told your *Lordfhips*, That the Precedent of *Henry* the Fourth that I offered to you (who was a Wife and Magnanimous Prince, yet upon the Addrefs of his Parliament, put away great part of his Family and Council at one time) is no proper Inftance ; becaufe he was an Ufurper, and had an ill Title and was bound to pleafe the People. *My Lords,*I meddle not with his Title,I am fure our *King* has a very undoubted one : But this, *My Lords*, you muft allow, That that Wife Prince, having need of the People, knew no better way to pleafe them, and to create a good Underftanding between them and him, than

1

2

---

1. *Earl's Bench:* the supporters of the earl (later marquis) of Halifax, George Savile (1633–1695), who led the fight against exclusion in the House of Lords.

2. *Henry the Fourth:* in 1403, Parliament asked that the king remove four members of his household; the king, though finding no fault with them, agreed to discharge them.

than to put away from Court and Council those
that were unacceptable to them. If our *King*
hath the fame necessity to please the People,
(tho' not the want of a Title) yet the President
holds good, That *a Wise Prince, when he hath
need of his People, will rather part with his Family and Counsellors than displease them.* My
Lords, this Noble *Lord* near me hath found
fault with that Precedent, that he supposes I
offered to your *Lordships* concerning the chargeable Ladies at Court : But I remember no such   3
thing I said. But if I must speak of 'em, I shall
say as the *Prophet* did to King *Saul,What means
the bleating of this kind of Cattel ?* And I hope   4
the *King* will make me the fame Answer,*That
he preserves them for Sacrifice, and means to deliver them up to please his People.* For there
must be in plain *English* a *Change* ; We must
neither have *Popish* Wife,nor *Popish* Favourite,
nor *Popish* Mistress, nor *Popish Councellor* at
Court, nor any *New Convert.* What I spoke was   5
about another *Lady* that belongs not to the   6
Court, but like *Sempronia* in *Catiline's* Con-   7
spiracy, does more Mischief than *Cethegus.*
In this time of Distress I could humbly advise
our *Prince* would take the fame Course that
the Duke of *Savoy* did,to suffer neither Strangers
nor Ambassadors to stay above some few Weeks
in this Country: For all the Strangers and
Ambassadors here have served the Plot and
Design against us. I am sure they have no
tye to be for us. But, *My Lords,* what I rose
up

---

3. *chargeable Ladies:* Charles II's mistresses.

4. *Cattle:* cf. I Samuel 15:14.

5. *New Convert:* K. H. D. Haley describes this passage as containing threats
against "Queen Catherine, Portsmouth, Mazarin, and Barrillon"—the king's wife,
two papist mistresses, and the French ambassador (Haley, p. 613).

6. *Lady:* the duchess of Mazarin, according to Haley (p. 613).

7. *Sempronia:* in Ben Jonson's *Cataline His Conspiracy* (1611) she is the "sulphu-
rous spirit" involved in Cataline's conspiracy against the Senate. *Cethegus* is a rash
young conspirator. Both are based upon historical figures. The play was popular
during the Restoration.

up to fpeak to was more efpecially to My *Lord*
of the *Earl's Bench* that fpoke laft, and its behind me ; who, as he has the greateft Influence in our prefent Councils, fo he hath let
fall to you the very Root of the Matter and
the Hinges upon which all turns. He tell you
that the *Houfe of Common*, have lately made
offers to the *King*. and he wonders we do not
accept the *King's* Anfwer to them, before we
enter into fo hot and high Debates. He tells
you, if the *King* b affured of Supplies, we
cannot doubt of his Complia: ce in this and all
we can ask: For otherwife the *King* fhould fall
into that, which is the worft Condition of a
Prince, to have his People have no Confi en e
in him. *My Lords*, this is th t I know they
wou'd put the *King* upon. and this is that we
muft be ruin'd by, if we may not with Plinn-
nefs and Freedom open our Cafe. *My Lords*,
it is a very hard thing to fay that we cannot
truft the *King*, and that we have already been
deceived fo often, that we fee plainly the ap-
prehenfions of Difcontent in the People is no
Argument at Court. And tho' our *Prince* be
in himfelf an Excellent Perfon that the eople
have the greateft Inclination imaginable to
Love ; yet we muft fay he is fuch a one, as no
Story affords us a Parallel of : How plain and
how many are the Proofs of the Defigns to
murder him ? How little is he apprehenfive of
it ? The Tranfactions between him and his
Brother are Admirable, and Incomprehenfible:

His

His Brother's Defigns being early known to aim at the Crown before his Majefty's Reftoration to this Kingdom. This match with the *Portugal Lady,* not like to have Children, contrived by the *Duke's* Father-in-Law, and no fooner effected, but the *Duke* and his Party make Proclamation to the World, that we are like to have no Children, but that he muft be the certain Heir. He takes his Seat in Parliament as Prince of *VVales,* his Guards about him, the Prince's Lodgings at *VVhitehall,* his Guards upon the fame Floor, without any Interpofition between him and the *King* ; fo that the *King* was in his Hands, and in his Power every Night ; all Offices and Preferments being beftowed by him, not a *Bifhop* made without him. This Prince changes his Religion to make himfelf a Party; and fuch a Party, that his Brother muft be fure to Die and be made away, to make room for him : Nothing could preferve him, but that which I hope he will never do, give greater earneft to that wicked Party than his Brother could : And after all, this Plot breaks out, plainly headed by the *Duke,* his Intereft, and his Defign. How the *King* has behaved Himfelf ever fince the breaking out of it the World knows ; we have expected every hour that the Court fhould joyn with the *Duke* againft us : And it is evident more has been done to make the Plot a *Presbyterian* Plot than to difcover it. The Prorogations; the Diffolutions, the Cutting fhort of

Parliaments,

---

8. *Portugal Lady:* the queen, Catherine of Braganza (in Portugal).

9. *Duke's Father-in-Law:* Edward Hyde, the earl of Clarendon. It was a common charge that Clarendon had purposely married Charles II to an infertile woman in order to make it possible for York, who married his daughter Anne, to inherit the throne.

10. *earnest:* pledge.

Parliaments, not suffering them to have time
or opportunity to look into any thing, have
shew'd what Reason we have to confide in
this Court. We are now come to a Parliament
again, but by what Fate or Counsel for my
part I cannot guess ; neither do I understand
the Riddle of it. The *Duke* is quitted and
sent away: The *House of Commons* have brought   11
up a Bill to disable him of the Crown, and I
think they are so far extreaml in the right ;
but your *Lordships* are wiser than I, and have
rejected it : Yet you have thought fit, and the
King Himself hath made the Proposition to
make such Expedients as shall render him but a
Nominal Prince. In the mean while where's   12
this *Duke,* that the *King* and both *Houses* have
declared unanimously thus dangerous ? Why?
he is in *Scotland,* raising Forces upon the *Terra
Firma,* that can enter dry-Foot upon us, without hazard of Wind or Seas the very place he
should be in to raise a Party to be ready, when
from hence he shall have notice : So that this
being the Case, where is the Trust ? We all
think the Business is so Ripe that they have
the Garrisons, the Arms, Ammunition, the
Seas, and Souldiery all in their Hands ; they
want but one good Sum of Money, to set up
and Crown the Work, and then they have no
further need of the People ; and I believe,
whether they are pleas'd or no, will be no
great trouble to them. *My Lords,* I hear of a
Bargain in the *House of Commons,* an Address
made

---

11. *sent away:* he left for Scotland on October 20, 1680.
12. *Nominal Prince:* the "Expedients" designed to disable York as a Catholic king
by legal limitations on his power.

and muft boldly fay it, and plainly, That the
Nation is betray'd if upon any terms we part
with our Money, till we are fure the *King* is 13
ours; have what Laws you will, and what
Conditions you will, they will be of no ufe,
but Waft-paper before *Eafter*, if the Court
has Money to fet up for *Popery*, and *Arbitrary Defigns* in the mean while: On the other
hand, give me leave to tell your *Lordfhips*,
the *King* hath no reafon to diftruft his People;
no Man can go home and fay,. That if the
King comply with his People, they will do
nothing for him, but tear all up from him:
We want a Government, and we want a Prince
that we may truft, even with the fpending of
half our Annual Revenues for fome time, for the
Prefervation of thefe Nations. The growing
Greatnefs of the *French* cannot be ftopt with
a little Expence, nor without a real and hearty
Union of the *King* and his People. It was
never known in *England* that our Princes wanted Supplies either for their foreign Defigns, or
for their Pleafures; nothing ever fhut our *Englifh* Purfes, but the Fears of having their Money ufed againft them.- The hour that the *King*
fhall fatisfie the People, that what we give is
not to make us Slaves and *Papifts*, he may
have whatever he will; and this your *Lordfhips* know, and all Mankind that know us:
Therefore let me plainly tell your *Lordfhips*,
the Arguments the prefent Minifters ufe, are
to deftroy the *King*, not to preferve him: For

F f   it

---

13. *Money:* i.e., to refuse appropriations until exclusion is accepted. One might
note that the king was present in the House to hear these threats; Shaftesbury
alludes to his presence on the following page.

if the *King* will firft fee what we will do for him, it is impoffible, if we are in our Senfes, we fhould do any'thing. But if he will tirft fhew that he is intirely ours, that he *Weds the Intereft and Religion of the Nation,* it is abfolutely impoffible he fhould want any thing he can ask, or we can give. But I plainly fee how the Argument will be ufed: *Sir, they will do nothing for you, what fhould you do with thefe Men?* But on the other hand, I am bold to fay, *Sir, you may have any thing of this Parliament, put away thefe Men, change your Principles, change your Court, and be your felf again;* for the *King* himfelf may have any thing of us. *My Lords,* if I have been too plain, I beg your Pardons; I thought it the Duty of a true Born *Englifhman* at this time to fpeak plainly or never. I am fure I mean well; and if any Man can anfwer and oppofe [Reafon to what I alledge, I beg that they would do it: For I do not defire or propofe any Queftion merely for Talking-fake. I beg this Debate may laft fome Days, and that we may go to the very Bottom of the Matter, and fee whether thefe things are fo or no; and what cure there is for the Evil that we are in ; and then the Refult of our Debates may produce fome proper Queftion. However we know who hears, and I am glad of this, that your *Lordfhips* have dealt fo honourably any fo clearly in the 14 *King's* Prefence and Hearing, that he can't fay he wants a right State of Things : He hath
it

---

14. *any:* and (misprint).

it before him, and may take Connfel as he thinks fit.

An Address to the
Honourable City of London (1681)

During most of 1680, there had been severe restrictions on the publication of opposition pamphlets, though some did appear, notably the "Black Box" assertions on Monmouth's legitimacy. But after Parliament was dissolved in January 1681, a new tide of election pamphlets streamed from the presses as the Whigs undertook a well-organized and financed campaign to elect another strongly exclusionist Parliament for the session coming in March at Oxford.

And they were successful, despite renewed Tory efforts to corrupt the electoral process through patronage. *An Address to the Honourable City of London,* published anonymously within a month of the end of the second Whig Parliament, praises the people of London for supporting exclusion and recounts the dangers of a "popish successor"— which include a possible French invasion, fire, poverty, and oppression. Parliament is the nation's only hope against these evils. The writer provides a "practical guide" for choosing candidates.

An Address to the Honourable CITY of LONDON, and all other CITIES, SHIRES, and CORPORATIONS, concerning their Choice of a new PARLIAMENT.

Hebr. 12. 16. *Lest there be any prophane person, as* Esau, *who for one Morsel of Meat sold his Birth-right.*

Gentlemen,

THE many and eminent dangers occurring to this Kingdom of late years from its intestine Treacheries and Basenefs, have produced that consternation, and that Jealousie in the minds of all good people, as render them diffident both of their Friends and Fortunes, knowing no more which way to dispose of their Estates, than their Affections: *A Kingdom divided within it self, can never stand* : and this was our condition; when those very men (the servants of the Publick) who ought to conduct and stand by us in the day of Battel, have been the Persons in the World most likely to betray us, and lead us up like Sheep to the Slaughter. Those *Danbean* Senators, from whose Wisdom so much was expected; those [1] Pensionary Tribunes of the People, in the late long Parliament, from whose integrity so much was hoped, have, instead of securing that Peace and Tranquility, that Religion and Property which all good men wish'd for, not only disturb'd the one, but hazarded ruining the other; *Quid non mortalia pectora cogit, auri sacra fam's?* our Temple [2] of *Janus* seemsto be already unlock'd, and we have every hour reason [3] to expect the *French* King should fling open the doors: And then, if two or three hundred *Dutch* Mariners could present us with such Horrour and apprehensions, as we all know they did at their Arrival in *Chatham* River, how much greater now will our distraction be, when [4] an Army of fifty or sixty thousand *French men* is Landed amongst us! When the Father must forsake his innocent and pretty Orphans, the Husband his disconsolate and helpless Widow, leaving them to be murder'd by the Papists at home, whilst he himself by his own death is compleating the Tragedy abroad! Are you not yet sensible of your condition? do you not yet perceive you approaching ruine? Think how the *French King* shakes his *Fasces* over us, when at the same time [5] the Treacherous *Papist* renders us naked to his correction! Think how entirely your happiness depends upon our Soveraign's Life;

B

---

1. *Danbean Senators:* the followers of the earl of Danby, the former lord treasurer, now in the Tower awaiting trial for high treason.
2. *Quid non mortalia pectora cogit, auri sacra fames?:* Virgil, *Aeneid,* III, 56–57. O sacred hunger of pernicious gold! / What bands of faith can impious lucre hold?—trans. John Dryden (1697).
3. *Temple of Janus:* in ancient Rome, it was opened in time of war, closed in peace.
4. *Chatham River:* in June 1677, the Dutch navy executed a daring raid up the Thames to the Medway, where it burned a number of English ships and caused a panic in the countryside.
5. *Fasces:* a bundle of rods bound up with an axe in the middle; a Roman ensign of authority.

Therefore by this Obſervation we may gueſs, who are fitteſt to be choſe Members of Parliament, and who are not.

Firſt, Avoid all ſuch as hold any Office of conſiderable value during pleaſure, 6 they being ſubject to be over-aw'd. For although a man wiſh well to his Country, and in the betraying thereof knows that at the long run he miſchieves his poſterity, if not himſelf, yet the narrowneſs of mens minds is ſuch, as makes them more tenderly apprehend a ſmall preſent damage, than a far greater hereafter. Such men muſt of neceſſity be under a great temptation and diſtraction, when their Conſciences and Intereſt look different ways, eſpecially having obſerv'd ſome men turn'd out of their Employs, after voting for the Intereſt of their Country, as Mr. *Garraway* was. Therefore ſince theſe men know before-hand the Inconveniencies, that attend the Truſt of a Member of Parliament faithfully diſcharg'd, 'tis very ſuſpicious and reflecting upon their honeſty, if any ſuch ſtand ; and I think we are bound in Charity, nor can we do them a greater courteſie, than to anſwer their Petition in the Lords Prayer, Not to lead them into temptation.

Secondly, Suſpect all thoſe (men of ill repute) *who in their Profeſſion or near Relations have any dependency upon the Court* ; for they (unworthily) gueſſing at the King by themſelves, are apt to vote right or wrong, as they imagine will moſt pleaſe the Prerogative party. And perhaps this fancy helpt the Earl of *Danby* to that favour, which hindred him from coming upon his Trial the former Seſſions. It is a hard matter for a Courtier to pleaſe that Miniſter who ſupports him, and thoſe whom he repreſents at the ſame time ; and if he endeavours to oblige both, he becomes ſuch an uncertain Weathercock, as moſt commonly he pleaſes neither. Wherefore the moſt prudent and honeſteſt of the Courtiers are obſerved to decline being Parliament-men, for this very Reaſon.

Thirdly, Suſpect all ſuch as ſpend much upon you in Entertainments at their Elections : for that (as I told you before) he who buys any Office, deſigns to make Money of it again. And then conſider with your ſelves, what Looſers you will be, if to laugh and be merry one day, the Perſon you chooſe ſhould give You and your Children occaſion to mourn for ever after! Think how juſtly the ancient Heathens may upbraid this baſeneſs of us Chriſtians, when, as they ſacrificed many of their Children, nay, and oftentimes their own Lives for the good of their Country; ſo on the contrary, do we ſacrifice both our Religion, Lives, and Country, for the pleaſure of one days debauchery.

Fourthly, Shun all ſuch men as are deſperately in Debt : for they needing Protection from paying of their Debts, are ſo afraid of being Diſſolv'd, as makes them ſubmit to any thing, rather than be left to the unmerciful Rage of their hungry Creditors, who have ſo long faſted for their Money. For all ſuch Perſons (though ſome of them may be look'd upon as honeſt fair-condition'd Gentlemen, and good Houſe-keepers) are in danger of being tempted to repair the decays of their own private Fortunes, by the Ruine of the Publick. Moreover, the chooſing of ſuch broken Fortunes, undoes Trade, ruines whole Families, and I have

7

8

9

---

6. *during pleaſure:* at the king's discretion.

7. *Mr. Garraway:* William Garraway (1616–1701), an M.P. from Chichester and leader of the Whig party. In 1674 he was dismissed from the post of commissioner of customs after he criticized Clarendon in Parliament.

8. *Sessions:* the king dissolved Parliament to prevent Danby from coming to trial.

9. *in Debt:* M.P.'s could not be jailed for debt while Parliament was in session.

have known it drive many men (contrary to their own inclinations) to wish never to fee Parliaments more in *England*. *ii.*

Fifthly, Avoid all fuch as have been known Favourers of Papifts, or Relations or Friends to any of the Lords in the Tower ; *Nay beware of any that fhall be recommended to you by fuch as are fo,* (let them be never fo Great men in your Countries) unlefs you intend to have their Friends to be their Judges. For when any perfon fhall out of a private Intereft of his own, Elect, or give his Voice for one who is either a Friend or Relation to *Him* that ftands Impeach'd by all the Commons of *England* of High-Treafon, he does in fuch a Cafe, as much as in him lies, endeavour to deftroy the Kingdom, by faving the Life of its Enemy ; for that if all other Electors fhould do the fame, he might live to perfect that Ruine amongft us, which otherwife he muft leave unfinifhed : An Act no lefs unnatural, than for a man to fell a Pardon to him that murder'd his own Father ! If the former wife Parliament thought it reafonable (as they did) to Vote *him a Betrayer of the Rights and Priviledges of the Commons of England,* who fhould dare to plead at Bar in behalf of the Earl of *Danby* ; let not thofe who choofe his neareft Relations and Friends for his Judges, think themfelves lefs faulty than he that fhould have pleaded for him after the aforefaid Vote, fince the defign of both is the fame, *viz.* the faving of his Life. Therefore if any do fo, may their fhame be their confufion.

Sixthly, Above all others choofe not any of thofe who have been juftly pointed at by the name of Penfioners, as being the worft and bafeft of Traytors ; who making Shipwrack of all Honour, Honefty, and good Confcience, fell their Votes for Offices, prefent Gratuities, or conftant Penfions. The firft notorious brood of thefe Vermin, were in the Old Long Parliament called by the name of *Self-feekers* ; but the late *Lord Treafure's* Creatures were in greater numbers, more voracious, and of more univerfal Obedience, or as the *French* call it, *Sans Referve.* They by the former excellent Houfe of Commons, are for their *Secret Service* branded by the open name of *Penfioners,* which they will hardly claw off, notwithftanding the Parliaments Diffolution, hath, as yet refcued them from other punifhment. However, that the Populacy might not fplit twice upon the fame Rock, my requeft is, that before they go to any Election, they would perufe Sir *Stephen Fox's* Catalogue both of fuch Perfons and Sums as he recollected in his memory, without the help of his Books which upon fome weighty Reafons (above us Vulgar peoples fearching into) was denied him. Now this *Penfionary* Inftitution of the Treafurers, was certainly of great advantage to himfelf, and moft pernicious to *England* ; for if he did really diftribute fuch fums as is pretended, then he might in a fhort time make and repeal what Laws he pleas'd ; or if he did not diftribute them, then to his own enriching, He might by an untrue accompt, divert a vaft Treafure into his own Purfe.

Seventhly and Laftly, As for you Citizens, Burgeffes, and Freemen of Corporations and Cities, I fhall fay but little to you in particular, more than what hath been faid already in general ; only, *whoever is unfit to be chofen Knight of the Shire, is likewife unfit to be chofen a Burgefs.* Neither let the more fpecious pretences of any man, (that fhall promife to build

D   you

10. *Lords in the Tower:* the five papist lords who were awaiting trial for treason.

11. *Him:* Danby.

12. *Pensioners:* hirelings paid by the Crown; also "Creatures"—see below.

13. *Sans Reserve:* unreservedly.

14. *Fox's Catalogue:* Fox (1631–1714) was lord commissioner of the treasury (which would pay the pensioners).

15. *Knight of the Shire:* member of Parliament from a shire or county.

16. *Burgess:* a member of Parliament from a town or city.

you a Town-Hall, or relieve your Poor with Mony,(or out of his adjacent Woods, deceive you any longer; for if so, wherein are you better
than your Horses, whom you catch every day, and clap a Bridle into
their Mouths, only by shewing them a few *Oats*, which they are never
like to Eat Even the very Mice are too wise to be taken by an old
Bait, but will first have the Trap new baited, before they'l meddle ; and
yet I have known a Corporation, which has been taken twice by the
same Bait But however suppose these men do really perform what they
promise, what compensation is that, if that the men you choose should
lay a good swinging Tax upon your Estates, without any real cause ; or
should give up the very Power you have of Taxing your selves, or sending your Representatives in Parliament, for one bad Parliament may
ruine us,) what good would the Mony for your Poor do you in such a
case, more than when you thereby reduced to Beggery, you might perhaps your selves the Gentry of the Country having no reason to relieve
you) be forced to come in for a small share of this their Hypocritical
Charity : An excellent reward for Folly.   Neither say, Oh, this is but
one man, and can have but one Voice ; he will do our Town a great deal
of good, and can do us but little hurt if he would.   For that, first, one or
two Voices have sometimes carried a Vote of great importance : and secondly, you know not the bad example this may give to otherNeighbor-
ing Corporations, and it all should do so, in what a miserable case would
you be ? since the Voices of the Burroughs make two thirds of the   17
House.   Lastly, no man can tell the influence that one cunning talkative
man hath over the rest of the House, especially over those that weigh
Words, more than Reason or Sense.   But I shall say no more upon this
subject. only desire you to remember *Esau*, who sold his Birth right for a   18
mess of Pottage, and could never afterwards recover it, though he sought
it with Tears : Also when once you had Elected such a corrupt Parliament, no Prince (but so just and gracious a Prince as ours) would suffer
you to get rid of 'em in hast, or at leastwise till they had done your business for you.

Having thus therefore shew'd you what persons you ought not to
choose, so now in the next place, the more clearly to perceive what kind
of persons our present necessity requires to be chosen, consider for what
ends they serve, and they are two : One is, the preservation of our Religion from *Popery* ; The other is, to preserve inviolably our *Liberty*,
and *Property*, according to our known Laws of the Land, without any
introduction of that absolute and arbitrary rule in other Countries,
which we are neither to imitate or regard.

First, Therefore as near as we can guess, *we ought to elect good Protestants towards God and just towards Man*. But forasmuch as in this corrupt
Age wherein we live, men are not so spiritual as they ought to be, it is
not amiss to seek for those, whose spiritual interests is seconded by a
temporal one. Wherefore the surest Champions for our Religion against
the Papacy, are our *Abby landed-men*; for notwithstanding the registred   19
Dispensation to *Harry* the Eighth from the Pope, for the seizing of those
Monasteries and Lands, yet of late they pretend that the Pope had not

pow-

---

17. *Burroughs:* boroughs—towns sending representatives to Parliament.
18. *Esau:* Genesis 25:24–34.
19. *Abby landed-men:* those who own lands confiscated from the Catholic Church.

power to alien them from rhe Church ; wherefore the prefent poffeffors can never truft or rely upon any new Promifes or actual Grants thereof, efpecially from him whofe everlafting and declared Maxim it is, *Never to keep Faith with Hereticks.* Undoubtedly to make eafy his afcent into the faddle, he will proffer many Affurances and Grants ; But if thefe Abby-landed men, be not the moft filly of all others, they will never be-lieve him ; for when he is once firmly fettled, then will with his Canon-Law diftinctions, like Fire under Quick-filver evaporate away all his promifes, and violently refume the Lands, glorifying in his own Bounty, if he require not the mean profits: — *habeat jam Roma Pudorem.* 20

Secondly, For our Liberty and Property, *men of fair Repute in their Coun-try, are of all others moft likely to prove the ftouteft Patriots, efpecially if in Pof-feffion or Reverfion they are men of good Eftates* ; for their Concern is the greater: And we find by experience of fuch as Travel into forreign parts, where themfelves have no Eftates, *Facile habetur paupertas fine damno* ; and accordingly when War and Confufion begins to arife, they appre-hend it not with the hundredth part of that anxiety, as they would do if the like fhould arife at home, where their whole livelyhood is at ftake. 21

Thirdly and laftly, I conceive it will not be amifs, if for the moft part you choofe the fame Members again that ferv'd you faithfully the laft time ; fince in fo doing, you will both take off that fear of Diffolutions, which is of fuch fatal confequence in a Parliament, as alfo oblige them to ferve you more chearfully ever after, when you have fo highly honoured them twice. Now to this purpofe, give me leave here to infert a Prefident worthy both the Confideration and Imitation of all the Shires and Cor-porations in *England* ; It is a moft generous Letter written (fince this late Prorogation to Sir *Gilbert Gerrard* and Sir *Henry Calverly* from the ho-neft Burgeffes of *North-Allerton* in *York-fhire,* (Dated *Jan.* 14.) in thefe Words : 22

Gentlemen,

The unexpected and fudden News of this days Poft preventing us from thofe due acknowledgments, which the Greatnefs of your Services for Publick Good have merited from us, we have no better way (now left us) to exprefs our Gratitude and the high refentments of your Actions before, and in the laft Seffions of Par-liament, than to manifeft our approbation thereof, by an Affurance that if a Diffo-lution of this prefent Parliament happen, (fince you have evidenced fo fufficient-ly your affection to His Majefties Royal Perfon, and your endeavours for prefer-ving the Proteftant Religion, our Lives and Liberties,) we are refolved (if you pleafe to comply with us) to continue you both as our Reprefentatives, and do there-fore humbly beg your acceptance thereof ; and farther, that you will continue your Station during this Prorogation, faithfully affuring you, that none of Us defire to give, or occafion you the Expence or Trouble of a Journey in order to your Electi-on, (if fuch happen) being fo fenfible of the too great expence you have been at already, in carefully difcharging the Truft and Confidence repofed in You: Sub-fcribed by above Sixty, whofe Worth and Loyalty deferve Immortal Fame, and to be Recorded as an Honourable Example both now and hereafter, for all other Corporations ; which being all the Advice I can give you in this Matter, I fhall conclude with defiring you not to be wea-ry 23

---

20. *habeat jam roma Pudorem:* Let Rome now show shame.
21. *Facile habetur paupertas sine damno:* Poverty is easily born without condemnation.
22. *Sir Henry Calverly:* both he and Gerard were reelected.
23. *resentments:* grateful appreciation and acknowledgment of services.

ry of well-doing, neither to be alarm'd or troubled at frequent Prorogation or Diffolutions ; fince if you perfift in the fame fteady courfe you
have already begun, it will but fall more heavily upon the heads of thofe
that are the contrivers of thefe Mifunderftandings between his Gracious
Majefty, and his moft faithful Subjects, for whofe happy union, as well
in opinion as affection, none can pray more heartily, than

Your moft Humble Servant,

and Fellow Subject,

C. B.

POST-SCRIPT.

WHat I have here written, I do declare before Almighty God, proceeded meerly from the earneft Zeal and defire I had of ferving my King
and Country ; hoping by this timely caution to the Vulgar, to procure
fuch Senators, as might add to the Luftre of our King, and fafety of our
Government, fuch as might keep the Ballance even, and prevent our
running either into Tyranny and Popery on the one hand, or into a Republick and Fanaticifm on the other : Such as might divert that ftorm
which threatens us, giving us that Peace and that Tranquility, which
all men, who have either Eftates or Families (like my felf) are bound
to pray for; fuch as might render to *Cefar* the things that are *Cefars*, and   24
to God the things that are God's, and to the People the things that are
the Peoples. For as I am govern'd by no private Faction or Intereft, but
purely by the dictates of my own Confcience and Reafon ; fo there is no
Government but our *Englifh* Monarchy, nor no Religion but what is pre-
fcribed in the Church of *England*, that I hope ever to fee prevail amongft
us, We have an old Proverb, and 'tis true as to our Condition, *Over Shoes
over Boots*; fo that now both City and Commons have proceeded thus   25
far in oppofing Popery, they cannot be fafe but in doing more ; for that
'twill be too late to repent, when a never-forgiving Popifh Succeffor fhall
come amongft us, with that Text in his mouth of St. *Luke* 19. 27. *But
thofe mine enemies which would not that I fhould reign over them, bring them hi-
ther and flay them before me.* -------- Wherefore to prevent all this ruine and
mifery, we cannot too often and too fincerely pray for the Life, Happinefs, and Profperity of our Sovereign, *Charles the Second,* whom God preferve both in this World and the next; which is the conftant Prayer of
his moft obedient and faithful Subject,

C. B.

F I N I S.

---

24. *Cesar:* Matthew 22:21; Mark 12:17; Luke 20:25.
25. *Over Shoes over Boots:* i.e., once in, venture all.

Vox Populi (1681)

Vox Populi: or, the Peoples Claim to their Parliaments Sitting, probably published a short time after *An Address to the Honourable City of London,* is more theoretical. J. R. Jones has referred to it as "the most clearly reasoned" of the Whig pamphlets (*The First Whigs* [London: Oxford University Press, 1961], p. 174). It also reveals the writer's considerable intensity as he argues for parliamentary power.

𝕮𝖔𝖝 𝕻𝖔𝖕𝖚𝖑𝖎 :

OR,

The PEOPLES Claim to their PARLIAMENTS Sitting, to Redress Grievances and to provide for the Common Safety, by the Known Laws and Constitutions of the Nation.

Recommended to the KING and PARLIAMENT at their meeting at *Oxford*, &c.

SInce the Wonderful Difcovery and undenyable Confirmation of that horrid Popifh Plot which defigned fo much ruine and mifchief to thefe Nations, in all things both Civil and Sacred, and the unanimous Sence and Cenfure of fo many Parliaments upon it, together with fo many publick Acts of Juftice upon fo many of the Traytors; it was comfortably hoped before thirty Months fhould have paft over after the Detection thereof, fome effectual Remedyes might have been apply'd to prevent the further attempts of the Papifts upon us, and better to have fecured the Proteftants in their Religion, Lives and Propertyes. But by fad experience we have found, that notwithftanding the Vigorous Endeavours of three of our Parliaments to provide proper and wholfome Laws to Anfwer both ends; yet fo prevalent has this Intereft been, under fo potent a head the *D*. of *Y*. as to ftifle 1 in the Birth all thofe hopeful Parliament-Endeavours; by thofe many Surprizing and Aftonifhing Prorogations and Diffolutions which they have procured, whereby our fears

A 2   and

---

1. *D. of Y.:* Duke of York.

and Dangers have Manifeſtly increaſed, and their Spirits heightned and incouraged to renew and Multiply freſh Plottings and Deſigns upon us.

But that our approaching Parliament may be more ſuc-ceſſeful for our Relief before it be too late, by being permit-ted to ſit to Redreſs our Grievances, and to perfect thoſe Good Bills which have been prepared by the former Parliaments to this purpoſe ; theſe following Common Law Maxims reſpect-ing King and Parliament, and the Common and Statute Laws themſelves (to prevent ſuch unnatural Diſappointments and Miſ-chiefs) providing for the ſitting of Parliaments till Grievances be redreſs'd, and publick Safety ſecured and provided for, are ten-dered to conſideration.

Some known Maxims taken out of the Law-Books.

1. Reſpecting the King.

That the Kings of England *can do nothing as Kings but what of right they ought to do.*

That the King can do no wrong, nor can he dye.

That the Kings Prerogative and the Subjects Liberty are deter-mined by Law.

That the King hath no Power but what the Law gives him.

That the King is ſo called from Ruling well, Rex a bene Re-gendo [viz. *according to Law*] *Becauſe he is a King whilſt he Rules well, but a Tyrant when he Oppreſſes.*

That Kings of England *never appear more in their glory, ſplendor and Majeſtick Soveraignty, than in Parliaments.*

That the Prerogative of the King cannot do wrong, nor be a Warrant to do wrong to any. Plowd. Comment. fol. 246.

2. Reſpecting the Parliament.

That Parliaments conſtitute and are layd in the Eſſence of the Government.

That a Parliament is that to the Common-Wealth which the Soul is to the Body, which is only able to apprehend and underſtand the ſymptoms of all Diſeaſes which threaten the Body politick.

That a Parliament is the Bulwark of our Liberty, the boundary which keeps us from the Innundation of Tyrannical Power, Arbi-trary and unbounded Will-Government.

That

---

2. *Parliament:* at Oxford (March 1681).

3. *nor can he dye:* when a king dies, his crown passes immediately to his successor.

4. *Comment. fol. 246:* Edmund Plowden, *Commentaries* (1659).

That Parliaments do make new, and abrogate Old Laws, Reform Grievances in the Common-Wealth, settle the Succession, grant subsidies; And in summe, may be called the great Phisitian of the Kingdom:

From whence it appears and is self evident if Parliaments are so absolutely necessary in this our constitution, That they must then have their certain stationary times of Session, and continuance, for providing Laws, essentially necessary for the being, as well as the well being of the People; and Redressing all publick Greivances, either by the want of Laws, or of the undue Execution of them in being, or otherwise: And suitable hereunto are those Provisions made by the Wisdom of our Ancestors as recorded by them both in the Common and Statute-Law:

First, What we find hereof in the *Common Law.*

The Common Law (saith my Lord *Coke*) *is that which is founded in the immutable Law and light of Nature, agreeable to the Law of God, requiring Order, Government, Subjection and Protection,* &c. *Containing ancient usages, Warrented by Holy Scripture, and because it is generally given to all, it is therefore called* Common. **5** Coke *lib.*7. *Rep.* p. 12, 13.

And further saith, *That in the Book called* The Mirror of Justice *appeareth the whole frame of the ancient common Laws of this Realm from the time of K.* Arthur, 516. *till near the Conquest; which Treats also of the Officers as well as the diversity and Distinction of the Courts of Justice* (*which are* Officinæ Legis *) and particularly of the High Court of Parliament by the name of Council General or Parliament;* so called from Parler-la-ment, *speaking judicially his mind:* **6** *Lib.*9. Preface. **7**

---

5. *Coke:* Sir Edmund Coke (1552–1633), *Institutes of the Laws of England* (1628; often reprinted).

6. *The Mirror of Justice:* The Book Called the Mirror of Justices (1646) by Andrew Horne (translated from French by W.H.).

7. *Officinae Legis:* of the law of business.

*The late
King's ad-
vice to his
Majesty.* Nor would he have him entertain any Averfion or Diflike
of Parliaments, which in their right Conftitution, with freedom
and honour, will never Injure or Diminish His Greatnefs,
but will rather be as interchangings of Love, Loyalty and
Confidence, between a Prince and his People.

It is true, fome Flatterers and Traytors have prefumed,
in defiance to their Countries Rights, to affert that fuch a
boundlefs *Prerogative* belongs to Kings. As did Chief Juftice
Trifilian,&c. in *R.2*'s. time; *Advifing him that he might Diffolve Parliaments at pleafure;* and, *that no Member fhould be
called to Parliament, nor any Act paft in either Houfe, without
His Approbation in the firft place;* and, *that who ever advis'd
otherwife were Traytors.* But this Advice you read was no
lefs Fatal to himfelf, than Pernicious to his Prince. *Bakers
Chron.* p. 147, 148, and 159.

8

9

King James *in his Speech to the Parliament* 1609. *Gives
them affurance, That he never meant to Govern by any Law, but
the Law of the Land; tho it be difputed among them, as if
he had an intention to alter the Law; and Govern by the
abfolute power of a King; but to put them out of doubt in
that matter, tells them, That all Kings who are not Tyrants,
or Perjured, will bound themfelves within the limits of their
Laws. And they that perfuade the contrary, are Vipers and
Pefts, both againft them and the Common-wealth.* Wilfon.
K. J. p. 46.

10

The Conclufion.

1. **I**F this be fo, That by fo great Authority (*viz.* fo many *Statutes* in force, The fundamentals of the Common Law, the Effentials of the Government it felf, *Magna
Charta*, The Kings Coronation Oath, fo many Laws of God
and Man;) the Parliament ought to fit to Redrefs Grievances and provide for Common Safety, efpecially in times of
Common

---

8. *Trisilian:* Sir Robert Tresilian, chief justice of the king's bench; he was impeached by Parliament and hanged at Tyburn in 1388.

9. *Bakers Chron.:* Sir Richard Baker, *A Chronicle of the Kings of England* (1643;
by 1696 it had reached its ninth edition).

10. *Wilson, K. J.:* Arthur Wilson, *The History of Great Britain, Being the Life and
Reign of King James the First* (1653).

Common Danger. (And that this is eminently fo, who can doubt, that will believe the King; fo many Parliaments, The Cloud of Witneffes, the Publick Judicatures, their own fenfe and experience of the manifold Mifchiefs which have been acted, and the apparent Ruine and Confufion that impends the Nation, by the reftlefs Attempts of a bloody Intereft, if fpeedy Remedy is not applyed.)

Then let it be Queri'd, Whether the People having thus the Knife at the Throat, Cities and Habitations Fired, and therein their Perfons fryed, Invafions and Infurrections threatned to Deftroy the King and Subjects, Church and State; and as fo lately told us, (upon Mr. *Fitz Harris's* commitment,) the prefent Defign on Foot was to Depofe and Kill the King; and their only remedy hoped for under God to give them Relief thus from time to time, Cut off, *viz.* Their Parliaments, who with fo much care, coft and pains are Elected, fent up, and Intrufted for their help, turned off *re infecta*, and rendred fo infignificant by thofe frequent Prorogations and Diffolutions.

Are they not therefore juftified in their important Cryes, in their many Humble Petitions to their King, Fervent Addreffes to their Members, earneft Claims for this their Birthright here Pleaded, which the Laws of the Kingdom, confonant to the Laws of God and Nature, has given them?

2. If fo, what then fhall be faid to thofe who advife to this high Violation of their Countries Rights, to the infringing fo many juft Laws, and expofing the Publick to thofe defperate hazards, if not a total Ruine?

If King *Alfred* (as *Andrew Horne* in his *Mirror of Juftice* tells us) hanged *Darling, Segnor, Cadwine, Cole,* and Forty Judges more, for Judging contrary to Law; and yet all thofe falfe Judgments were but in particular and private Cafes; What Death do thofe Men deferve, who offer this violence to the Law it felf, and all the Sacred Rights of their Country? If the Lord Chief Juftice *Thorp* in *Ed.* 3's time, for receiving the Bribery of One hundred pounds was adjudged to be Hanged as one that had made the King break his Oath to the People; How much more guilty are they of making the King break his Coronation Oath that perfuade

11. *Fitz Harris:* William Fitzharris, at this time in prison awaiting trial for treason and claiming to have important information about the plot. See Introduction (p. 11).

12. *re infecta:* by something which is not done.

13. *King Alfred:* Alfred the Great (849–901); this story of his hanging the unjust judges is regarded as mythical. It was given in a tract entitled *The Triumph of Justice over Unjust Judges* (1681).

14. *Lord Chief Justice Thorp;* in 1350 he was convicted of corruption and sentenced to be hanged, but Edward III remitted his sentence, though his goods and lands were seized.

fwade him to Act againſt all the Laws for holding Parliaments, and paſſing Laws therein, which he is ſo ſolemnly
ſworn to do? And if the Lord Chief Juſtice *Treſillian* was
Hanged, Drawn, and Quartered for Adviſing the King to Act
contrary to ſome Statutes only; what do thoſe deſerve
that adviſe the King to Act not only againſt ſome, but againſt
all theſe Ancient Laws and Statutes of the Realm?

And if *Blake*, the King's *Council*, but for Aſſiſting in the Matter, and   15
drawing up Indictments, by the King's Command, contrary to Law,
though, it's likely, he might plead the King's Order for it; yet if he was
Hang'd, Drawn and Quartered for that, What Juſtice is due to them that
aſſiſt in the Total Deſtruction of all the Laws of the Nation, and, as much
as in them lies, their King and Countrey too? And if *Usk* the Under-   16
Sheriff, (whoſe Office it is to Execute the Laws) for but endeavoring to
aid *Treſilian*, *Blake*, and their Accomplices, againſt ſome of the Laws, was
alſo, with Five more, Hang'd, Drawn and Quartered; What Puniſhment
may they deſerve, that Aid and Endeavor the Subverſion of all the Laws
of the Kingdom? And if *Empſon* and *Dudley* in *Henry* the Eighth's   17
Time, though Two of the King's Privy Council, were Hanged, for procuring and executing an Act of Parliament contrary to the Fundamental Laws of the Kingdom, and to the great Vexation of the People; ſo
that though they had an Act of Parliament on their ſide, yet that Act being againſt the known Lands of the Land, were Hang'd, as Traytors, for
putting that Statute in Execution: Then what ſhall become of thoſe
who have no ſuch Act to ſhelter themſelves under, and who ſhall Act not
only contrary to, but to the deſtruction of the Fundamental Laws of the
Kingdom? And how harmonious ſuch Juſtice will be, the Text tells us,
Deut. 27. 17. *Curſed be he that removeth his Neighbors Land-mark: and
all the People ſhall ſay*, Amen.

What Senſe our late Worthy Parliament had of the Horrid Crime of
ſuch Malefactors, was expreſſed in one of their laſt Votes, the day of
their Prorogation, *viz.*

Lunæ 10 *Die Januarii*, 1680.   18

☞ Reſolved,

*That whoſoever Adviſed His Majeſty to Prorogue this Parliament to
any other purpoſe, than to the paſſing of a Bill for the Excluſion of James
Duke of* York, *is a Betrayer of the King, the Proteſtant Religion, and of
the Kingdom of* England; *A Promoter of the French Intereſt, and a
Penſioner to* France.

*That this preſent Seſſion may have a happy Iſſue, to anſwer the
great ends of Parliaments, and therein our preſent Exigencies
and Neceſſities, is the inceſſant Cry and longing Expectation of
all the Proteſtants in the Land.*

---

15. *Blake:* John Blake, a lawyer.

16. *Usk:* Thomas Usk, the author of "The Testament of Love," was condemned
by Parliament for plotting against the duke of Gloucester; he was executed on
March 4, 1388.

17. *Empson and Dudley:* Sir Richard Empson and Edmund Dudley were condemned for treason after becoming notorious for abusing their positions as tax
collectors. Both died in 1510.

18. *Lunae 10 Die Januarii, 1680:* Monday, January 10, 1681; as the new year
began on March 25, this date is actually 1681 in the modern calendar.

PART SIX

Countermeasures

Richard Langhorn's
Memoirs (1679)

One of the first means used by Catholics to bring their case before the public is represented by Richard Langhorn's *Memoirs*. After Langhorn's execution for treason on July 14, 1679, his friends published his final writings. Similar final statements appeared from other Catholic victims of Oates and the plot hysteria. And despite the strong anti-Catholic feelings of the time, they made an impression on the public, which felt that a man's last words deserved special respect. In addition, the dignity and piety of the Catholics who went to the scaffold provided a moving sight to the crowds that observed their executions.

Langhorn's work is especially interesting because his death was delayed for a month (he was convicted on June 14) in the hope that he would confess. His account of the cruel pressures exerted against him as he waited for death could not be flattering to Shaftesbury or his followers. Langhorn also wrote a number of devotional poems (not included here); whatever their literary merit, they exhibited his sincerity and piety, as did the account, reprinted from the end of the tract, of his execution.

BEing adjudged to dye by a Publick Judgment, for the Crime of High-Treason, [1] Charged and Sworn against me at my Tryal by two Witnesses, namely Mr. *Oates* and Mr. *Bedloe*; And having both before my Tryal, and after the Judgment given, declared my Innocency to All with whom I have had the Liberty to converse since my first Imprisonment, I take it to be my Duty to leave a Testimony under my Hand, for the farther Justification of my Innocency, and of the Truth, against all those Calumnies which have been, and may be laboured by ill Men to be cast upon me; And the rather, because I do not know whether it will be allowed me to speak with freedom at my death; or if that should be permitted, yet I well know that what I may then say, may be misrepresented to the prejudice of Truth

I am not in the mean time ignorant, what prejudice I lie under, and how difficult it is for me to express my self in such words, as may gain Belief with the World But my design being only to satisfie good Men, who accustom themselves to judge according to the Rules of right Reason; And as they would have others judge of them; I shall not much care for the Censure of the Multitude.

The Crime which I am Charged, is the most heinous of all Crimes ; But whether I am in Truth Guilty, can only lie within the knowledge of the Great God, who is the Searcher of all Hearts, my own Conscience, and the Consciences of my before-named Accusers. My God, I am sure, knows my Innocency, and will acquit me at the great day of Judgment. My Conscience with great Joy and Peace bears me witness, that I am so perfectly innocent of the Treason for which I stand Condemned, That it invokes Almighty God to witness, that I was never in the whole course of my life guilty of so much as one Disloyal Thought against m, Sovereign Lord King *C H A R L E S* the Second, whom I here own in the presence of God, to be my True and Lawful King and Sovereign, taking the words in the same sense in which they are taken and intended, in the Oath commonly called , *The Oath of Allegiance.*

As to all other Persons who have judged , or shall take upon them to judge of me, whether I am Guilty or not Guilty of that Crime, of which I here profess my self to be Innocent, I am sure that according to Reason they must disclaim, to make any Judgment upon science or strict knowledge; And must own, if that they can make no other Judgment, than what must be grounded upon their Belief, which can never have, or pretend to have any greater or higher certainty, than the Motives of the Credibility upon which it is built and grounded.

I do not, nor would I be taken to arraign the Justice of the King, of the Government, of the Judges, before whom I was Tryed ; or of the Jury who gave the Verdict upon which Judgment was given against me, whilest I pretend to examine the motives of Credibility upon which a Judgment of Belief in this Case is to be grounded In the mean time I hope that neither His Majesty, nor my Lords the Judges, nor my Jury will take it ill, if I presume to say, That neither the Judges, nor the Juries of *England* do, or ever did claim to be guided in their Proceedings in Cases of this nature, by any Spirit of Infallibility. The Lord *Coke*, in his Pleas of the Crown, reports a sad, but very true Case of a Person Condemned [2] and Executed for the Murther of a Girl, who, after the Execution of the Party so Condemned, was found to be living, and in perfect health. And I think it is well known to most Men of our Times, that even since His now Majesties Happy Restauration to His Crown and Dignities, there hapned a more sad Accident, where three Persons, *viz.* the Mother and two Sons were Condemned, Executed, and Hanged in Chains, for the Murther of a Person, who was afterwards found to be living, and never to have been any wayes assaulted, or hurt by those who were Executed for his Murther. Here then there were innocent Persons Condemned and Executed by Publick Verdicts and Judgments ; And what hath happened, may again happen: and yet the Juries, the Judges, the Justice, the King and Government no way blemished, they proceed, and must always be taken to proceed according to the Rules of Law and Justice. But there was certainly great Faults somewhere in those two Notorious Cases before mentioned: as there is likewise in my Case, supposing it to be true what I here affirm in the presence of God, to be true in relation to my Innocency , notwithstanding the Judgment given against me.

B   Having

---

1. *High Treason:* the trial was on June 14, 1679 at the Old Bailey; he was sentenced to death upon conviction.

2. *Pleas of the Crown:* the third part of Sir Edmund Coke's *Institutes of the Laws of England* (1644, and frequently reprinted).

Having therefore difclaimed, as I here again do, all Intentions of Arraigning the Juftice of my King, my Judges, or my Jury, I will recommend to be confidered the Motives of which a right Judgment grounded upon Belief, is to be made by Men not by affed by Paffion or Prejudice, touching my being Guilty or Innocent of that horrid Crime, of which by Judgment of Law I ftand Condemned; which Motives of Credibility can only be truly and clearly known and reprefented, by a juft, true, and fincere ftating of my Cafe, with all its Circumftances, with as much brevity as it is capable of, which I here give as followeth.

The firft news which I had, and the firft mention which I ever heard of this Plot and Treafon againft His Majefty, for which fo many have been lately Executed, and for which I ftand Condemned, was on the 9th of September laft, when I heard feveral Priefts were taken, and in Cuftody, being Charged by one Mr. Oates for High Treafon. On Monday come feven-night after, being the 7th of October, I was my felf feized on in my Chamber in the Temple, by a Meffenger of the Council, by vertue of a Warrant under the hands of Four Privy Councillors, iffued out againft John Langhorne Efq; my name being Richard, I told the Meffenger that he could not feize me by vertue of that Warrant. To which he anfwered, That he believed me the Perfon intended, and would run the hazard; whereupon I fubmitted, and went with him to Newgate. And though upon my coming thither, I told the chief Gaoler Captain Richardfon, that he could not juftifie the detaining of my Perfon by vertue of that Warrant; He not only told me, that he would run the hazard of it, but immediately made me a clofe Prifoner, and continued me fo, with the utmoft ftrictnefs, for about eight Months. From hence it muft in all reafon be agreed, that there being a full Week paffed from the time wherein I heard of Perfons being Committed for the Plot, to the time of my being feized, I muft be a perfect Mad-man to appear publickly, and not to flie or conceal my felf, if I were confcious of any the leaft imaginable Guilt. And the fame conclufion muft neceffarily follow, upon my fo quiet fubmitting my felf upon a Warrant made againft one of another name, to one who had no Title by his Warrant to make me a Prifoner. And it may reafonably alfo be conceived, that Mr. Oates, upon whofe fole Information (as I have fince heard) that Warrant was iffued, was not fo well acquainted with me as at my Tryal he fwore himfelf to be, fince he knew not my right Chriftian name, of which fcarce any Perfons were ignorant, who ever had any manner of Converfation or Bufinefs with me.

After Michaelmas Term, having continued under the before-mentioned clofe Imprifonment for two Months, without ever having been fo much as Examined, or told what I was Committed for; I confidered that too long a filence on my part, might poffibly be rather taken for a Sullennefs, than Patience. And that there being a Seffions then very near, it imported me to prevent, as far as I could, that I fhould not be furprized by a Tryal; and hurried from my clofe imprifonment to a Bar, without being permitted to fpeak with any of my Friends, or to prepare for my Tryal. Hereupon I addreffed my felf to the faid Captain Richardfon, to procure leave to addrefs a Petition to His Majefty; and having leave, I did about the 10th day of December, deliver a Petition to my faid Keeper, to be Humbly prefented by him to His Majefty, there being no poffibility for me to put the fame into any other hand to be delivered. Whether this Petition did ever come to His Majefty, or not, I could not know with certainty, but I believe it did; the fubftance of it was, to reprefent the miferies of my clofe Imprifonment, together with my Innocency, and total Ignorance of all particular matters with which I could be Charged; and to pray, that I might be admitted to an Examination; and confronted with my Accufers, as I conceive the Law required, to the End I might juftifie my felf before His Majefty, and be difcharged, if there fhould appear no juft Caufe for my being longer detained; or otherwife, that by knowing what was Charged againft me, I might be enabled to make my juft Defence at my Tryal; and might for that purpofe have the liberty of the Gaol, and of fpeaking freely with my Friends, and of fending for fuch Witneffes as I fhould have occafion to ufe for my juft Defence; and might not be furprized and hurried to a Tryal, without any poffibility of being able to make any Defence.

To this Petition I could never obtain any Anfwer; but about the 16th day of December, I was fent for down out of my Chamber, into Captain Richardfon's Houfe, where I found three Noble Lords of Parliament, who profeffed to come to me in Charity, as I believe they did.

3

---

3. *Michaelmas Term:* a session of the High Court of Justice beginning soon after September 29, the Feast of St. Michael.

did. These Noble Lords, when I was brought into their presence, were pleased to tell me, That I stood Charged with High Treason, (but of what in particular, they did not say) and that there was great and evident Proof against me, which would most certainly take away my Life. And that they had heard so good a Character of me in the World, That they were moved in Charity and Compassion to come to me, to advise me to make a free and full Confession of the Plot and Treason against His Majesty and the Government, with which I stood Charged, and thereby save my Life. And they were pleased to offer me to become my Mediators to a Pardon, for the saving of my Life, and of my Estate, in case I would make such Confession. I was much amazed to hear of such a Charge against me, when my Conscience cleared me from all Guilt of that nature, so much as in thought. I therefore asked their Lordships, Whether from the Character they had received of me in the World, they did believe me to be an Honest man? To which it was answered by one of their Lordships, That their Answer to that Question of mine was to be distinguishing, viz. That I had so good and unblemished a Reputation in the World, that if I were to give Evidence in any Concern of Ten or twenty thousand Pounds, he should value my Evidence as highly as any Mans Evidence whatsoever; But that in this present Case, if I should swear my Innocency, or that I knew nothing of the Plot or Treason with which I was Charged, his Lordship would not believe one word that I should swear. This Answer made me see, That it would be in vain for me to make any Asseverations to their Lordships of my Innocence and Ignorance of any Plot designed against His Majesty; wherefore omitting that, I humbly represented my condition to their Lordships, as to my close Imprisonment, and my never having been Examined, so as to make me capable of making a just Defence, by a fore knowledge of what was Charged against me. And I told them, That although it was supposed by the Law, that in Criminal Cases the Affirmative was to be proved by the King's Witnesses, and that a Negative could not be proved; yet it was known by all, that there might in many Cases such Affirmatives be proved by the Prisoner as to many circumstances, as might clearly prove the Affirmative, sworn by the King's Witnesses, to be impossible to be true. And that for this Reason, it I should be surprized by a sudden Tryal, without knowing what was Charged against me and the circumstances of the Charge; and without having the liberty of the Gaol, and of any Friends coming freely to me, in order to my preparing for my Tryal, and for my just Defence, it would be the same thing as to murder me. To all which, one of the said Lords reply'd (it was the Earl of Shaftsbury) That he took this way of close Imprisonment to be Illegal, and that to be so surprized by a Tryal, would be the same thing as to cut my Throat; and his Lordship did thereupon tell me, That, care should be taken, that I should have a just liberty and freedom in the Gaol for my Friends to come to me, and should not be surprized by a Tryal, as I feared to be.

This Promise of this Noble Lord gave me great comfort; but notwithstanding this, my close Imprisonment continued. My opinion was, that I was forgotten; and therefore I did several times send to Captain *Richardson*, to put their Lordships in mind of it; and when that was without effect, I apprehended that Captain *Richardson* neglected me. But I find since, that those Lords must have been understood to have intended to move the House of Lords, in relation to the making good of that Promise; and that by the Dissolving of that Parliament, (which hapned shortly after, though unknown then to me) there was no possibility for the making of such motion.

My close Imprisonment continuing in *January* or *February* following, my poor Wife procured leave from His Majesty to see me; but not otherwise, than in the presence of my Keeper. Upon her coming, I bemoaned my self to her, that I was totally ignorant of what was Charged against me; and had still a continuance of my Fear, that I should be surprized with a Tryal, without being able to make any Defence. My Wife, much troubled to hear this, could not give me any answer to remove my apprehension, because Captain *Richardson* was present; but against the time of her next coming to me, she procured an Abstract to be made of the several Narratives of Mr *Colemans* and Mr. *Irelands* Tryals; and when she came next, she endeavoured to give it to me, to the end I might from thence know what was at those Tryals given in Evidence relating to me. But Captain *Richardson* discovering her intention, took the Paper; and though he told me he would restore it to her, he carried it to the Privy Council, and would not permit my Wife to see me any more.

Upon

Upon the delivery of the before mentioned Paper to the Council, (which was on the first day of *March*) a most worthy Friend of mine had Licence from His Majesty to come to me, to exhort me to confess my knowledge of the Plot, to represent unto me my danger, if I refused ; and to give me hopes of a free Pardon, in case I complied therein. In truth he represented my condition to me so dismally, that had not Almighty God been very merciful unto me, his discourses would have been of sufficient force to have deprived me of my understanding. In short, he both told me I was to expect no Mercy, without a discovery made by me of the Plot, and that there was two or three express Witnesses against me, who had been believed already by several Juries; and that it was unreasonable in me to expect, that other Juries should not believe what former Juries had believed. He added, That the whole People were so possessed of a full belief of the Plot, from the Testimony of those Witnesses, and of such strange an Abhorrence against all of my Religion, that whatever could be said against me, would be believed by every Jury ; and whatever I should pretend to give in Evidence for my Defence, would be disbelieved and rejected, though an Angel should come from Heaven to confirm it. To all which I gave answer, That my Trust and Reliance was in my God, and onely in Him, that I had no doubt but my God, who knew my Innocency, would stand by me and assist me, and find some way for the justification of my Innocency, which to him I did averr and declare in the Presence of God, and by invoking his Divine Majesty, to testifie the Truth of what I so averred and declared, with all the Solemnity that I could use, and that can be used by a Christian in any case of like nature. I told him that there must be two several Persons perjured, or I must be safe ; and I could not think that two Persons should conspire in Perjury, for the destroying of so inconsiderable a Person as I knew my self to be. And I added, that in case my God should so far withdraw his Grace from me, by abandoning me to a Reprobate Sense, as to leave me to submit to the Temptation of charging other Persons falsly with any Crime or Plot, by which I should endanger the Lives of others, for the saving of my own Life, I was totally ignorant how to frame a Plot that should seem credible ; and could not in possibility frame any thing that could agree with what was at the present affirmed by my Accusers, I being totally ignorant of what they had affirmed.

After this Person had left me, I was in the beginning of *March*, and about one or two days before the meeting of the now Parliament, again sent for down into Captain *Richardson*'s House, where I found two most Honourable Lords of His Majesties Council, who gave me the same Exhortation and Invitation, in order to a discovery of the Plot, as I had received before from my other Friend; with this great addition, That their Lordships shew'd me an Order of Council to secure me of my Pardon, in case I should make such Discovery; but with this Condition, that I must make it then, or else the assurance of Pardon, promised by that Order, to be void.

My Conscience being clear and innocent, I made the same Answers to these Noble Lords, as I had done to the former Person who had been sent to me ; whereupon, before their departure, they delivered into my hands that Paper which my Wife had formerly prepared for me, it being (as I found) the Opinion of His Majesty, and of the Council, that I should have it.

Upon all these Circumstances duely considered, I hope it will appear to every charitable Judgment, That if I had been in the least measure conscious to my self of any Treason, I must (as I have said before) be esteemed to have totally lost my understanding, and to have become a perfect Lunatique, in refusing to Discover what (in case I had been Guilty) I could not but see would be proved against me, especially when my Discovery was so fully secured, of producing me a Pardon.

My close Imprisonment continued until two or three days before *Whitsunday*, about 4 which time it was allowed to some of my Friends to come to me with freedom, in order to my preparing for my Tryal, which was appointed to be at the end of *Whitson-week*. By these Friends, I had the Printed Narrative brought to me of all the former Tryals relating to this Plot, but I could have no light (otherwise than from them) of what would be Charged against me in Evidence.

I found it given in Evidence by Mr. *Oats* at Mr. *Coleman*'s Tryal, That he communicated the substance of a Treasonable Consult unto me, on the 25th of *April* 1678. The very next
day

---

4. *Whitsunday:* the seventh Sunday after Easter, Whitsun-week is the week beginning on Whitsunday.

day (as he then fwore) *after the Confult*, and faw feveral Commiffions then in my Cham-ber lying before me; and that after that time, he had never feen me. And I was glad to find that he had (as I conceive by what he then fwore) lockt himfelf up by his Oath to a time, and could not, without Perjury, charge any thing againft me as done after that time. And fo far as I could make any Judgment of what was depofed by Mr. *Bedloe* againft me at Mr. *Ireland*'s Tryal, touching my Regiftring the Confults of the Jefuits, I conceived it was only intended by him upon his hear-fay. This was the whole (fo far as I could ga-ther from the printed Narrative) of what appeared to be charged. I did remember the name of *Oates*, having once by his hand received a Letter; but I did not remember his Per-fon. And as for Mr. *Bedloe*, I did not remember ever at any time to have heard his name.

I found alfo from the faid Narratives, That the Court had declared both thofe Witneffes to be Ill Men. And as to Mr. *Oates*, I found that he had owned himfelf to have been firft a Proteftant, then a Roman Catholique; and now upon this Charge laid by him upon me, and others, of more Value in the World by much, than my poor felf) to profefs himfelf again to be a Proteftant. I alfo found, That upon comparing the feveral Evidences which he had given againft others, he had apparently contradicted himfelf, and affirmed feveral things which could not fubfift to be all true, becaufe they were contradictory one to the other. And as to Mr. *Bedloe*, I found by the Narrative of Mr. *Reading*'s Tryal, That he fwore himfelf at that Tryal to be flatly Perjured, when he gave Evidence againft Mr *Whitebread* and Mr. *Fenwyck* at Mr. *Ireland*'s Tryal; for being then fworn to fpeak the Truth, the whole Truth, and nothing but the Truth againft the faid Mr. *Whitebread* and *Fenwyck*. And having then affirmed upon his faid Oath, That he was a Stranger to them, and knew no-thing to give in Evidence againft them, he did at the faid Tryal of Mr. *Reading*, fwear that it was impoffible that he fhould be fuch a Stranger to Mr. *Whitebread* and Mr. *Fenwyck*, as he affirmed himfelf to be at their Tryals, when he was fworn to give Evidence againft them. I was alfo informed, (and there was a Witnefs to prove the fame) That when at one of the former Tryals Witneffes were tendred, to prove that Mr. *Bedloe* was a very Ill Man, and that for that Reafon no Credit was to be given to him. He anfwered in the Court publickly, That they might fave their labour to prove how Ill he had been, for he readily owned the worft things that could be faid of him; but that having the King's Pardon, he was fafe. And as to both Mr. *Oates*, and Mr. *Bedloe*, I was informed from good hands:

1. That they had owned themfelves (with what Truth I will not undertake to fay) Guilty of the fame Treafon that they now charged upon me and others; and this was evi-dent, from what they fwore at every Tryal.

2. That they had received their Pardons more than once each of them.

3. That they had received great Rewards for the Evidences by them given againft others in the fame cafe.

4. That they expected greater and farther Rewards for the Evidence to be given againft me, and others.

All which, I conceived, would render their Evidence unfit to be credited by any Jury, if not wholly invalid in Law.

Having gained thefe Lights, after my long Imprifonment, I did with very great longing expect my Tryal, and with great joy went to it when the day came, (which was *Saturday* in *Whitfun-Week*, being the 14th of *June* now paft) though in my paffage from the Gaol to the Court, I found my felf condemned by the Multitude before my Tryal, which (I thank my God) put me in remembrance of what my blefled Jefus fuffered, from the like Vote of the People.

I fhall forbear to repeat the Particulars of my Tryal, becaufe I will give no occafion to think, That I have any intention to Arraign the Juftice of my King, or of the Government, or of my Judges, or Jury; onely I fhall crave leave to obferve thefe following Particulars, *viz.*

I. *That the Two firft Witneffes which were Sworn for the King, Depofed nothing againft me; Thofe were Mr.*Dugdale, *and Mr.* Prance. 6

II. Th...

---

5. *Mr. Reading's Tryal:* Nathaniel Reading was tried on April 24, 1679, for bribing Bedloe to suppress his evidence against the Jesuits Whitebread and Fenwick. His conviction in effect confirmed Bedloe as a perjurer.

6. *Dugdale, Prance:* these two testified only to the general existence of the plot at Langhorn's trial.

II. *That Mr.* Oates, *who was the Third Witnefs Sworn for the King, and the firft whofe Evidence charged me, Depofed, That he had two feveral Communications with me fince the Month of* April 1 6 7 8. *namely, in* July *and* Auguft 1 6 7 8. *whereas at the Tryal of Mr.* Coleman, *he had exprefly Sworn, That after the Month of* April 1 6 7 8. *he had never feen me to his knowledge or remembrance.*

III. *That Mr.* Bedloe *Depofed, That as he and Mr.* Coleman *were together walking in my Chamber in the* Temple, *he faw me Entring feveral Treafonable Letters into a Book in my Study; and that the faid Book was a great Book, lying upon the Desk in my Study : Whereas every perfon who knows my faid Chamber, and the fcituation of my Study, cannot but know, that it is impoffible to look out of my Chamber into my Study, fo as to fee any one Writing there, and that I never had at any time any Desk in my Study.*

What paffed farther at my Tryal I forbear to mention, for the Reafon before given, but refer to fuch Narrative of my Tryal, as I hear is publifhed in Print; which if it be truly 7 made, I thank the Reporter for his Juftice; if untruly, I then beg of God to pardon the Reporter's Injuftice. In the mean time I do here, in the Prefence of the Great God, who is the God of Truth, and the Searcher of all Hearts, Declare and Proteft:

1. That as to Mr. *Bedloe*, I do not know, remember or believe, that I ever faw him, or heard him fpeak, before that time that he appeared in the faid Court, to give Evidence againft me at my faid Tryal.

2. That I did never fee or fpeak with Mr. *Oates* at any time fince the Month of *November* 1 6 7 7. fo that I can with great Truth affirm, and do affirm, in the Prefence of the All-knowing God, That whatever was given in Evidence againft me by the faid *Bedloe*, was utterly falfe and untrue. As likewife whatever was given againft me in Evidence by the faid *Oates*, as fpoken by himfelf, or by me, in the Months of *April, July* and *Auguft, 1678*. or at any other times after the Month of *November* 1677. As alfo what was fworn in Evidence againft me by the faid *Oates*, at his firft coming to me in the Month of *November* 1677. which related to my prejudice; and which I could have proved to be falfe by a very good Witnefs, in cafe I could have forefeen, that Mr. *Oates* would have had the confidence to have given any thing in Evidence againft me, as pre ended to have been fpoken by me at 8 that time. But Mr. *Oates*, at the Tryal of Mr. *Coleman*, gave a clear evidence of his skill in this kind of Fencing, and of his great care and cunning, to prevent that no Perfon, whofe Life he defigns to take away by his Evidence, fhall ever be able to know what he intends to fwear, or confequently to produce any Witnefs to difcover or difprove his Perjuries: For being then upon his Oath, and being interrogated what he had informed againft Mr *Coleman* before His Majefty and the Council at Mr. *Coleman*'s Examination there, before he was Committed to *Newgate*, Mr. *Oates* did not blufh to fwear, That he did only at that time inform what he judged fufficient, whereupon to ground Mr. *Coleman*'s Commitment; and concealed what he had farther to fay, left he fhould by faying it, enable Mr. *Coleman* to produce Witnefles as to the circumftances of time and place, to difprove what Mr. *Oates* fhould fay againft him, or to the like effect.

Add to all this, that which Mr. *Oates* anfwered at my Tryal, when interrogated by me, (and to my beft remembrance *Bedloe* gave the like anfwer to the fame queftion) what Gratification or Reward he had received, for his pretended Difcovery of this by him pretended Plot, and for giving Evidence againft fuch as had been Tryed thereupon; and particularly, whether he had not received the Sum of 500 *l.* and did not expect to receive a farther Gratification for his farther Services therein? He boldly anfwered, That he was fo far from having received any fuch Sum, or any Reward for his faid Services, that he was out of Purfe 750 *l.* of his own Monies, in the profecution of the fame. Which, how great an Untruth that is, I refer to His Majefty, and thofe who manage His Majefties Monies and Treafury; and to all who knew the moft extream Poverty of thefe two Perfons, *Oates* and *Bedloe*, before they relieved their Wants, and found the way to fupply their Neceffities, by charging thofe Perfons with Treafon who have been Executed, or remain ftill Prifoners upon their Accufations. 9

After

---

7. *Narrative of my trial: The Tryal of Richard Langhorne, Esq.* (1679).

8. *pre ended:* pretended (misprint).

9. *their accusations:* according to John Kenyon, Oates received relatively little in return for his "services": about £10 a week for expenses until May of 1681, when his allowance was reduced to £2; in September it was stopped. In addition he received a little more than £400 from the government. Bedloe received about as much, plus £500 for "discovering" Godfrey's murderers, the unfortunate Green, Berry, and Hill (Kenyon, p. 242).

(7)

After Judgment was given against me, upon the Verdict found upon the Evidence of these two Men, there were two Persons came to me to the Gaol, as sent by the Earl of *Shaftesbury*, or his Order, to propose something to me in Charity, for the saving of my Life. The first thing by them proposed to be done by me for that end, was a Discovery to be made by me of the Plot and Treason for which I stood Condemned. But when I had satisfied them so far, as to my Solemn Protestations made in the Presence of God, were of force to satisfie them touching my Innocency, and my total Ignorance of any Plot or Treason ever at any time designed against His Majesty, other than the late Unparallel'd Treason and Rebellion, which was before His Majesties Happy Restauration. They were pleased to propose farther, That it was well known, that I had been made use of as a Councel for the Jesuits, and in that Capacity could not but know what Estates they had in *England*, or at least a very great part of those Estates; and that if I would freely make a Discovery of such Estates of that nature as should be of a considerable value, I should thereby obtain my Pardon; the granting of which, upon such Discovery, might be well justified to the Parliament at their next Meeting. **10**

Having well weighed this latter Proposal, and considered, That it would be a Sin against Truth, to deny that I had knowledge of such Estates; and that all the Scandal which could be taken by my Discovery of them, could not be so great, as my Denial would be offensive to God. And having no Doubt, but that my frank and sincere discovering and owning what was within my knowledge, though to the Displeasure of those who were to be concerned therein, would make it evident to all Honest and Judicious persons, That in case I knew any of the Plot, or of any Treason intended against His Majesty, (the concealment of which by me would be a Sin unto Damnation) I would without Difficulty discover the same, for the saving of my Soul, as well as of my Life, since I was ready to make a Discovery of such Estates, the concealment of which could be no Sin against God nor the King. I freely engaged my self to Discover all that I knew touching such Estates , for the Service of His Majesty ; and the Persons by whom the same was so proposed, went from me, with a resolution, to report my ready compliance therein unto his said Lordship: **11**

After this, I did by some Friends prevail to have a Report made to His Majesty, of what had passed between those two Persons and me, with which His Majesty seemed (as I was informed) to be well satisfied, and directed, That I should send unto, and intrust His Majesty with so much as I could remember (without having resort to Writings) of those Estates, which I with all readiness did : And I took that Command from His Majesty, to be an evident implied promise of a Pardon, for the securing of my Life. This Engagement of mine, to make this Discovery, occasioned a Reprieve to be granted me for some dayes; but after the said Reprieve granted, my Lord of *Shaftesbury* was pleased to intimate unto me by one of the aforesaid Persons, by whom it was first proposed unto me to make such Discovery, That no Pardon should be granted to me, without a full Discovery made by me of the Plot. And his Lordship was also pleased to come to Captain *Richardson*'s house, and sending for me thither, to tell me to this effect, viz. That as my Parts and Reputation in the World had made me fit for Employment, so I might rest secure, That in case I would make a full Discovery of the Plot, I should be put into as good a Post, both as to Honour as Estate, as my own Heart could wish; but if I failed to do that, no Discovery of Estates could or should procure my Pardon. I laboured, what I could, by Solemn Protestations to satisfie his Lordship of my Innocency, and my total Ignorance of any Plot or Treason whatsoever ; and this I did so fully, (as I conceived) That in case Almighty God should have so far withdrawn his Grace from me, as to leave me to a Reprobate Sense, and to permit against truth, to have pretended a knowledge of a Plot, to the prejudice of any person, meerly for the saving of my own poor Life, and the obtaining those advantages with which I was tempted, I ought not in any measure to have been believed. But blessed be my God, who hath by his Grace so far strengthned, as to enable me rather to choose and lose my Life in Innocency, and save my Soul, than by Falsities to lose my Soul, and become Guilty of the Blood of others, against whom I could not with Truth testifie any thing of any Crime.

After his said Lordship had given me the Temptation before-mentioned, I had several Persons applied to me, with Discourses tending wholly to make me despair of Pardon, unless I would discover a Plot ; and to perswade me, that it was not Honourable nor Honest for me

to

10. *Unparallel'd Treason:* the Civil War that led to the execution of Charles I.

11. *Estates:* as a result of his disclosures, the Jesuits lost their estates (Kenyon, p. 209).

to difcover any Eftates, which His Majefty might feize on, in cafe I did not know, That the Owners of the faid Eftates were Traytors. But I took all thefe Difcourfes to fignifie no more than a Repentance, for having propofed to me to make a Difcovery of Eftates: And therefore having fent fuch Difcovery unto His Majefty, as I was able to make upon my Memory ; I laboured by my Friends, and did obtain a farther Reprieve, together with an Order, requiring to fend into the Council by a day limited, fuch Difcovery as I could make; and a Licence to have all my Writings and Papers in my Chamber perufed by fuch as I nominated, and according to fuch Direction as I fhould give, for the Letter enabling me to perfect fuch Difcovery. This was conceived by me, and my Friends, to be intended by His Majefty, as an Affurance of a Pardon, it being to engage the whole Council, as His Majefty was pleafed to engage Himfelf before, when He Commanded me to truft Him ; and it feemed evident, that this Difcovery required, muft be a Difcovery of Eftates, otherwife the perufal of Papers and Writings had been to no purpofe.

In Obedience to the faid laft mentioned Command, I applied with all Diligence to compleat my Difcovery, my Papers and Writings were examined by my Friends, and my Difcovery was perfected, and delivered in unto the Council, at the precife day for that purpofe limited, and it amounted to the value (as I computed the fame) of between Twenty and thirty thoufand Pounds *Sterling*, and was annexed to a Petition, wherein I declared my Innocency and Ignorance of any Treafon or Plot, and my fincere dealing as to my faid Difcovery; and offered to fubmit my felf to be examined upon Interrogatories upon Oath, or to undergo any Tryal of any Teft, for the giving fatisfaction, that the Difcovery then by me made was complete, and that I knew of no other Lands belonging in any wayes to the Jefuits, other than what I had then and there Difcovered : and likewife for the purging of my felf touching any other matter, upon which it fhould be thought fit to Examine me. And in my faid Difcovery, I exprefied every thing with fuch certainty as to the Names of the Eftates, and the Places where they lay, and the Values (fo far as I was able to give the fame) and the Perfons (fo far as I knew) concerned therein, that it was eafie to feize the fame immediately for the ufe of His Majefty : So that I thereby did all that was in my power, in order to my giving a perfect Obedience to the faid Commands of His Majefty, and to what was thereby required from me. And my Friends, as well as my felf, had no Doubt, but that as Almighty God requires no more from us, for the obtaining his pardon of our Sins, and the falvation of our Souls, than what His Divine Majefty knows to be poffible for us to do on our parts : fo the King's Majefty, and His Council, would require no more from me, for the faving of my poor Life, and the obtaining of my Pardon, than what was poffible for me on my part to do. I alfo looked upon the Publick Honour and Faith to be now firmly engaged for the fecurity of my Life, and the granting of a Pardon to me, I having fully performed my part, of that which was the Condition. And it being clear, that when once my Difcovery was delivered in, and read in Council, it ceafed to be a Secret, and that nothing therein contained, could afterwards remain as a thing undifcovered. It was likewife evident that by this Act I had done (as I believed) more than any other fingle perfon now living, who is meerly a Lay-man, could do for the Service of His Majefty. And that if there were any fuch Plot, as is affirmed by *Oates* and *Bedloe*, and that any perfon now charged therewith, had knowledge thereof, and fhould be required, as I had been, to difcover what he knows for the faving of his Life, he would hardly be induced to make fuch Difcovery, in cafe my Life fhould be taken away, after my fo free Difcovery of all that was within my knowledge to be difcovered, was in obedience to fo great a Command delivered out of my hands. However I refted fatisfied, That in cafe my Life fhould be taken away for the Crime for which I ftand Condemned, and after my Obedience given to His Majefties Commands, in making the faid Difcovery, I fhould dye with this great comfort. That I fhould have a double Martyrdom. Firft, as dying perfectly Innocent of the Crime for which I fhould lofe my Life. And fecondly, as choofing rather to dye, than to fin againft my God, and my Neighbor, by charging others falfly, and becoming guilty of their Blood, and of the Ruine of their Families, by accufing them of a Crime, of which my own Confcience muft bear me witnefs, that I did never know them, or any of them Guilty; but on the contrary, believe them to be perfectly Innocent. *Whereas* if I had on the other fide denied my felf to have known any thing of thofe Eftates, which I was required to difcover.

cover, I muſt have ſinned againſt the God of Truth, by affirming a Lye. And if Confeſſing, That I had knowledge of ſuch Eſtates, I ſhould rather have choſen to dye, than to have made a Diſcovery of ſuch my knowledge for the ſaving of my Life, I ſhould have appeared (in ſome ſort at leaſt) guilty of my own Blood, through my obſtinacy.

Upon the delivering of this Diſcovery, and the reading of it in the Council, the Lord Viſcount *Hallifax* produced a Letter written to him (as his Lordſhip affirmed) from the Earl of *Roſcommon* from *Bruxels*, in which Letter the ſaid Earl taking notice, that he had heard of my being Reprieved, affirmed himſelf to be much ſatisfied, That my Life ſhould be ſaved ; and gave this Reaſon, That my Life might be uſeful to the Publick, or to the like effect. Theſe words were taken to my great Diſadvantage, and to import, as if the Earl of *Roſcommon* did know, That I was able to make a Diſcovery of the Plot. And though the words might well bear a more kind ſenſe, and did not, without forcing, ſo much as incline to that unkind Interpretation; yet upon the reading of that Letter, my Diſcovery was rejected, after having been Publickly read, and ordered to be ſent unto me by a Clark of the Council, and notice to be given to me, That by an Order of Council, I was Reprieved onely until the 14th day of *July* ; and that if before that day I did not make a Diſcovery of the Plot, I was to expect no farther mercy.

My Friends were more aſtoniſhed at this Order than my ſelf was, and being now in this condition, I preſumed yet once more, to addreſs a Petition, in which I prayed, That my Life might be ſaved, though to be ſpent in Baniſhment ; and to the end that I might do all that in me lay, to expreſs and declare my Innocency, I did, to that Petition, annex this following Declaration, and Proteſtation, *viz.*

I *Do Solemnly and Sincerely , in the Preſence of Almighty God , Profeſs, Teſtifie, and Declare , as followeth :* That is to ſay,

I. *That I do believe, and own my my Moſt Gracious Sovereign Lord the King's Majeſty, King* CHARLES II. *to be my True and Lawful Sovereign King , in the ſame Senſe and Latitude, to all Intents and Purpoſes, as in the Oath commonly called ,* The Oath of Allegiance , *His ſaid Majeſty is expreſſed to be King of this Realm of* England.

II. *That I do in my Soul believe , That neither the Pope, nor any Prince, Potentate , or Foreign Authority, nor the People of* England, *nor any Authority out of this Kingdom, or within the ſame, hath or have any Right to diſpoſſeſs His ſaid Majeſty of the Crown and Government of* England, *or to Depoſe Him therefrom, for any Cauſe , or pretended Cauſe whatſoever ; Or to give Licence to me, or to any other of His Majeſties Subjects whatſoever, to bear Arms againſt His Majeſty, or to take away His Life, or to do Him any Bodily Harm ; Or to diſturb the Government of this Kingdom, as it is now Eſtabliſhed by Law ; Or to Alter, or go about to Alter the ſaid Government, or the Religion now Eſtabliſhed in* England, *by any way of Force.*

III. *That I neither am, nor ever was at any time Guilty, ſo much as in my moſt ſecret Thoughts, of any Treaſon, or Miſpriſion of Treaſon whatſoever.*

IV. *That I do Believe, That if I did know, or ſhould know of any Treaſon, or Treaſonable Deſign that was, or is intended, or ſhould be intended againſt His ſaid Majeſty , or the Government of this His Majeſties Kingdom, or for the Alteration by Force , Advice, or otherwiſe, of the ſaid Government, or of the Religion now Eſtabliſhed in this Kingdom, and ſhould conceal, and not diſcover, the ſame unto His ſaid Majeſty, or His Majeſties Council or Miniſters, or ſome of them, That ſuch Concealment would be to me a Sin unto Death, and Eternal Damnation.*

D   And

12

13

---

12. *Roscommon:* Wentworth Dillon (1633–1685), the fourth earl and a Protestant; he is known for his poetry and criticism.

13. *Misprision:* here, concealment of treason.

And I do Solemnly, in the Presence of God, Profess, Testifie, and Declare, That as I hope for Salvation, or expect any benefit by the Blood and Passion of Jesus Christ, I do make this Declaration, and every Part thereof, in the Plain and Ordinary Sense of the Words, wherein the same stands written, as they are commonly understood by English *Protestants, and the Courts of Justice of* England, *without any Evasion, or Equivocation, or Delusion, or Mental Reservation whatsoever. And without any Dispensation, or Pardon, or Absolution already granted to me, for this, or any other purpose, by the* 'Pope, *or any other Authority or Person whatsoever, or without any hope of any such Dispensation. And without thinking or believing that I am, or can be acquitted before God or Man, or absolved of this* 'Declaration, *or any part thereof, although the Pope, or any other Person or Persons, or Power whatsoever, should Dispense with, or Annul the same, or Declare that it was, or is Null or Void from the beginning.*

This, with my Petition, was Presented to His Majesty in Council on, *Thursday*, the 10th of *July* instant; and after the reading of my Petition, my said Protestation and Declaration was (as I am informed) begun to be read, but when the person that read the same, came to read that part of it, in which I aver my Innocency, he was not (as I am informed) permitted to read farther ; and it was declared, That I was to expect no farther mercy, unless I would make a Discovery of the Plot, which (God is my Witness) I cannot do, because I know nothing of it directly or indirectly.

And now having related all the particular Circumstances of my Case, so far as my memory can recollect them ; and made such Protestations and Declarations as is before mentioned, I shall only recommend to be considered by all impartial Judgments, those solemn and serious Protestations which were made by those others, who have lost their Lives already upon the Evidence given against them, by the same Mr. *Oates* and Mr. *Bedloe* , and pray that it may be duely weighed, Whether the Solemn Oaths and Protestations of sober Men, made by them immediately before their respective Deaths, and this Protestation of mine before mentioned, made at a time, when my Confession and Discovery of a Plot or Treason against my King (in case I had been privy unto, or known such Plot or Treason) would not only have saved my Life, and secured me of a Pardon; but would also have entituled me unto, and (in all probability) put me into the full possession of Preferments and Advantages, greater than I ever (I thank my God) coveted ; Be not more considerable to move a Belief of my Innocency, than the Evidence given against me by my Accusers before-mentioned, to move a Belief of my Guilt? It is said, it is not upon the bare Oaths of those two Witnesses, but upon the Verdict of the Twelve Jurors, that I am found Guilty. I am sure that every judicious Person , who understands our Proceedings in our Law of *England*, in all Cases of this Nature, doth know, and can answer, That the Verdict of the Twelve Jurors is grounded wholly upon the Evidence given by the Witnesses. The Jurors Belief of the Witnesses produced and sworn to give Evidence against me, was the foundation of their Verdict, and justifies them in Law ; and the Verdict given by the Jurors, doth in Law justifie the Judgment given by the Judges, for the taking away of my Belief. And I beseech God that the same Rule of Law, may, at the great and terrible day of Judgment, acquit as well the Jurors, who gave that Verdict, as the Judges, who gave that Judgment, from all Guilt of my Blood. But I must again refer it to the Consciences of all unbyassed, judicious, and good Men, whether in Christian Charity, the motives of Credibility founded upon such Judgment, the Verdict, which was solely grounded upon the Evidence of Mr. *Oates* and Mr. *Bedloe*, be of greater force to a good and charitable Conscience to pronounce me Guilty, than the several other motives which I have here represented, will be found to pronounce me Innocent ?

It will no way concern me as to my own particular, whether the world shall adjudge me Innocent, or not; it is sufficient for me, That my Conscience doth with great Joy and
Peace

Peace acquit me. And that the God of all Truth, my deareſt Jeſus, who is Truth it ſelf, doth know me to be Innocent. And that the Conſciences of thoſe moſt Unhappy Men, Mr. *Oates* and Mr. *Pedloe*, will at the laſt day, when the ſecrets of all hearts ſhall be made manifeſt, be compelled, to the Glory of God, and their own ſhame, To proclaim me Innocent. I beſeech Almighty God to give thoſe miſerable Men a true and ſincere Repentance for the Sin which they have committed, and by which they have drawn upon themſelves, the Guilt of my Innocent Blood.

I do here profeſs my ſelf to dye a Member of the Holy Catholique and Apoſtolique Church, of which, the Biſhop of *Rome* is the Supreme Viſible Head of Government on Earth, as the Succeſſor of the Holy Apoſtle St *Peter*. And of which Church our bleſſed Lord Jeſus is the Supreme, Inviſible Head, of influence to Guide, Govern, and direct the ſame by his Holy Spirit. And I do take my Religion to be the ſole Cauſe of my being the Object of the Malice of my Enemies, who are the Cauſers of my Death.

If what I here ſay be any wayes disbelieved becauſe of my Religion, I humbly recommend it to the conſideration of ſober Men, whether ſuch disbelief upon this ground, be not,

1. To caſt a Reproach and Blemiſh upon the Honour and Reputation of all our moſt Pious Anceſtors, and our whole Nation, who lived and dyed before the 20th Year of King *Henry* VIII. and who did all live and dye in the ſame Faith, and Members of the ſame Church, of which by God's Grace I am now a Member, though unworthy.

2. To caſt a like Reproach upon all the Princes, States and People of the World, who are Members of the ſame Church.

3. To give a Juſt Occaſion to the ſame Princes, States and People, never to give Credit to any thing affirmed or ſworn by any *Engliſh* Proteſtant; and conſequently,

4. To lay a Foundation for the total deſtroying of all Trade, as well as Converſation, with all thoſe Princes, States and People.

We muſt learn to do unto others, as we would have others do unto us. And it is not a good Anſwer to ſay, That this Disbelief is only in relation to the Jeſuits, and thoſe who make uſe of them : For there is ſcarce any Prince of this Religion now living, who doth not make uſe of a Jeſuit for his Ghoſtly Father ; which will likewiſe be a clear Evidence, That thoſe Princes (known to all the World not to be Fools or Mad-men) have not an Opinion, That the Doctrines and Principles of the Jeſuits, are any wayes Pernicious and Dangerous to Government, as the Pulpits of *England* repute them to be. And certainly if an *Engliſh* Proteſtant ſhould in *France*, caſt the two Execrable Murthers of thoſe two Kings 14 of that Kingdom, who were killed by *Clement* and *Ravillack*, upon the Jeſuits, or as an effect of any Doctrine of our Church, That Church, and that Order, would with much greater eaſe clear themſelves from ſuch a Reproach, than our *Engliſh* Proteſtants could clear themſelves, in caſe the Murther of Queen *Mary* of *Scotland* (our King's Great Grand- 15 Mother) or of our laſt moſt excellent Prince King *CHARLES* I. ſhould be caſt as a 16 Reproach upon the Doctrines of the Proteſtant Church of *England*, or of any other Party profeſſing Proteſtancy, theſe Murthers being committed under the Solemn Shew and Formalities of Publick Juſtice ; when it is well known, That *Clement* and *Ravillack* were only two private Villains, who were diſowned by all the World. Nor do there want Authors, who call themſelves, and are reputed to be Proteſtants, who, in their Publick Writings, juſtifie theſe two Murthers, of Queen *Mary*, and King *Charles* I. Nay, there may, peradventure, be found more Authors, reputed Proteſtants, who juſtifie the People to have a Power to Depoſe, and take away the Lives of Kings, than there are found Authors, reputed to be Catholicks, who aſſert the Pope to have Power to Depoſe Princes. Yet, God forbid,

---

14. *Execrable Murders:* of Henry III and Henry IV of France (see p. 120).

15. *Queen Mary of Scotland:* Mary Stuart, a Catholic, executed after being imprisoned in England by Elizabeth I, on February 8, 1587.

16. *CHARLES I:* condemned to death by a Protestant Parliament and executed on January 30, 1649.

forbid, That I fhould call thefe Pofitions, or Opinions, the Doctrines of the Church of *England*; I impute thefe Actions, to the Paffions of wicked and ambitious Men ; and thefe Doctrines, to thofe onely, who write or own them ; and certainly the fame Charity can-not, without Sin, be denied to us, by all fober Judgments. But if this Juftice be denied unto me and thofe of my Religion, I befeech God to pardon fuch as are fo uncharitable; And I do moft heartily, and from my Soul, forgive thofe who want this Charity, as I do the before named Mr. *Oates* and Mr. *Bedloe*, and all others, who are any wayes guilty of my Death, or of my not obtaining my Pardon, or of rejoycing at the fhedding of my Inno-cent Blood ; and all who have done me any Injury whatfoever , *S W E E T J E S U S Forgive Them, They know not what they do.*

July 12.
1679.

Richard   Langhorne.

Here Langhorn's anonymous editor gives an account of his behavior at the scaffold.

17

HAving given you now Reader the Speech at length, which Mr. *Langhorne* had prepared (for the Reason he mentions) against his Execution, it will not be, perchance, ungrateful to you, to know, that when he came down from his Chamber at *Newgate* , to be put into the Sledge, he had it with him, but the Sheriff (*telling him, that he must use no* **18** *Papers at the Gallows*) took it away, so that he repeated there so much of it only as he could remember ; therefore to satisfie the Curiosity of those also, that would know what and how much that was, I shall here give you the Particulars, with some other things that occurr'd, before he was turned over.

When the Hangman was putting the Rope over his Head, he took it into his hands, and kissed it. Afterwards said :

I do not know whether you will allow me liberty of Speech, or no; and the Noise of the People being so great, that I believe it is impossible to speak to be heard.

SILENCE was Commanded.

Mr. L. *I would gladly speak to Mr. Sheriff* HOW ; who coming up to him, he addressed himself thus :

Mr. Sheriff. *I having some doubt, whether I should be suffered to speak, in relation to my Innocency and Loyalty, I did, for that Reason, prepare what I had to say, and what I i. tended to say in Writing, and it is delivered into your hands, Mr. Sheriff ; and therefore for the particular and precise Words and Expressions, I do refer my self to that, and I hope you will be so just to my Memory, that you will permit it to be seen.*
I shall therefore make only a short Preface, and I do declare, in the Presence of the Eternal God, and as I hope to be saved by the Merits and Death of my dear Jesus, That I am not Guilty directly or indirectly, of any Crime that was sworn against me ; I do not speak this to Arraign the Court of Publick Justice, either Judges or Jury, but those Men that did swear it ; and the Jury had liberty to believe, or not believe, as they pleased ; And I do likewise say , with the same Averrment, That I did never in my Life see any Commissions or Patent, or any Writing, or any other Thing, under the hand of Johannes Paulus de Oliva, &c.   **19**
S. Nor under no other hand.
L. *No, nor under any other hand, of any Commission or Patents, for the Raising of an Army, or any Thing else against the King.*
S. What was the Patents for ? for Nothing !
L. *I never saw any, nor do I believe there was any : And whereas I have read in a Narra-* **20 21** *tive, that I sent a Commission by my Son, to the Lord Arundel* of Warder, *and that I deliver'd another to the Lord* Petre (*or* Peters) *with my own hands, I take God to Witness, that I never saw him in my life, or ever, to my knowledge, saw the face of that Lord ; nor did I send or know of any thing that was sent to my Lord* Arundel of Warder, *of that nature.*
S Shorten your business, you have, Mr. *Langhorne*, and your Party, so many wayes to Equivocate, and after Absolution you may say any thing.
L. *I refer my self to that Paper I gave you, Mr. Sheriff.*
S. I think it is not fit to be Printed. I will do you no wrong
L *I do not think you will.*   **22**
S. You have already printed a Paper, or some body for you.
L. Sir, *I did not Print it, and it was done without any Direction or Permission of mine.*

The Lord preserve His Majesty from all manner of Treason, and preserve Him from falling into such Hands, as His Royal Father, of Glorious Memory, fell under ; I pray God to forgive my Enemies, as I freely do those that Accused me, those that Witnessed against me ; and all others that either desired my Blood, or rejoyce at the shedding of it ; and all Persons that have any wayes concern'd themselves with me, I freely forgive them with all my Soul, and beg my dear Jesus to forgive them, and all others. God Almighty bless you, and bless the whole Na-
G   *tion,*

tion, and the Government, and preserve it from all Evil and Mischief that I am afraid is coming on it, for the shedding of Innocent Blood. Sweet Jesus, lay not my Innocent Blood to their Charge.

I shall say no more now Publickly.

Asked the Executioner, *Whether the Rope was right or no?* He said, Yes ; and he asked him, Whether he did forgive him ? To which Mr. *Langhorne* said, *I freely do.*

I shall now recommend my self to God in Private.

S. You may have liberty.

The Writer. The Lord have Mercy on your Soul.

L. The Lord in Heaven reward your Charity.

Croft himself, pray'd again.

Blessed Jesus, into thy Hands I recommend my Soul and Spirit, now at this instant take me into Paradice ; I am desirous to be with my Jesus ; I am ready, and you need stay no longer for me.

F I N I S.

17. *11:* a misprint for 21. The omitted section contains Langhorn's verse, in which he meditates on death and affirms his faith.

18. *Sheriff:* Sir Richard How. The two London sheriffs were in charge of executions.

19. *Johannes Paulus de Olivia:* Gian Paolo Olivia (1600–1681), the eleventh director-general of the Society of Jesus.

20. *a Narrative:* Oates's *True Narrative.*

21. *Lord Arundel of Warder:* one of the five lords in the Tower, as was Lord Petre.

22. *a Paper: The Petition and Declaration of Richard Langhorne*; the brief preface from the publisher is dated July 11, 1679. It is hostile to Langhorn.

185

Sir Roger L'Estrange's
A Further Discovery of the Plot (1680)
and *The Observator* (July 20, 1681)

L'Estrange's *A Further Discovery of the Plot* (1680)

The court wished to move against the opposition press during the Exclusion Crisis, but it soon discovered that attempts to suppress the Whig writers and printers were usually futile. They published under the protection of Parliament when it was in session, and the lapsing of the "Printing Act" in 1679 enabled Shaftesbury to establish presses "everywhere." It is said that Sir Francis North, the lord keeper of the great seal, advised the king in 1681 to fight back by employing his own writers to outdo his enemies (J. G. Muddiman, *The King's Journalist, 1659–1689* [London: John Lane, 1923], pp. 213 and 233). This strategy was made to order for Roger L'Estrange, who became the chief Tory propagandist of the period and proved to be more than a match for his opponents in energy, dedication, and harshness.

Born in 1616, L'Estrange lived for almost eighty-eight years, an ardent royalist and Anglican, and an eager, voluminous controversialist. During the Civil War, he was captured by the parliamentary forces, tried for treason, and sentenced to death; he waited for execution in Newgate prison for almost four years before he finally escaped. Afterwards, he continued his unflagging support of the royalist cause, with innumerable tracts defending the monarchy and himself, attacking the republicans and dissenters (including Milton), and opposing religious toleration. In 1663, King Charles appointed him surveyor of the imprimery, with the power to act against the authors and printers of seditious or libelous books. He had at least one printer sent to the gallows.

In addition, he was granted the sole privilege of printing a newsletter, *The Intelligencer,* which appeared on Mondays and was supplemented on Thursdays by *The News.* These continued until 1666. But his greatest subjects were the Popish Plot and the question of exclusion. Beginning in 1679, he produced countless tracts attacking Shaftesbury and the exclusionists; he frequently wrote answers to their tracts, including Marvell's *An Account of the Growth of Popery* and Charles Blount's *An Appeal from the Country to the City.* His *History of the Plot* (1680) is a report on the plot trials, but *A Further Discovery of the Plot* (1680) contains considerable irony at Oates's expense. Though he does not openly deny the plot, which would have been too dangerous, he does undermine it. The first twenty-two pages of this pamphlet are devoted to an elaborately ironic dedication to Titus Oates—matching Oates's audacity in dedicating his *True Narrative* to the king—in which he defends his own *History*. The main text, given here, attempts to turn the energies generated by the plot against the dissenters, who were among the plot's chief supporters. Since both dissenting Protestants and Catholics refused the oaths required by the Test Acts, both, he argues, must be regarded with equal suspicion. For this and other efforts, L'Estrange was attacked in print and in the law courts as a covert papist. In November 1680, fearing that Parliament would impeach him, he fled the country. But in the following February, "the Dog Towzer"—the most famous of the names his enemies had for him—was back at home. In April, he founded his best known newspaper, *The Observator.*

L'Estrange did not cease his efforts against Oates until he was instrumental in getting the prime witness convicted of perjury in 1685. In that same year, James II knighted L'Estrange for his services. After 1688, he was repeatedly imprisoned for his hostility to William III, but he survived nevertheless until 1704. He was a good musician in private life and a respected man of letters, who translated the fables of Aesop and a number of other works. Although his achievements were narrowed by rigid partisanship and intolerance, he made his way through life with rough wit and boundless energy.

A Further Difcovery of the PLOT, Drawn from the NARRATIVE and DEPOSITIONS of Dr. *TITUS OATES*, &c.

AS it cannot be deny'd, but that the Kings Witnef-fes have ventur'd as far, and done as much as men could do, (under their Circumftances) to make out the Truth of a *Damnable*, and *Hellifh Popifh Plot* upon the *Life* of his *Sacred Majefty*, our *Religion* and *Civil Go-vernment* : So neither muft it be deny'd, on the other hand, but that the Juftice and Wifdom of this Nation have emprov'd all Difcoveries, by the ftricteft Inquifiti-on, and fcrutiny imaginable ; and done all that was pof-fible alfo toward the fuppreffing of the Confpiracy, by the higheft Inftances of Political zeal and Rigour. In-fomuch, that after fo many Priefts and Jefuits, and o-ther Leading men of that Party removed by the ftroke of *Publique Juftice* ; fo many of them under *Confinement* ; fo many more reduced to fhift for themfelves *beyond the seas*, befide the fevere Penalties of the *Law* upon the reft, with all forts of Encouragement, both for their *detection* and *punifhment* : After all this care taken (I fay) to tear up the accurfed Plot by the *Root*, We are yet affured, that (all this notwithftanding) the Plot is ftill carried on with *Confidence*, and *Vigour*. And this we have, even from thofe very Perfons themfelves that formerly wrought in the fame Mine with the Confpirators ; till through the Grace of a better Light they came to govern them-felves by other Meafures. *This* is a truth no more to be

D   *doubted,*

acuoted, then that of the *Plot* it *felf* ; which has ftood the Tryall of fo many *Solemn* and *Publique Tefts* : Befide that we have the fame Authority for the One as for the Other ; only the Circumftances not being brought into Proof, the matter of Fact lies a little more in the Dark.

Whether or no the Plot *goes on ftill*, after all this Havock made of the *Papifts*, is the Common fubject of every *Coffee houfe Difcourfe*. They that muft be prefum'd to know beft, are of opinion that it does ; and thofe that are upon the *Negative*, reafon the point after this manner. *What* ? (fay they) *Is it a* Plot *that will work without hands* ? *Where are the* Papifts, *the* Inftruments *that fhould drive it on* ? *Are they in the* Aire *or* under Ground ; *or are they* Invifible? *For as they are now difpers'd, and broken, (befide the Terrour that overawes them)* there are *at leaft* three Thoufand Proteftants, *in fight, to* one Papift. ¹ But do they ask where they *are*, becaufe we cannot *fee* them ? Why do they not rather ask where they are *Not* ? becaufe they may be any where, and we not *know* them : For, as I have been told by perfons of Great Quality, they'l indure all *fhapes*, and Exercife all *Profeffions*. They fpeak of *one Jefuit* that cry'd *work for a Cooper* ; another ² that wrought upon the Trade of a *Shoo maker* ; *Priefts* in *Red coats* Innumerable : And it is obferv'd that ³ upon the bringing of the Late Plot to Light, all the little *Frenchmen* with their *Marionets* or *Puppet-fhows* vanifh'd in a trice : which gave a fufpition that they were only a kind of *Itinerant Agents* for the *Faction* : To fay nothing of their skill and Induftry, in the managing of all our Divifions, and difcontents, to the advantage of their own Party. Thefe are ftories (I know) that are much more eafily *Contradicted*, then *Prov'd* : and therefore with out laying any ftreffe at all upon *Common Fame*, or *Hearfay*, I fhall now apply my felf to *that farther Difcovery of the Plot*, which I have promis'd in my Title ; and fupport

---

1. *one Papist:* John Miller estimates that the Catholics made up between 1.1 and 1.2 percent of the entire population of five or five and a half million, or about 60,000 people (Miller, p. 11).

2. *Cooper:* a maker of casks or tubs.

3. *Red coats:* in the army.

fupport my undertaking, upon the Authority of Dr. *Oates* himfelf ; with a refpect both to the Validity of his *Teftimony* , and to the weight of his *Obfervations* ; being a Perfon that hath dived deeper into the *Myftery* of this Iniquity (with favour of the reft) then any other man.

As to the Hellifh Defign upon the Life of our Gracious Sovereign, by *Piftol*, *Sword*, or *Poyfon*, we hope that the Neck of that *Particular Plot* is broken, to all Intents and purpofes : But we are beholden alfo to Dr. *Oates* for the Difcovery of *Other* and of *Farther Plots* that are ftill carry'd on by the fame reftleffe Party ; tending to the *defaming* of his *Majefties Perfon*, and *Government* ; the *Subverfion* of our *Eftablifh'd Religion*, and the *Difturbance* of the *Publick Peace*. So that unlefs the remaining, and the ftill growing *Difficulties*, and *Hazzards* be encounter'd with *Timely* and *Effectual Remedies*, the work of our Deliverance is but half done, and we fhall yet run a rifque of being ruin'd at laft even in the very Port.

Dr. *Oates* tells us in his *Narrative, Printed by Authority of Parliament*, that the Pope, *Society* of Jefus, *and their* Confederates *in this* Plot, have a Defign to reduce *England*, *Scotland*, and *Ireland*, to the *Romifh Religion* and *Obedience*, by the *Sword* : *Pag.* 63. which they hope to accomplifh, among Other means, *by difaffecting the Kings beft Friends at home and abroad, and Subjects, againft his Perfon and Government ; charging him with Tyranny, and Defigns of Oppreffing, Governing by the Sword, and without Parliaments*, Pa. 67.

By Afperfing, Deriding, Expofing, and declaiming againft his Perfon, Councils, and Actions in Parliaments, and elfewhere , by Mifreporting, and raifing Falfe News of his Affairs; by difaffecting his Majefties Allyes, Holland, Spain, *the* German Emperor, *and* Princes *by Falfe Intelligence. By* Seditious Preachers, *and* Catechifts, *fet up, fent out,*

Maintained,

Maintained, and directed what to Preach in their Own, or other Private, or Publick Conventicles, and Field Meetings. [4] *By setting up false pretended Titles to the Succession of the Crown; and Animating Different Parties, one against another, on this or such like False pretences, to Arm and put the People in blood, upon the Kings Death.*

We have found Dr. *Oates's Observations* (as to these particulars,) so punctually true, that every syllable of what he has here deliver'd, is from point to point, the very matter now in Agitation. For there's not a day passes without a Libell upon his Majesties *Authority, Administration, Designes,* and solemn *Resolutions* of *State,* and *Council;* belying the Condition of his Affairs, and endeavouring to create *Distrusts,* and *Jeloufies* among Forreign Princes, and States, by *False Intelligence;* animating, and *Exciting* of *Turbulent Factions,* and *anticipating* of *Confederacies,* to involve us all in Blood; upon a *Remote* and *Undutifull* S U P P O S I T I O N of the KINGS DEATH. And finally, we have sedition *Preach'd* as well as *written,* and our *Conventicles* both instructed themselves, and instructing Others, in the Methods and Principles of Rebellion, this may suffice for the Doctors Judgment upon the present State of things, which in truth looks liker a *Revelation,* then a *Conjecture.*

As to his Reflexions upon the Interest which the *Papists* had in our Past troubles; these are his words in his Preface to the aforesaid *Narrative.*

Who beside these were the First Authours and Contrivers of the late Unnatural War, by their Known Diabolical Art of enflaming Parties, and Passions against each other? And (addressing to the King) of your Royal Fathers Unspeakable sufferings, and Barbarous Usage? It was these that brought him to his End, and flourish'd swords, and Trumpets over his dead Body, whom they durst not approach when Living. The Putney Projectours (says he) *were in most, if not all* [5]
the

---

4. *Conventicles:* meetings of nonconformist Protestants for worship.

5. *Putney Projectors:* radical members of the army who at Putney in late 1647 proposed sweeping democratic changes in the government to Cromwell.

the Councils, *that* contriv'd *his* Ruine. *What broke the* Uxbridge Treaty, *but the* Romiſh Intereſt, *and* Policy? 6
Who continu'd to baffle all deſigns of Peace, *and* Settlement
to this Nation, *and* Proſperity *to his Majeſties Family, but*
thoſe Incendiaries, Milton *was a known frequenter of a* 7
Popiſh Club; *who more forward to ſet up* Cromwell, *and
to put the Crown of our Kings upon his Head, then* Papiſts?
And his new fangled Government was contriv'd by a Popiſh
Prieſt; *and* Lambert *a* Papiſt, *for above theſe* Thirty 8
years.

I have inſerted theſe Paſſages as a Curioſity in the Hiſtory of thoſe times; which may perhaps have eſcap'd
other men as well as my ſelf. For though I never made
any Queſtion, but that the Church of *England,* as it ſtands
Eſtabliſhed by Law, in the *Purity* of *Doctrine,* and the
Venerable *Sobriety* of *Diſcipline,* was ever an *Eye ſore* to
the Church of *Rome*; yet I was of Opinion too, that a
Licentious Vein of *Ambition* and *Schiſm* among our ſelves,
had carry'd a great ſtroke alſo in that *Fatal Revolution.*
But however, this is a point wherein a man may without
loſs of Honour, or Credit, admit the poſſibility of his
being in a Miſtake. Wherefore we ſhall now (with the
Doctors Leave) advance to plain matter of *Fact,* whereupon we have his *Depoſition* ; the only Caſe wherein
a man may, without Vanity pronounce himſelf within
a degree of *Infallible.*

We finde Pag. 8. that Richard Nicholas Blundell *had* 9
every day in the Week his ſeveral places in the City of London, *where he taught the Youth Treaſonable, and Malicious
Doctrine, againſt the Intereſt, and Perſon of his Sacred Majeſty.*

Alſo (Pag. 25.) that Richard Aſhby *had a Conference* 10
for the ſending of New Meſſengers into Scotland, *to promote the Commotions there ; and to inform the People, of
the great* Tyranny *they did ly under, by reaſon of their being
deny'd the* Liberty *of their* Conſcience; *and that not being*
to

---

6. *Uxbridge Treaty:* an unsuccessful attempt to reach a peaceful agreement between Parliament and King Charles I in January 1645.

7. *Milton:* quoted from Oates's dedication to his *True Narrative.*

8. *Lambert:* John Lambert (1619–1683), the Cromwellean general condemned
for treason at the Restoration, was at this time living in exile in Guernsey.

9. *Blundell:* see also Oates's *True Narrative,* p. 43.

10. *Ashby:* see also Oates's *True Narrative,* p. 29.

to be procured but by the sword, they must take that Course to purchase their Liberty: By which means (sayd the Fathers thus Assembled) we shall weaken both the Presbyterian, *and the* Episcopal Faction. *At which Conference, the* D E P O- N E N T *was* P R E S E N T, *and heard the Words.*

And again, *Two Messengers were sent into* Scotland, *One by the Name of* Father Moore, *and the Other by the Name of* Father Saunders *alias* Brown, *with Instructions to carry themselves like NON-CONFORMIST MINI- STERS; and to* Preach *to the* Disaffected *Scots, the Necessity of taking up the Sword for the Defence of* Liberty *of* Conscience. These *the* D E P O N E N T *saw* Dispatch'd, *&c.*

Take notice, in the *First* place, that here's a *Designe* carry'd on for the *Destruction* of the *King*, and the *Embroyling* of the *Government. Secondly*, the pretence of the Quarrel is to be matter of *Liberty* and *Conscience. Thirdly*, it is to be promoted by *Popish Emissaries*, in the *Councils*, and *Conventicles* of the *Non-Conformists. Fourthly*, the means by which the *Papists* propound to compass their Ends, are by making *Interests* with the *Separatists*, under the Disguise of *Ministers*, and *Teachers*, respectively of the several Parties they have to do withall. And *Fifthly*, Let me recommend this Particular to your *special Remark*, that Dr. *Oates*, throughout the whole Course of his *Depositions*, charges no part of the *Popish Design* upon any *Intelligence*, or *Communication* with the Church of *England*; but makes it only to be a practice upon the *Dissenters* from the *English Communion*, to transport them into *Tumults*, and *Distempers* against both *Church* and *State*.

We have here in few words, a *Scheme* of the whole business ; Here's the *Designe*, the *Pretext*, the *Instruments* and the *Methods*: and upon the whole matter, here is the Church of *England* acquitted, as to any point of *unwarrantable affinity* with the Principles or Practises of the

the Church *of Rome* ; however that *Tefty Frenchman* is
pleas'd to fpeculate in *his Fanatical Reve'ryes* upon our
approaches to That *Communion* : Wherein it may be a
Queſtion, whether he is more out in his *Hiſtory*, or in his
Morals. We are, in ſhoi t, very much obliged to the
Doĉtor, for clearing our Church to all Gainſayers,from
thoſe obloquies which by both the Extremes are indiffe-
rently caſt upon us.

It muſt not be any longer a ſuppoſition, that which
Dr.*Oates* has given us his *Oath* for ; ſo that taking it for
granted, that there is ſuch a Projeĉt on foot, that the
Papiſts are in the *bottom* of it ; and that it is promoted
by the Seĉtaries, only as *Paſſive Agents* that are blindly
bringing about the others ends : the Queſtion is now how
the Government may fairly diſcriminate the *Proteſtants*
from the *Papiſts* ; being ſo blended in their *Intereſt*, as
well as in their Councils ; and mask'd under ſuch *Re-
ſemblances*, the *One*, of the *Other*, that they are not eaſily
to be diſtinguiſhed. It cannot be expeĉted that a pretending *Proteſtant* ſhall own himſelf to be a *Papiſt* ; ſo
that there's no believing any man in the Caſe. And
then the *Epithete* of a *Reputed ſo or ſo*, is ſo ſlender an Evidence, that many a Reputed *Papiſt* is found to be a *True
Proteſtant*, and many a *Reputed Proteſtant* as true a *Papiſt*.
The known and Legall Expedient which has been hitherto found Competent enough to anſwer the Reaſon
and Intent of State, is the *Teſt* of the *Two Oaths* of *Allegiance* and *Supremacy* : and yet this very proviſion will
not reach all caſes : For there are many *Papiſts* that will
Take them without any difficulty ; and there are ſeverall
that call themſelves *Proteſtants*, that will as obſtinately
refuſe them. Now though the *Latter (Primo Eliz.)* was
a *Proviſion for the aboliſhing of Foreign Power*, and the *Former (Tertio Jac.)* an Aĉt for the diſcovering and repreſ-
ſing of *Popiſh Recuſants* ; the Scope and Equity yet of Both
theſe Proviſions. has a regard to the ſecuring of the Government

11

12

13

---

11. *Sectaries:* members of any of the sects of Protestant dissenters.
12. *Primo Eliz.:* the Oath of Supremacy (1559) denied that any foreign potentate could have ecclesiastical power in England.
13. *Tertio Jac.:* the Oath of Allegiance (1606) renounced the doctrine that the Pope could depose kings.

ternment againſt any ſort of people, and againſt any Pretenſions whatſoever: ſo that whoever Refuſes, up-on a *Lawfull Tender*, to take theſe *Oathes*, he's a *Papiſt* in 14
the eye of the *Law*, let his Perſwaſion be what it will? For it is the only Priviledge of Omniſcience to reade the Heart: or if (for diſcourſe ſake) we ſhould ſuppoſe him to be no *dapiſt*, he is yet in the proſpect of *Common Reaſon*, liable to that Impoſition, becauſe it is exacted as a Proof of his *Allegiance*, not of his Faith ; and men of *Different Judgements* in *Religion* may yet *agree* in *Common Principles* of *Diſloyalty*.

And then again, there's no appealing in this *Caſe* from the *Prudence* and *Caution* of the *Law* (which is all-ways preſum'd to intend the *Common Good*) to the Teſti-mony of a *Friend* or *Neighbour* in favour of a *Recuſation*. 15
For the *Law* is a *General Rule*, that takes no notice of any *Exceptions* to it. The *Law* requires me to *Take Theſe Oaths* in proof of my *Allegiance* to the Government ; and my anſwer is, *that I am a very Honeſt man, but I cannot take them*. What is this to the *Law*, that takes no Cognizance of my *Honeſty*, but of my *Obedience* ? And this *Rule* holds in Common, as well to the *Papiſt* as to the *Prote-ſtant Recuſant* ; They both vouch for their own *Loyalty*, and at the ſame time they do both of them Refuſe to comply with the *Law*. The Common way of Reply in this Caſe, is to caſt it in a mans Teeth ; *But what ? will you make no difference betwixt a* Papiſt *that refuſes and a* Proteſtant? Yes, I would, if you would but ſhew me how I may certainly know the One from the Other. Who knows not that *Intereſt governs the World* ? and that for Reaſons beſt known to themſelves, he that is a *Proteſtant* in his heart may be induced rather to appear a *Papiſt* ; and the Other, though a *Papiſt* in *his heart*, may find it his Intereſt yet to ſeem a Proteſtant? But we'l yield that Point too; and put the Caſe, that the *Law* ſhould be relax'd, on the behalf of any man living, Does not
This

---

14. *Oathes:* oaths.
15. *Recusation:* an appeal in law based on the judge's prejudice.

195

This open a Gap (let him be never fo Honeſt) to the
admittance of ten Thouſand men that may plead *Honeſty*
too, and yet betray their Duties? And is it not better
then, that ſome few particulars ſhould ſuffer by keeping *firm* to the *Law*, then that the whole ſhould be endanger'd by Remitting it? ſo that there is neither *Reaſon*
nor *Safety*, nor *Equity*, in ſuch a *Relaxation*, nor any regard of *Common Juſtice* and *Duty* in demanding it.

But what if it be ſaid, that it is not the *Thing Sworn*,
but the *Oath it ſelf,* that is *Scrupled?* and that there are
ſeveral ſorts of Perſwaſions that will not bear any ſwear-
ing at all? This I muſt confeſs, is a Caſe ſomewhat   16
nice, and unhappy, to thoſe people that are ſo ſtraight-
lac'd in that *Particular*: But then, on the Other ſide, it
is to the *Government* the moſt *dangerous* of all *Pretenſions*,
and lets in all the *Prieſts* and *Jeſuits* in Nature, under
That Colour. So that now take it both ways; If the
Law be *partially* Executed, the *Jeſuits* and *Prieſts* will
ſhelter themſelves under *That Indulgence:* Or, if the *Law*
ſhould be ſuſpended, out of a reſpect to thoſe that would
be thought to make a *Conſcience* of an *Oath*, the *Prieſts*
would all flow into *Thoſe Parties* that ſhould be *exempted*
from *this Teſt*, and carry on their *Deſignes* without either
Triall or *danger.*

Now to wind up this Diſcourſe, in a plain and clear
Dilemma. It muſt be granted, either that the *Papiſts have*
a Deſign upon the *King, Religion,* and *Government*, and
that they advance it by acting the Parts of *Quakers, Ana-*
baptiſts, Presbyterians, and *Other Sectaries;* or *not.* No man,
I preſume will dare to Queſtion the Truth of the Doctors Depoſition; for in ſo doing he would imply a   17
ſtrange abuſe impos'd upon the Nation. But on the o-
ther ſide, admitting it to be true; there can be no ſecurity to this Government, without either *diſſolving* all
ſeparate Meetings, or bringing all *Diſſenters* to this *Legal*   18
Teſt; for otherwiſe, the *Papiſts* have all ſorts of *Liberty*,
                                    E   and

---

16. *any swearing:* as with the Quakers.
17. *Doctors:* i.e., Oates's—L'Estrange maliciously insists on his spurious degree.
18. *separate Meetings:* the dissenters' conventicles.
19. Page (31) misnumbered (25).

and *Security* in herding themselves among the *Conventicles*; where upon the beating of a Bush, it will be an even wager whether you start a *Jesuit*, or a *Fanatick*. And in effect, in this case, there is not much difference betwixt them, where the *Jesuit* plays the *Fanatick*, and the *Fanatick* the *Jesuit*.

If the main assertion be true, there's no way of finding out the *Papists*, but by *this Test* : and the *Dissenters* themselves, if they would have *Popery* ferretted out in good Earnest, cannot chuse but encourage the Proposition. Either they *have* Priests among them or they have *not* : If they *have*, why do they not do the best they can to find them out ? if they have *not*, why do they say they *have* ? And again, either the *Non-Conformists* are influenc'd by the *Jesuits* or they are *not* : If they *be*, why do they not do all that is possible toward the *Purging* of their *Congregations* ? If they be *not* so Influenc'd, why do they pretend that they *are*, and so *set the Saddle upon the wrong Horse* ? And yet again ; either it is *possible* to clear their *Conventicles* of this dangerous Mixture, or it is *not* : If it be *Possible*, why do they still *complain* of it, and *do nothing in't* ? If it be *Impossible*, there is no way of *Extirpating* Popery, but by rooting out *Fanaticism*.

Let the World judge now, with what injustice, the *Order*, and the *Rituals* of the Church of *England* are charg'd with a Tincture of *Superstition*, and Popery, when upon Manifest proof, the *Calumniators themselves* of our *Ecclesiastical State* are, throughout the *whole Body* of them, tainted with this *Leaven*. We are now come to the *Bottom* of the *Popish* Plot. *This Liberty of wandering from the Rule, is the* Trojan Horse, *which under* a Religious colour, *we have entertain'd within our* Walls ; *with* Discord, *and* Destruction *in the Belly of him.*

A 3

L'Estrange's *The Observator* (July 20, 1681)

The Observator lasted—often in three or four numbers per week and eventually in three different series—until 1687. The format was a satiric dialogue, with speakers named Whig and Tory—later rechristened *Observator and Trimmer*. In the issue reprinted here, one finds the speakers arguing over the Whig petitions for a new Parliament and the trials of Stephen Colledge and Edward Fitzharris. The "Whig" is notably candid, from the Tory point of view, in admitting his designs to destroy the king's power. Here one can see that L'Estrange was capable of writing, as Lord Macaulay commented, with "keenness and vigour," but equally apparent is his tendency to become mired in the infinite details of the controversies, a circumstance that led Macaulay to describe his diction as "disfigured by a mean and flippant jargon" (*The History of England* [London: Longmans, Green, and Co., 1896], I, 393).

Wednesday, July 20 1681.

WHIG. THe very *Name* of an Address is *Scandalous.*

To. Troth in my Opinion an *Address* sounds every jot as well as a *Petition.* But you are Gall'd at the *Matter* and the *Intent* of these Addresses ; and then ye Pick a Quarrell with the Poor *Syllables.*

Wh. Janeway's Historicall Account of the Rise and Progress of Addressing will shew you that *Oliver* was the first Contriver of 'em ; and so the Practise was Continued under *Richard* ; the *Councill of State* ; the *Army* ; and that upon the *Deposing* of *Richard*, all the Addressers *forsook* him.

To. And if Mr. *Janeway* had been pleas'd to give ye *the History of Petitioning* too ;(that is to say of giving *Libells* the name of *Petitions*) he might have trac'd it through every step of the late Rebellion ; for that was the Device that gave Life and Motion to our troubles. Does not his Majesty himself (*Exact Collections, P.*536.) tell us of the *Alarms the Faction gave the City to put them into Arms,* and their calling the *Kings Actions,* the *Designs of the Papists* ? Their sending their Emissaryes up and down the Nation with *Petitions, ready drawn* to Infuse *Fears* and *Jealousies* into the minds of the People. And was it not by the force of *Petitions,* that the *War* was rais'd, the *Government Dissolved,* and the *King brought to the Scaffold?*

And beside. D'ye make no difference betwixt the applications of *Loyall Subjects,* & of *Rebells* ? Betwixt Addresses for the *Preserving* of the Kings Person and *Authority*; the *Law* ; *Religion* ; *Propertyes,* and *Libertyes* of the Nation ; and Addresses for *Destroying* them all ? They us'd the word *Deposing* too as well as *Addressing.* And why may not *We* continue the *One,* as well as *You* continue the *Other* ? And again ; we only write and speak according to *Oliver's Grammer* and *Alphabet* ; & you govern your selves by his *Doctrine,* and *Principles* ; for your way of *Colledging* a Prince is the very same thing with their *Deposing* of him. But come, Let us have it without any more ado. What is it really that you would be at in these *Petitions?*

Wh. I'le tell ye then ; and you shall be as Free with me in the Design of your *Addresses.*

There's nothing to be done without a House of Commons for our Purpose ; and there's no Compassing of that, without first gaining the People ; For *Factious Electors* will be sure to Chuse a *Factious Representative.* And upon this Consideration it is, that all our Petitions to the *King* ,on the behalf of the *People,* are in the nature of *Complaints* to the *Subjects* against his *Majesties Proceedings:* For we do only *ask* that of the King which we are sure he neither *Can* nor *Will* ever *Grant* ; and, at the same time, Endeavour to Possess the *Multitude,* that they are Utterly Ruin'd without it. And this is a Fair Step (you'l say) toward the *Lessening* of his *Majesties Credit,* and the *Advancing* of our *Own.* And take notice, that we still Couple, the Calling of a *Parliament* with the *Disinheriting* of the *Duke* ; so that we leave the King no way to Gratify his *People,* but by offering Violence to his *Conscience.*

To. Well! But you may Petition till your Hearts ake, if the King may Chuse whether he will yield, or not ; And over and above, if he be utterly Resolv'd against it.

Wh. Do not mistake your self ; for we'le Weather that Point too. When the People are once Perswaded *that* a thing is *Profitable,* and *Convenient*; there will be little Difficulty to Possess them likewise that it is *Necessary,* and *Lawfull* : Wherefore the next step after the Disposing of their *Desires,* and *Affections,* must be to work upon their *Judgments,* and *Opinions* ; and so Train them on, by degrees, from *Petitions* to *Expostulations* ; and so to the *Demanding* of those things as of *Right,* which were lookt upon before as only Matters of *Grace,* and *Favour.* To this End, we have set up the old *Statutes* of the 4. and 36. of *Ed.* 3. for the *Holding* of *Annuall Parliaments,* and likewise referr'd the People to 2. *Ri.* 2. Nu. 28. for the *Continuing* of them, without *Prorogation,* or *Dissolution,* till all the *Petitions,* and *Bills* before them were *Answer'd* and *Redressed* (*Vindication of the Two last Parliaments,* p.1.)

To. Very Good. And what will this avayl ye?

Wh. This serves us both ways. First, If the King does *not* Call a Parliament, the People will Challenge it as their *Due,* and *Quarrel* upon't if it be not done. 2ly, In Case of his Majesties *Summoning* a Parliament, They'l assume a Right, on the other hand, of *Continuing* it.

To. With what Face can you Impose this upon the People for *Law* ? First, as to the *Annuall Parliaments,* Those two Statutes of *Ed.* 3. are Determin'd by 16. *Car.* 2. *Cap.* 1. for the *Holding of a Parliament once in Three years at least* ; with a regard to those Statutes. And 2ly, there's no such thing in that of *Ri.* 2. as *Petitions Answer'd* and *REDRESS'D.* The very words upon the Roll are these [*Il plest au Roy que des tielles Petitions baille en Parlement des choses que ailloirs ne purront estre terminez, bone et resonable responce soit fait et donez devant departir de Parlement.*] *It is the Kings Pleasure that a Good and Reasonable Answer be made and Given before the Dissolution of the Parliament, upon such Petitions Deliver'd in Parliament as cannot be determin'd elsewhere.* Now nothing can be clearer then that the Intent of this Statute reaches only to such Bills and Petitions as shall be Ready for the Kings Sanction, at what time soever he shall think fit to Dissolve the said Parliament : For otherwise ; what signifies the *Royall Authority* of *Dissolving Parliaments,* if it shall ly in the Power of any *One Member of the House of Commons* to *Perpetuate* them ? For Bills and Petitions may be kept afoot to Eternity. And

1. *Address:* a Tory document supporting the King.

2. *Petition:* these were Whig instruments calling for new sessions of Parliament and, by implication, exclusion.

3. *Janeway:* Richard Janeway was a Whig journalist and publisher known as "Dick implement." His publications included *The Impartial Protestant Intelligence* and *The True Protestant Mercury.*

4. *Addressing:* published in 1681.

5. *Oliver:* Cromwell, who ruled as Lord Protector from 1653 to 1658.

6. *Richard:* Cromwell's son who attempted to succeed him, 1658–1659.

7. *Exact Collections: An Exact Collection of all Remonstrances, Declarations, Votes, Orders . . .* (1643). The reference is to "His Majesties Declaration" of August 12, 1642, issued by King Charles I.

8. *Colledging:* a reference to Stephen Colledge, at this time awaiting trial for fomenting rebellion at Oxford; his trial took place the following month (August 17) and he was executed on September 2, 1681.

9. *Possess:* persuade or convince.

10. *last Parliaments: A Just and Modest Vindication of the Proceedings of the Two Last Parliaments* (1681): this cites the statutes mentioned above.

11. *16 Car. 2 Cap. 1:* the Second Triennial Act (1664).

then for any Obligation upon the King to RE-
DRESS matters, as the *Vindicator* would have it.
First, the King can do more, at that rate, then a
Clark of the House to *Attest* and *Record their Procee-
dings*. And 2ly, it was so far from the True meaning of that *Statute*; [*Num.* 34. 52. and 55. of the
same Parliament] that his Majesty gave these *Three
Answers to Three Petitions*. First, Concerning *Sheriffs*.
[*His Majesty will advise with his Councell*.] 2ly, Concerning *Par--- --- ---ing will Consider on't*] And
3ly, upon a Petition about the Restraint of Excess in
apparrel: [*The King can Consider of it till the next Parliament*.] So that these two suggestions of yours are
meerly *Abuse*, and *Imposture*.

Wh. Now be you as Clear with me, and tell me
the True Scope and Business of your *Addresses*.

To. There are a sort of Murmuring, seditious and
Unthankfull People (I speak of *LIBELLERS* not
PETITIONERS) that make it their Business to be
perpetually finding fault with his Majesty, the Kings
Ministers, the Law and the Government; and these
men, what with artificiall Scandalls, Holy Pretences
and False Musters of the Number and Strength of
the Party, make a shift to *Fool* the *Weaker* sort of his
Majestys subjects out of their *Allegeance*, and endeavour *to Affright Others*. Now the Drift of our *Address is to* Obviate all these Designs; by opposing
Numbers to Numbers; the *Resolution* of *Defending* the
King, the *Law*, and the *Government*, to the *Contrivance*. that are set afoot for their *Overthrow* and
Ruine ; to give a Loyall Evidence of our *Thankfulness* to his Majesty for all his Royall Graces and Favours to his People ; and finally to Govern our
selves, in all our actions with a *submissive* and *peaceable
Resignation*, and *Obedience*. These *Addresses* carry no
Scimiters, Blunderbusses, Pistolls & *Coats of Mail* in the
Bellyes of 'em ; unless where Authority Commands
them for the Service of the *Established Religion*, their
Prince and *Country*. Here are none of your *Jesuiticall
True-Protestant Reserves*, and *Equivocations*.

Wh. I know your Meaning, but you'l hear another Story perhaps, though they found the Bill at
Oxford, when *College* comes to his Tryall. What
will you say if some of those that brought it in *Ignoramus*, here at *London*, shall come in as Witnesses against the *Kings Evidence* ? I heard somebody speak
Bug-words about that Business to'ther day. Nay the
Curtises the *Janeways* and the *Baldwins* tell ye downright, that the *Witnesses* were *Snborn'd* ; *Contradicted*
themselves ; *Confess'd* that they were *Set on* ; and
Effectually *Disclaim'd* their *Evidence* : and that the
Paper Expos'd by Dr. *Hawkins* as the *Confession* of
Mr. *Fitz-Harris*, was an *Absolute* Forgery.

To. Dr. *Oates* I can assure ye wou'd never have put
up these Indiguities upon the *Kings Evidence*.

Wh. Now we talk of a Dr. what's become of the
Dr. there of——*Nova Scotia* I think ?

To. He may be of *Utopia* for ought I know. What's
his *Profession* ? *Law* ? *Physick* ? *Divinity* ? or what is't ?

Wh. He should be a *Civilian* methinks, by the
Arguments I have heard him use for *Cutting off the
Succession*, and *Divorcing the Queen* ; and yet by his
Allegory upon the *Body Politique*, and the *Body Natural*, I fancy sometimes he shou'd be a *Physitian*.

To. Oh ! Now I Guess where ye are, He has a
Wonderfull Faculty (they say) at opening a *Vein*,
and giving a *Glister*, and I am told he has got an
Estate by't. If it be the Person I mean, 'tis a *Tall botterish look'd man* ; His Eyes are Commonly Bludshotten.

Wh. The very same. I took him for a *Divine* at
first ; till I heard him treat *Two Persons* of the *Trinity*, at a Rate as if he had taken 'em for *Jesuites*.

To. You have many of that Odd kind of People
among the *United Dissenters*. But what makes you
so Curious to know what's become of him ?

Wh. I am about to Purchase an Estate for *Three
Lives* ; and I wou'd Gladly take his Advice along
with me.

To. Why pre'thee he's no *Conveyancer*.

Wh. No ; But he's a Wonderfull *Phisiognomist*
and shall give a better Judgment by a mans face
whether he be *Long*, or *Short-liv'd*, than all the
Doctors of the *College* shall do by his *Pulse, or Water*.
He has certainly a strange *Fore-sight*.

To. I have heard as much ; and that he'l tell ye,
not only the *Time*, and the *Disease*; but the very
manner, the *Place Where* and *How* a man is to Dye.

Wh. What wou'd I give now for a Cast of his
Skill upon *Stephen College* ; if a body cou'd but tell
where to meet with him ?

Wh. 'Tis but getting an *Advertisment* into the
Observator, or *Heraclitus*, for notice to be left at
Dicks Coffee House, or the *Queens Head*, and the
Business is done.

Wh. You are a stranger I perceive to the Order
of the Committee in *Pater-Noster-Row* yonder of
Thursday night last.

To. I heard something of a Consultation there,
for the Propagating of *True Protestant Principles*, and
the suppressing of your *Tory* and *Tantivy Pamphlets* ;
but I cou'd make neither Head nor Tayl on't. *H.V.*
and *T. C.* were there (they say) and severall Ladies
of Condition, over a Treat of *Cold Chickens, Westphaly-Hams*, and *Sturgeon* : and *Drink*, more then they
cou'd carry away with 'em.

Wh. You are somewhat near the matter. It was
there Resolv'd upon the Question, that the *Society
of News-mongers* should be obl'g'd from time to time
to Furnish the *True Protestant Mercuries* and *Hawkers* with *Good Marketable Papers*, and *Intelligence*,
upon Condition that the said *Mercuries* and *Hawkers* should stand Engag'd, not to *Publish*, or *Expose*
any *Observators, Heraclitus's*, or any other books or
Papers of *that Stamp*, any further then to serve a *Customer* in the way of *Trade*. SIGNED *Andrews,
Clarke, Miller, Boate, Budds Agent, Jackson* ; *MERCURIES* ; *cum Multis aliis. R. Janeway Chair-man.
H.V.* and *T. C. Deputies* from the *Society*.

To. And this was really the Bus'ness ?

Wh. Yes Yes ; It was so ; and we have been as
Carefull too about the Ordering of our *Common
News-Letters*, Every man has his *Post* assign'd him,
and his Instructions how to manage his *Intelligence*.
These Papers are presently all over the Kingdom,
as fast as the Post can carry 'um : And agreeing all in
a Tale, They have the old Proverb to Vouch for
their Credit, *That which* One man *says*, may *be True* ;
but that *which* Every body *says*, must needs *be True*.

London, Printed for *Joanna Brome* at the Gun in S. *Pauls* Church-yard.

12. *REDRESS:* the following words are "matters as."

13. *of that:* the following word is "statute."

14. *Concerning:* the following word is "Parliament."

15. *Kings' Evidence:* at Colledge's trial, Oates was to appear for the defense, contradicting and impugning the testimony of Dugdale and others who were the King's evidence, for the prosecution.

16. *Bug-words:* threatening language, meant to terrify.

17. *Baldwins:* Richard Baldwin (1633?–1698) was, like Janeway, a Whig journalist and printer.

18. *Forgery:* Hawkins, the chaplain of the Tower, had published Edward Fitzharris's *Confession* after his execution for treason on July 1, 1681. In it, Fitzharris claimed that the Whig sheriffs, Bethel and Cornish, had suborned him to testify about the plot.

19. *Civilian:* an authority on civil law.

20. *Cutting off the:* the following word is "Succession."

21. *Glister:* a medicine injected into the rectum.

22. *Whitterish:* pale.

23. *Conveyancer:* a lawyer who prepares documents for the conveyance of property.

24. *Phisiognomist:* one who reads the character or foretells the future from the face.

25. *water:* urine.

26. *Heraclitus: Heraclitus Ridens,* another Tory paper issued by John Flatman between February 1, 1681 and August 22, 1682.

27. *Dick's Coffee House:* on Fleet Street (originally called Richard's); it was owned by Richard Torvor or Turver, who opened it in 1680. Coffee houses were centers of political discussion and intrigue.

28. *Queen's Head:* a tavern on Pater-Noster Row, just north of St. Paul's. The area was associated with stationers, journalists, and booksellers, including Richard Janeway.

29. *Tantivy:* a supporter of the duke of York; see p. 92n.

30. *H.V. and T.C.:* Janeway's *The True Protestant Mercury,* the Whig paper, was described as "Printed for H.V. and T.C." in the first twelve numbers.

31. *cum Multis aliis:* with many others.

Engraved by R. Cooper.

KING CHARLES THE SECOND.

OB. 1685.

FROM THE ORIGINAL OF SIR PETER LELY, IN THE COLLECTION OF

THE MOST NOBLE THE MARQUIS OF HERTFORD.

Portrait of King Charles II. From Edmund Lodge, *Portraits of Illustrious Personages of Great Britain* (1823–34), vol. 9.

His Majesties Declaration
(April 8, 1681)

King Charles II, whose shrewdness and firmness against exclusion had been so disastrously underestimated by his opponents, began his own assault on public opinion immediately after he dissolved the Oxford Parliament in March 1681. On April 8, he issued his royal "Declaration," in which he condemned the conduct of the exclusionists in Parliament and defended his own actions. It was ordered to be read from every pulpit in the land. Of course there were Whig replies and Tory rejoinders, one of which, *His Majesties Declaration Defended* (1681), is ascribed to Dryden, but the main result seemed to be an outpouring of loyal support for the king. The court was deluged with addresses of thanks—the Tory counterpart to the earlier Whig petitions.

According to Godfrey Davies ("The Conclusion of Dryden's *Absalom and Achitophel*," *Huntington Library Quarterly* 10 [1946], 69–82), Dryden based King David's final speech upon this work, some of whose arguments he appropriated.

His Majesties
DECLARATION
To all His Loving Subjects,

Touching

The CAUSES & REASONS
That moved Him to Dissolve

The Two last

PARLIAMENTS.

I T was with exceeding great trouble, that We were brought to the Dissolving of the Two last Parliaments, without more benefit to Our People by the Calling of them : But having done Our part, in giving so many opportunities of providing for their Good, it cannot be justly imputed to Us, that the Success hath not answered Our Expectation.

We cannot at this time but take notice of the particular Causes of Our Dissatisfaction, which at the beginning of the last Parliament, We did recommend to their care to avoid, and expected We should have had no new Cause to remember them.

A 2   W9

206

We Open'd the laſt Parliament which was held
at Weſtminſter, with as Gracious Expreſſions of Our   1
readineſs to ſatisfie the Deſires of Our Good Subjects, and to ſecure them againſt all their juſt Fears,
as the weighty Conſideration, either of preſerving
the Eſtabliſh'd Religion, and the Liberty and Property of Our Subjects at home, or of Supporting
Our Neighbours and Allyes abroad, could fill Our
heart with, or poſſibly require from Us.

And We do ſolemnly Declare, That We did
Intend, as far as would have conſiſted with the very Being of the Government, to have Comply'd
with any thing, that could have been propos'd to
Us to accompliſh thoſe Ends.

We ask'd of them the Supporting the Alliances
We had made for the preſervation of the General
Peace in Chriſtendom; We recommended to them
the further Examination of the Plot; We deſir'd
their advice and aſſiſtance concerning the preſervation of *Tanger*; We offer'd to concur in any Re-   2
medies that could be propoſed for the Security of
the Proteſtant Religion, that might conſiſt with preſerving the Succeſſion of the Crown, in its due and
legal Courſe of Deſcent; to all which We met with
moſt unſuitable Returns from the Houſe of Commons: Addreſſes, in the nature of Remonſtrances,
rather than of Anſwers; Arbitrary Orders for ta-   3
king Our Subjects into Cuſtody, for Matters that
had no relation to Priviledges of Parliament;
Strange illegal Votes, declaring divers eminent
Perſons to be enemies to the King and Kingdom,
without any Order or Proceſs of Law, any hearing
of their Defence, or any Proof ſo much as offer'd
againſt them.   Beſides

---

1. *Westminster:* on October 21, 1680.

2. *Tanger:* Tangier, which had come into the possession of England as a result of Charles's marriage with Catherine of Braganza in 1662, was currently under attack by the Moors. The king had requested funds for its defense, but by 1683 the English garrison had to be abandoned.

3. *Arbitrary Orders:* after the defeat of the Second Exclusion Bill in the House of Lords in November 1680, the Commons passed a resolution demanding the removal of Halifax, the leader of its opponents, and ordered the impeachment of several ministers and judges.

Befides thefe Proceedings, they voted as followeth on the 7th of *January* laft ;

Refolved, *That whofoever fhall Lend or caufe to be
Lent by way of Advance, any Money upon the Branches of
the Kings Revenue, arifing by Cuftoms, Excife, or Hearth-
money, fhall be adjudged to hinder the Sitting of Parliaments,
and fhall be refponfible for the fame in Parliament.*

Refolved, *That whofoever fhall buy any Tally of An-
ticipation upon any part of the King's Revenue, or whofoever fhall pay any fuch Tally hereafter to be ftruck, fhall
be adjudged to hinder the Sitting of Parliaments, and fhall
be refponfible for the fame in Parliament.*

Which Votes, inftead of giving Us Affiftance to
fupport Our Allyes, or enable Us to preferve *Tanger*, tended rather to difable Us from Contributing
towards either, by Our Own Revenue or Credit ;
not onely expofing Us to all Dangers that might
happen either at home, or abroad ; but endeavouring to deprive Us of the Poffibility of Supporting the Government it felf, and to reduce Us
to a more helplefs Condition then the meaneft of
Our Subjects.

And on the 10th of the fame Month they pɪft
another Vote, in thefe words,

Refolved, *That it is the Opinion of this Houfe, That
the Profecution of Proteftant Diffenters upon the Penal
Laws, is at this time grievous to the Subject, a weakening
of the Proteftant Intereft, an Encouragement to Popery,
and dangerous to the Peace of the Kingdom.*

B   B;

By which Vote, without any regard to the Laws eſtabliſh'd, they aſſumed to themſelves a Power of Suſpending Acts of Parliament ; whereas Our Judges and Miniſters of Juſtice neither can, nor ought, in reverence to the Votes of either or both the Houſes, break the Oathes they have taken, for the due and impartial Execution of Our Laws; which by Experience have been found to be the beſt Support, both of the Proteſtant Intereſt, and of the Peace of the Kingdom.

Theſe were ſome of the unwarrantable Proceedings of that Houſe of Commons, which were the occaſion of Our parting with that Parliament.

Which We had no ſooner Diſſolv'd, but We caus'd another to be forthwith Aſſembled at *Oxford* ; at the Opening of which, We thought it neceſſary to give Them warning of the Errors of the former, in hopes to have prevented the like Miſcarriages ; and We requir'd of Them to make the Laws of the Land their Rule, as We did, and do reſolve, they ſhall be Ours : We further added, That what We had formerly and ſo often Declared concerning the Succeſſion, We could not depart from : But to remove all reaſonable Fears that might ariſe from the Poſſibility of a Popiſh Succeſſor's coming to the Crown, if Means could be found, that in ſuch a Caſe, the Adminiſtration of the Government might remain in Proteſtant Hands, We were ready to hearken to any Expedient, by which the Religion Eſtabliſh'd might be Preſerv'd, and the Monarchy not Deſtroy'd.

But contrary to Our Offers and Expectation, We ſaw, that no Expedient would be entertain'd but that of a total Excluſion, which We had

had fo often declar'd, was a Point, that in Our
Own Royal Judgment, fo nearly concern'd Us
both in Honour, Juftice, and Confcience, that We
could never confent to it : In fhort, We cannot,
after the fad Experience We have had of the late
Civil Wars, that Murder'd Our Father of Bleffed
Memory, and ruin'd the Monarchy, confent to a
Law, that fhall eftablifh another moft Unnatural
War, or at leaft make it neceffary to maintain a
Standing Force for the Preferving the Government   4
and the Peace of the Kingdom.

And We have reafon to believe, by what pafs'd
in the laft Parliament at *Weftminfter*, that if We
could have been brought to give Our Confent to a
Bill of Exclufion, the Intent was not to reft there,
but to pafs further, and to attempt fome other
Great and Important Changes even in Prefent.

The Bufinefs of *Fitz-Harris*,who was Impeach'd   5
by the Houfe of Commons of High Treafon, and
by the Houfe of Lords referr'd to the ordinary
Courfe of Law, was on the fudden carried on to
that extremity, by the Votes which the Commons
pafs'd on the 26th of *March* laft, that there was
no poffibility left of a Reconciliation.

The Votes were thefe,

Die Sabbati 26° Martii, poft Meridiem.   6

Refolved, *That it is the undoubted Right of the Commons in Parliament Affembled, to Impeach before the
Lords in Parliament any Peer or Commoner, for Treafon,
or any other Crime or Mifdemeanor; and that the refufal
of the Lords to proceed in Parliament upon fuch Impeachment, is a denial of Juftice, and a violation of the Conftitution of Parliaments.*

Refolved,

---

4. *Standing Force:* a standing army in peacetime was distrusted as a possible agent
of domestic repression.

5. *Fitz-Harris:* Edward Fitzharris had been indicted for publishing a seditious
pamphlet; under pressure to confess, he claimed to have substantial information
about the plot, and it was to exploit him as a witness that the Commons wished to
impeach him.

6. *post Meridiem:* Saturday afternoon, March 26, 1681.

Refolved, That in the cafe of Edward Fitz-Harris, _who by the Commons hath been Impeach'd of High Treafon before the Lords, with a Declaration, That in convenient time they would bring up the Articles againft him for the Lords to Refolve, That the faid_ Fitz-Harris _fhould be proceeded with according to the courfe of Common Law, and not by way of Impeachment at this time, is a Denial of Juftice, and a Violation of the Conftitution of Parliaments, and an Obftruction to the further Difcovery of the Popifh Plot, and of great danger to His Majefties Perfon, and the Proteftant Religion._

Refolved, _That for any Inferiour Court to Proceed againft_ Edward Fitz-Harris, _or any other Perfon lying under an Impeachment in Parliament, for the fame Crimes, for which he or they ftand Impeach'd, is a high Breach of the Priviledge of Parliament._

It was a Matter extremely fenfible to Us, to find an Impeachment made ufe of to delay a Tryal, that We had directed againft a profefs'd Papift, charg'd with Treafons againft Us of an extraordinary Nature : And certainly the Houfe of Peers did themfelves Right in refufing to give countenance to fuch a Proceeding.

But when either of the Houfes are fo far tranfported, as to Vote the Proceedings of the other to be a Denial of Juftice, a Violation of the Conftitution of Parliaments, of Danger to Our Perfon and the Proteftant Religon, without Conferences firft had to examine upon what Grounds fuch Proceedings were made, and how far they might be juftified ; This puts the two Houfes out of capacity of tranfacting bufinefs together, and confequently is

the

the greatest Violation of the Constitution of Parliaments.

This was the Case, and every day's continuance being like to produce new Instances of further Heat and Anger between the two Houses, to the disappointment of all Publick Ends, for which they were Call'd, We found it necessary to put an end to this Parliament likewise.

But notwithstanding all this, let not the restless Malice of ill Men, who are labouring to poyson Our People, some out of fondness of their Old Beloved Commonwealth-Principles, and some out of anger at their being disappointed in the particular Designs they had for the accomplishment of their own Ambition and Greatness, perswade any of Our Good Subjects, that We intend to lay aside the use of Parliaments : For We do still Declare, That no Irregularities in Parliaments, shall ever make Us out of Love with Parliaments, which We look upon as the best Method for healing the Distempers of the Kingdom, and the onely Means to preserve the Monarchy in that due Credit and Respect which it ought to have both at home and abroad.

And for this Cause We are Resolved, by the Blessing of God, to have frequent Parliaments ; and both in and out of Parliament, to use Our utmost Endeavours to extirpate Popery, and to Redress all the Grievances of Our good Subjects, and in all things to Govern according to the Laws of the Kingdom.

And We hope that a little time will so far open the Eyes of all Our good Subjects, that Our next

C   meeting

meeting in Parliament, shall perfect all that Settlement and Peace which shall be found wanting either in Church or State.

To which, as We shall Contribute Our utmost Endeavours, so We assure Our Self, That We shall be Assisted therein by the Loyalty and good Affections of all those who consider the Rise and Progress of the late Troubles and Confusions, and desire to preserve their Countrey from a Relapse.

And who cannot but remember, That Religion, Liberty and Property were all lost and gone, when the Monarchy was shaken off, and could never be reviv'd till that was restored.

Given at Our Court at Whitehall *the Eighth day of* April 1681.

The Trial of Stephen Colledge
(1681)

This trial represents an important element in the "Stuart Revenge"—the court's efforts to pursue the exclusionist leaders as traitors. Colledge, "the Protestant Joiner," was accused in 1681 of inciting rebels to arms in Oxford during the last Parliament. After a London Grand Jury—packed by Sheriffs Bethel and Cornish—threw out these charges on July 8, the government moved the case to Oxford, because, it claimed, the offenses had been committed there. More important, there a sympathetic Tory jury lost no time in convicting Colledge, who was soon executed. After this success, the Tory party hoped to convict Shaftesbury himself of high treason; since July, he had been in the Tower awaiting trial. Fortunately for him, his trial could not be moved to Oxford.

The version of Colledge's trial reprinted here is from a collection of Lord Stafford's *Works* published in 1681 by an anonymous supporter. This author is aware of the irony represented by Colledge's trial, for several of the key witnesses against Stafford, who had been convicted of treason and executed some eight months earlier, were now fighting among themselves and discrediting each other's testimony. The main body of the book is a defense of the Catholics and a collection of Stafford's writings in which he protests his innocence.

A N

APPENDIX,

Containing fome Remarques upon the late Tryal of

Stephen Colledge,

In Relation to the Chief Witneffes againft my

Lord STAFFORD.

Here annexed for the more Ample Satisfaction of the
Reader in that Particular.

HAving in fome meafure performed what I purpofed, and pro-   1
mifed in the front of this *Treatife*; I might well have here
put a ftop to my Pen, had not an extraordinary Accident,
raifed new matter of Reflections upon the *King's Evidence*
in point of *Credit*, and feemed to call me to a fhort Survey of it, in
the clofe of my Difcourfe.

The *Judgments* of the *Almighty* are incomprehenfible; And St. *Paul*
had good reafon to Cry out, as it were in an Extafy, O *The depth of* ^{Ro.ri 11. 33.}
the riches both of the Wifdom and Knowledge of God; *How unfearchable
are his Judgments, and his ways paft finding out*; Who could ever have
imagined, That the three direct and main *Witneffes* againft my Lord *Stafford* at his *Tryal*, fhould all convene together at another, of a quite contrary ftamp; And this in fo fatal a conjuncture, as to confound, and
deftroy by open *Perjury* each others *Teftimony*? My *Lord* (as you have   2
feen) endeavoured to fhew the *Infamy* of the *Witneffes*: The *Contradictions* in their *Evidence*: The *Incoherence* of parts: And *Incredibility*
of *circumftances*, throughout the whole *Charge*. To make out which
he alledged many preffing *Arguments*, and produced many *Subftantial
Witneffes*, both *Catholicks* and *Proteftants*, in his behalf: Nothing feemed wanting, fave only his *Adverfaries themfelves, againft themfelves*,
to compleat his *Evidence*. And here it is the *Divine Goodnefs* (fay the
Papifts) who is the *Defender of Innocence*, and *Fountain of Truth*, hath
wonderfully manifefted what manner of *Men*, my *Lord's Accufers* were,
and what Credit ought to be given them; Even by the proper *Teftimony* of their own *Mouths*; Herein alfo fulfilling in fome fort, what my
Lord himfelf (Prophetically) foretold in his laft *Speech*, (*viz.*) *I have
a great confidence that it will pleafe Almighty God*; *And that he will in a
fhort time bring Truth to Light*. *Then all the World will fee and know,
what Injury they* (Oates, Dugdale, *and* Turbervil,) *have done me*.   3

To

---

1. *Treatife:* mainly a defense of Lord Stafford who had been convicted of high
treason by the House of Lords (November 30–December 7, 1680); he was executed
on December 29.

2. *My Lord:* Stafford, who conducted his own defense with considerable vigor,
though the trial began on his sixty-ninth birthday.

3. *Oates, Dugdale, and Turberville:* the chief witnesses against Lord Stafford. Stephen Dugdale (1640?–1683) provided the most specific information about Stafford's
involvement in the plot and Edward Turberville (1648?–1681) accused Stafford of
trying to enlist him to assassinate the king.

To give a brief account of this affair, There are few who have not heard of the late *Tryal* of *Stephen Colledge*, Sirnamed the *Protestant Joyner* (a man very active in the Death of my *Lord Stafford*, and a zealous defender of *Dugdales Honesty*.) He was *Impeached, Arraigned, Condemned,* and *Executed for High Treason*; In Speaking *Treasonable Words*; And having by a designed *combination* with others, appeared in *Arms* to *Seize the Kings Person* at Oxford. The *Witnesses* against him were, *Smith, Dugdale, Turbervil, Haines*, Mr. *Maisters*, and Sir *William Jennings*.

It is not my intent here, to *Fpitomize Colledges* whole *Tryal*; Nor to give my Censure or Verdict upon it; But only to inform the *Reader* of some Passages which chiefly relate to the main *Witnesses* against my *Lord Stafford*; And which are now become the Subject of Surprize, and Astonishment to all Considering Persons.

Please then to Note, That *Stephen Dugdale*, and *Edward Turbervil*, (two of the Principal *Witnesses* upon whose *Testimony* my *Lord* was *Found Guilty*,) and *John Smith*, otherwise called *Narrative Smith*,(who at my *Lords Tryal* seemed the only plausible *Deponent*, as to the *Plot in General*) gave respective *Evidence* against this *Colledge* at Oxford, as followeth.

Page 18. &c. . 'Stephen *Dugdale* Swore First. Mr. *Colledge* told him; That the 'King was a *Papist*, That he was as deep in the *Plot* as any Papist of 'them all (which the Papists themselves also confess.) That he had an 'hand in Sir *Edmundbury Godfreys death*; That he was a *Rogue* ; That 'nothing was to be expected from him but *Popery*, and *Arbitrary Go-* 'vernment. And that the *Clergy of England* were *Papists in Masquerade*, 'Secondly, That *Colledge* had framed several notorious *Libels* against 'the *King* to render him contemptible. And raised *Arms* with intent 'to *seize His Sacred Person* at Oxford, &c.

Page 19. &c. '*Turbervil* Swore, He heard *Colledge* say; First. That there was 'no good to be expected from the *King*. For that he and his Family 'were *Papists*, and had ever been such. Secondly, That His Party 'would *Seize the King*, and secure Him, till he came to those terms 'they would have of him. Thirdly, That the *Parliament* which cut off 'the late *King's* Head, did nothing but what they had just cause 'for, &c.

Page 27. '*Smith* Swore ; First. That *Colledge* told him, There were Moneys 'collected to buy Arms and Amuniton to bring the *King to Submission* 'to *His People* ; Adding thereunto, That he wondered Old *Rowley* '(meaning the *King*) did not consider how easily His *Fathers Head* 'came to the Block, which he doubted not would be the end of *Rowley* 'at last. Secondly, That *Colledge* had provided himself of a great 'Sword, Pistols, Blunderbuss, with Back, *Breast, and Head-Peice. 'And that he heard him say, The *City* was provided, and ready with 'Powder and Bullets : That he would be one who should *Seize the* 'King in case he secured any of the Members of *Parliament*. And that 'if any man, nay even *Rowley* himself should attempt to seize upon his 'Arms, *He would be the death of him*, &c.

4

In direct Opposition to these witnesses, *Colledge* produced *Titus Oates* (the third principal Witness against my *Lord Stafford*. And first Grand discoverer of the *Popish Plot*) who gave attestation against the said several Witnesses, after this manner.

'Against

---

4. *Old Rowley:* the nickname derived from the king's horse, Rowley; it connotes sexual prowess.

'A Gainſt *Dugdale*. *Oates* depoſed ; That the ſaid *Oates* diſcourſing Page 49, &c. 5
'upon occaſion with *Dugdale* concerning his being an intended
'Evidence againſt my Lord *Shaftsbury* and others. *Dugdale* replied, There
'is no body hath any cauſe to make any ſuch report of me ; For *I call*
'*God to Witneſs* I know nothing againſt any Proteſtant in *England*. But
'afterwards *Dugdale* having Sworn matters of High-Treaſon againſt
'*Colledge*, before the Grand-Jury at the *Old-Baily* ; and being here-
'upon charged by *Oates*, as having gone againſt his Conſcience and
'contrary to what he had declared to him. *Dugdale* anſwered. *It was*
'*all long of Collonel* Warcup, *for (ſaid he) I could get no money elſe* ;   6
'*And he promiſed I ſhould have a place in the* Cuſtom-Houſe.

'In oppoſition to this Teſtimony, *Dugdale* Swore ; *Upon the Oath* Page 50.
'*he had taken, and As he hoped for Salvation, It was not true*

'Againſt the ſame *Dugdale*, *Oates* farther depoſed. That *Dugdale*
'did confeſs he had an old *Clap* ; yet gave out he was Poyſoned ; * • viz *By the*   7
'which ſham paſſed throughout the Kingdom in our Intelligences ; But Papiſts.   8
'in Truth (ſaid *Oates*) it was the *Pox*: As I will make appear by
'the * Phyſician that cured him. • Dr. Lower.

'In oppoſition to which *Dugdale* proteſted, If any Doctor would Page 50.
'come forth, and ſay he cured him of a Clap, or any ſuch thing ; He
'*would ſtand Guilty of all that is imputed to him.*

Page 48.

'A Gainſt *Turbervil* alſo *Oates* gave Evidence in theſe words. A little
'before the Witneſſes were Sworn againſt *Colledge* at the *Old-Baily*,
'I *(Oates)* met with Mr. *Turbervil*. I was in a Coach ; But ſeeing
'Mr. *Turbervil* ; I ſtept out of the Coach, and ſpoke with him ; For
'hearing that he was a Witneſs, I did ask him, whether he was a Wit-
'neſs or no againſt *Colledge ?* Mr. *Turbervil* ſaid, He would break any
'ones head, that ſhould ſay ſo againſt him ; for he *neither was a Witneſs* ;
'*nor could give any Evidence againſt him*. So after he came from *Oxon*,   9
'I met with Mr. *Turbervil* again ; And hearing he had been there ;
'I asked him, if he had Sworn any thing againſt *Colledge ?* He ſaid, yes ;
'He had been ſworn before the Grand-Jury. Said I ; Did not you
'tell me ſo and ſo ? Why (ſaid he) *The Proteſtant Citizens have de-*
'*ſerted us* ; *And God Damm him, He would not ſtarve*. Theſe very
'words he ſeveral times repeated ; But when I asked him, what he
'had ſworn ? he ſaid ; I am not bound to ſatisfie Peoples Curioſities.
'*Upon the word of a Prieſt* (ſaid *Oates*) *what I ſay is true* ; *As I am a*
'*Miniſter, I ſpeak it ſincerely* ; *In the preſence of God* ; *This Gentle-*
'*man did ſay theſe words to me* ; which made me affraid of the Man ;
'And I went my ways, and never ſpoke with him afterwards, nor durſt
'I ; For I thought, *He that would Swear and curſe, after that rate, was*
'*not fit to be talked with.*

'In oppoſition to all which, *Turbervil* ſwore, That he met Dr. *Oates*
'juſt at his Lodgings ; And the Dr. alighted out of his Coach, and
'ſpoke to him, and invited him to come to his old Friends. For he
'told him ; *They had ſome Jealouſie that he was not true to them* ; And he   10
'farther told him ; If he would come to the *King's Head Clubb*, he
'ſhould be received with a great deal of Kindneſs. But never af-
'terwards (ſaid *Turbervil*) did I ſpeak with the Doctor a Tittle about
'any Evidence ; *Upon my Oath (added he) I did not* ; *And truly I*
'*always looked upon Dr.* Oates *as a very* Ill Man, *and never would con-*
'*verſe much with him.*   V   'Againſt

---

5. *p. 49, &c.*: refers to the printed account of the trial, *The Arraignment, Trial,
and Condemnation of Stephen Colledge* (1681).

6. *Collonel Warcup:* Edmund Warcup, a justice of the peace active in taking
evidence from plot witnesses.

7. *Clap:* gonorrhea.

8. *Intelligencies:* newspapers.

9. *Oxon:* Oxford.

10. *Jealousie:* suspicion.

Prg: 49.

'A Gainſt *Smith*, *Oates* gave this atteſtation ; (*viz.*) To my know-
'ledge Mr. *Colledge* and Mr. *Smith* had ſome provoking words paſ-
'ſed betwixt them at *Richards Coffee-houſe*. And Mr. *Smith* comes out,
'an I Swears, *God Damm him he would have* Colledges *Bloud* ; So when I
'met him, ſaid I, Mr. *Smith*, you profeſs your ſelf to be a *Prieſt*, and
'have ſtood at the *Altar*: And now you intend to take upon you, the
'*Miniſtery of the Church of England*; And theſe words do not become
'a *Miniſter of the Goſpel*, His reply was ; *God Damn the Goſpel*.
'*This is truth* (ſaid *Oates*) *I ſpeak it in the preſence of God and Man*.
'The whole ſubſtance of this atteſtation, *Smith* abſolutely forſwore,
'ſaying ; *Not one word of this is true, upon my Oath*. Then addreſſing
'himſelf to *Oates*. 'Tis a wonderful thing (ſaid he) you ſhould ſay
'this of me, *but I will ſufficiently prove it againſt you* ; *That you have*
'*confounded the Goſpel, And denied the Divinity too*.

This is the Sum of the Evidence given as well by Dr. *Oates* againſt
Dugdale, *Turbervil and Smith*; as by *Dugdale*, *Turbervil and Smith*
againſt Dr: *Oates*. From which fatal manner of ſelf-condemning and
Perjuring each other ; The Papiſts (with two good conſequence) draw
theſe deductions.
Either *Oates* atteſting theſe things againſt the aforenamed Witneſſes,
In the word of a Prieſt ; *As he was a Miniſter of the Goſpel, Sincerly* ;
In the preſence of God and Man, &c. Did give true Evidence, or not ;
If he did ; Then are *Dugdale* ; *Turbervil*, *and Smith*, both in their
Teſtimony againſt *Colledge*, and in their ſeveral Oaths here againſt
Oates, doubly forſworn. But if *Oates* did not give here *true* Evidence
(as the other three poſitively Swear he did not) then is he guilty of
manifeſt *Perjury*. So that from the reciprocal Teſtimony of each other,
in this matter ; It is an undenyable demonſtration ; Either *Oates* (the
Pillar of the *Plot*,) or *Dugdale*, *Turbervil*, *and Smith*, (the joynt
Supporters of it,) or Both, and All, are Perjur'd Men, and can juſtly
Challenge no right of beleif, or credit to any thing, they ever did,

Page 50.

or ſhall ſwear. Hence the *Attorney General* in this very Tryal inge-
niouſly complained: '*It is an unhappy thing That Dr.* Oates *ſhould come*
'*in againſt theſe Men that ſupported his Evidence before*. And Mr. Ser-

Page 94. & 97.

'jeant *Jefferies* rightly inculcated to the Jury ; *If Dugdale Smith and*
'*Turbervil, be not to be believed, you Perjure* (ſaid he) *three Men, And*
'*(in them) trip up the Heels of all the Evidence and Diſcovery of the*
'*Plot*. In like manner : The Papiſts argue: If *Oates* alſo, be
not to be believed ; the whole Fabrick of the *Plot* Falls. What ? Dr.
Oates? the *Quondam Top-Evidence*, *The prime Diſcoverer* ; *The Saviour*
of the King, and Nation from Popiſh Maſſacre ; He ſwear falſe ? He
not to be believed ? What Account ſhall be given to *God, and the*
World, for the *Bloud-ſhed*, and the Severities uſed, upon his Sole, or
chief Evidence ? Yet it is impoſſible, if *Dugdale, Smith, and Turbervil*,
Swear not falſe, *Oates* ſhould Swear true ; Or if he Swear not falſe ;
They ſhould Swear true ; And as it is impoſſible, both ſhould Swear
true ; So is it next to impoſſible, (if either Swear falſe) the *Plot* ſhould
be true. However, moſt aſſuredly one part of the Witneſſes againſt
my *Lord Stafford* (without which the other could never have found
credit,) are here, by their very *Compartners*, proved *Perjur'd Men*.

11

12

13

It

---

11. *Attorney General:* Sir Robert Sawyer (1633–1692).

12. *Mr. Serjeant Jefferies:* Sir George Jeffreys (1645–1689). Both Jeffreys and
Sawyer were acting as prosecutors for the Crown.

13. *Quondam:* heretofore (Latin).

IT is objected They might all of them peradventure have sworn true before; Though some of them for certain Swear false now.

The Papists *answer*: So might they all of them for certain have sworn false before, though some of them peradventure swear true now. We are not to Judge of Men's past, or future proceedings in order to *Justice*, by what they possibly might be, but by what they probably were, or will be; And to make a rational Judgment herein, we have no other Rule to guide us in the knowledge of covert *intentions*, then the Test of *Overt* actions. Seing therefore these Witnesses are proved actually Perjur'd; We have no rational ground to believe, but that upon the same motives, and in the same concurence of Circumstances, they both did, and will commit the same Crimes.

Men of lost Consciences, and desperate Fortunes, allured by gain, and encouraged by Indemnities, regard not what, when, nor how they Swear. And my *Lord Stafford* had just Cause to say, 'If it be permit- Page 45. 'ted these Men daily to frame new accusations: If easy Credit be given 'to all their *Fables*: And whatever they shall from time to time *In-* '*vent*, may pass for good *Evidence*: Who can be secure? At this rate 'they may by degrees, *Impeach the whole Nation*, (both *Catholicks* and '*Protestants*,) for Crimes which neither they nor any Man else, ever 'yet dream't on.

It is also objected by *Colledge's* Party; That *Dugdale*, *Smith*, and *Turbervil*, are *Papists* in *Masquerade*; and now made use on to Sham off the *Popish Plot*, by turning it upon the *Presbyterians*; Wherefore though credit may be given them when they Swear against *Papists*, yet the same credit ought to be denyed, when they bear *Testimony* against his *Majesties* true *Protestant Subjects*.

The *Papists answer*: First, Granted, that *Dugdale*, *Smith*, and *Turbervil* be real *Papists*; how is it proved they were imployed to Sham off the *Plot*? Why may not *Papists*, be good *Witnesses* against the *Presbyterians*, in point of *Treason*, without Suspition of a *Sham*? Is *Treason* a thing so strange, and unheard of amongst the *Presbyterians*? Or why should credit be given to the *Witnesses* when they Swear against the *Papists*, (who are only charged with a *Design to Kill the King*,) And Credit be denyed to the same *Witnesses*, when they Swear against those *who actually Killed the King*? Secondly, What the least Argument, or Appearence, is there, that *Dugdale*, *Smith*, and *Turbervil* are *Papists*, or *Popishly affected*? They profess the *Protestant Religion*; They frequent the *Protestant Church*, They receive the *Protestant Communion*, They take all *Oaths*, and *Tests* can be required of them, (as was acknowledged in this very *Tryal*.) They practise neither *Fasting*, *Pennance*, nor other works of *Supererrogation*, (the *Symptomes* of 14 *Popery*.) They pursue their former *Design of Swearing against the* Page 85. Papists, with as much obstinacy, and violence as ever; (as was likewise proved in this *Tryal*.) And is it possible the *Papists* should imploy, in their *Shams* and *Intrigues*, (if they had any) the very *Persons* who at the same time make it their *Trade* and *Lively-hood*, to *cut their Throats*? Indeed if any of the *Witnesses* against my *Lord Stafford* be Page 90. *Popishly* affected, It is Dr. *Oates*, *Whose present Disparagement of his fellow* Evidence, *look's* (said Mr. Sollicitor General,) *as if he were a-* 15 *gain returning to St. Omers.* *Lastly*, 16

---

14. *Supererrogation:* in Catholic doctrine, the performance of good works beyond what God commands or requires, which constitute a store of merit.

15. *Mr. Sollicitor General:* Henage Finch (1621–1682), created earl of Nottingham in this year (1681).

16. *St. Omers:* the Catholic school Oates attended after his "conversion."

Laſtly, It is argued; The *Jury,* bringing in *Colledge Guilty of high Treaſon,* by that very Verdict, cleared *Dugdale, Smith,* and *Turbervil* of the *Perjury,* charged upon them by Dr. *Oates.*

It is anſwered: Firſt, The *Jury* brought in their Verdict againſt *Colledge,* not upon the ſole *Teſtimony* of *Dugdale, Smith,* and *Turbervil;* but more eſpecially, upon the *Evidence* given by Sir *William Jennings,* and Mr. *Maiſters,* Perſons of known worth and honeſty; As alſo upon pregnant proof made, (and acknowledged in a manner by *Colledge* himſelf;) That he by Combination with others, appeared in open *Arms,* at an appointed time, and place, ready for, and Deſigning, *publique Acts of Hoſtility,* in the very preſence of the *King,* yet without his *Knowledge* or *Authority;* which by the *Law* is adjudged *Treaſon.* 2ly. The *Papiſts* do not undertake to make good *Oates's* Charge of *Perjury* againſt *Dugdale, Smith* and *Turbervil;* Nor theirs, againſt him: But only to ſhew, that the guilt of this *Horrid Crime* lyeth amongſt them; And conſequently, whether it be charged upon *Oates,* as the Chief *Swearing-Maſter,* and Original Author of the *Plot;* Or upon *Dugdale, Smith,* and *Turbervil,* as his *Pedants* and *Acceſſaries* in the *Impoſture;* Or (as is moſt rational) upon Both, and All of them; It follow's, That the *Lord Stafford dyed by Perjury;* And *Roman Catholicks* have wrongfully ſuffered by their Villanies, the loſs of their *Fortunes;* their *Eſtates,* their *Liberties,* their *Lives.*

Luke 19. Verſe 22.

Out of thine own Mouth will I Judge thee, Thou Wicked Servant.

THus I have here Briefly and Impartially ſet down, what occur's to me on this occaſion; And now for an *Appology* to the whole *Treatiſe:* Being the *Papiſts,* as well as all other *Men,* have a natural right, when *Impeached,* to defend their *Innocence,* I hope it will not be Imputed a fault in me, to have *Rehearſed* ſome of their *Arguments,* as they lay within the *Limits,* and *Sphere* of my *Deſign.* If any Perſons of *Depraved Judgments,* ſhall from hence draw ſiniſter *Reflections* upon the *Juſtice* of the *Nation.* I declare they abuſe both the *Government,* themſelves, and *Me,* by ſuch their unjuſt *Paraphraſe.*

F I N I S.

The History of the Association (1682)

The papers given here represent the only tangible evidence presented against the earl of Shaftesbury at his trial for treason on November 24, 1681. This draft of a Protestant association was allegedly found in Thanet House, Shaftesbury's London residence, when he was arrested on June 2. It was a plan for a parliamentary cabal to work against the succession of the duke of York, "by force of arms if need so require."

Yet like the testimony of the disreputable Irish informers brought against Shaftesbury before the Grand Jury, this document did not make for a very strong case, as it was neither signed nor dated and was not in Shaftesbury's hand. And indeed the jury was unlikely to find a true bill in any case, as it had been packed with Whigs by the newly installed sheriffs, Pilkington and Shute. The brief account of the trial given by Narcissus Luttrell suggests the tensions released when Shaftesbury, still a popular hero in London, was not indicted:

> The jury crosse examined the witnesses, and found them vary in severall matters; after which they withdrew for about two hours, and then came in and returned the bill Ignoramus; at which there was a very great shout, that made even the court shake. The witnesses were affraid to goe home, and therefore had, by order of the court, a guard from the sheriffs to see them safe home for fear of the rabble; and at night were ringing of bells and bonefires in severall parts of the citty. (Luttrell, I, 146)

Afterward, Tory propagandists printed this document as part of a general assault on Shaftesbury and the "*Ignoramus* Jury." Shaftesbury was depicted as a dangerous intriguer and the "association" compared to a similar parliamentary alliance of 1643, in order to raise again the familiar charge that the Whigs were leading the country into civil war.

This material is taken from an anonymous pamphlet on Shaftesbury's activities in the Exclusion Crisis, *The History of the Association* (London, 1682), pp. 18–22.

Then this Paper was Read as followeth.   1

WE the *Knights,* &c. *finding to the grief of our Hearts, the Popifh Priefts and Jefuits, with the Papifts and their Ad-herents and Abettors have for feveral years laft paft, perfued a moft pernicious and hellifh Plot, to root out the True Proteftant Religion as a peftilent Herefie, to take away the Life of our Gracious King, to fubvert our Laws and Liberties, and to fet up Arbitrary Power and Popery.*

And it being notorious that they have been highly en-couraged by the Countenance and Protection given and procured for them by **J. D. of Y.** *and by their Expe-ctations of his fucceeding to the Crown, and that through crafty Popifh Councils his defign hath fo far prevailed, that he hath created many and great Dependents upon him by his beftowing Offices and Preferments both in Church and State.*   2

It appearing alfo to us, That by his Influence Merce-nary Forces have been levied and kept on foot for his fe-cret defignes contrary to our Laws ; the Officers there-of having been named and appointed by him, to the ap-parent hazard of his Majefties Perfon, our Religion, and Government, if the danger had not been timely fore-feen by feveral Parliaments, and part of thofe Forces with great difficulty, caufed by them to be disbanded at the Kingdoms great Expence : And it being evident, that notwithftanding all the continual endeavours of the Parliament to deliver his Majefty from the Councils, and out of the Power of the faid D. yet His Intereft in the Miniftry of State and others have been fo preva-lent, that Parliaments have been unreafonably Proro-gued   3

<hr>

1. *was Read:* i.e., introduced as evidence at Shaftesbury's trial.
2. *J.D. of Y.:* James, duke of York.
3. *disbanded:* in 1678, Parliament had sought to purge the army of popish of-ficers, and most of the army was disbanded in 1679.

gued and Diſſolved when they have been in hot purſuit of
the Popiſh Conſpiracies, and ill Miniſters of State their
Aſſiſtants.

And that the ſaid D. in order to reduce all into his
own power hath procured the Garriſons, the Army and
Ammunition, all the power of the Seas and Soldiery,
and Lands belonging to theſe three Kingdoms to be put
into the hands of his Party and their Adherents, even
in oppoſition to the Advice and Order of the laſt Parliament

And as we conſidering with heavy Hearts how greatly
the Strength, Reputation and Treaſ re of the King-   4
dom both at Sea and Land is Waſted and Conſumed, and
loſt by the intricate expenſive management of theſe wicked deſtructive Deſignes ; and finding the ſame Councils
after exemplary Juſtice upon ſome of the Conſpirators,   5
to be ſtill purſued with the utmeſt deviliſh Malice, and
deſire of Revenge; whereby his Majeſty is in continual
hazard of being Murdered to make way for the ſaid D.'s
Advancement to the Crown, and the whole Kingdom in
ſuch caſe is deſtitute of all Security of their Religion,
Laws, Eſtates, and Liberty, (ad experience in the
Caſe, Queen Mary having proved the wiſeſt Laws to   6
be of little force to keep out Popery and Tyranny under
a Popiſh Prince.

We have therefore endeavoured in a Parliamentary
way by a Bill for the purpoſe to Bar and Exclude the ſaid
Duke from the Succeſſion to the Crown, and to Baniſh
him for ever out of theſe Kingdoms of England and
Ireland. But the firſt means of the King and Kingdoms Safety being utterly rejected, and we left almoſt in
Deſpair of obtaining any real and effectual ſecurity,
and knowing our ſelves to be intruſted to Adviſe an Act
                                                      for

---

4. *Reputation and:* the following word is "Treasure."

5. *Conspirators:* i.e., those Catholics executed for the plot.

6. *Queen Mary:* "Bloody Mary" who persecuted Protestants during her reign
(1553–1558).

*for the preservation of His Majesty and the Kingdom,
and being perswaded in our Consciences that the dangers
aforesaid are so eminent and pressing, that there ought
to be no delay of the best means that are in power to secure the Kingdom against them. We have thought fit
to propose to all true Protestants an Union amongst
themselves by solemn and sacred promise of mutual
Defence and Assistance in the preservation of the true
protestant Religion, His Majesties Person and Royal
State and our Lawes, Liberties and Properties, and
we hold it our bounden Duty to joyn our selves for the
same intent in a Declaration of our United Affections
and Resolutions in the Form insuing.*

I A. B. Do in the presence of God solemnly Promise, Vow, and
Protest to maintain and defend to the utmost of my power,
with my Person and Estate, the true Protestant Religion, a-
gain Popery and all Popish Superstition, Idolatry, or Innovation, and all those who do or shall endeavour to spread or advance
it within this Kingdom.

I will also, as far as in me lies, Maintain and defend his Majesties Royal Person and Estate; as also the Power and Priviledg
of Parliaments, the lawful Rights and Liberties of the Subject
against all incroachments and Usurpation of Arbitrary power
whatsoever, and endeavour entirely to Disband all such Mer-
cenary Forces as we have reason to believe were Raised to Advance it, and are still kept up in and about the City of London, to the great Amazement and Terror of all the good People
of the Land.

Moreover J. D of Y. Having publickly professed and owned
the Popish Religion, and notoriously given Life and Birth to
the Damnable and Hellish Plots of the Papists against his Majesties Person, the Protestant Religion, and the Government of
this Kingdom; I will never consent that the said J D of Y.
or any other, who is or hath been a Papist, or any ways adher'd
to the Papists in their wicked Designs, be admitted to the Succession of the Crown of England, But by all lawful means and
by force of Arms, if need so require, according to my Abilities,
oppose him, and endeavour to subdue, Expel and Destroy him,
if

if he come into England, or the Dominions thereof, and seek by force to set up his pretended Title, and all such as shall Adhere unto him, or raise any War, Tumult, or Sedition for him, or by his Command, as publick Enemies of our Laws, Religion and Country.

To this end we and every one of us whose hands are here under written, do most willingly bind our selves and every one of us unto the other, joyntly and severally, in the bond of one firm and Loyal Society or Association, and do promise and vow before God, That with our joynt and particular Forces, we will oppose and pursue unto Destruction all such as upon any Title whatsoever shall oppose the Just and Righteous Ends of this Association, and Maintain, Protect and Defend all such as shall enter into it in the just performance of the true intent and meaning of it, And lest this Just and Pious work should be any ways obstructed or hindred for want of Discipline and Conduct, or any evil minded persons under pretence of raising Forces for the service of this Association, should attempt or commit Disorders; we will follow such Orders as we shall from time to time receive from this present Parliament, whilst it shall be sitting, or the Major part of the Members of both Houses subscribing this Association, when it shall be Prorogued or Dissolved: And obey such Officers as shall by them be set over us in the several Countries Cities, and Burroughs, until the next meeting of this or another Parliament; and will then shew the same Obedience and Submission unto it, and those who shall be of it.

Neither will we for any respect of Persons or Causes, or for Fear, or Reward separate our selves from this Association, or fail in the Prosecution thereof during our Lives, upon pain of being by the rest of us prosecuted. and suppressed as Perjured Persons, and Publick Enemies to God, the King, and our Native Country.

To which Pains and Punishment we do voluntarily submit our
G   selves,

*felves , and every one of us without benefit of any Colour or Pre-
tence to excufe us.*

> In Witnefs of all which Premifes to be in-
> violably kept , we do this prefent Writ-
> ing put our Hands and Seals , and fhall
> be moft ready to accept and admit any
> others hereafter into this Society and Af-
> fociation.

This contrived peice of fcandalous Treafon, is that which was faid, or
rather fworn to have been found in the Earl of *Shaftfbury's* Study. Now,
whether the Paper were really in the Hair Trunk, or put into the Velvet 7
Bagg among other loofe Papers, is a difpute of another Nature. However
the Paper being found, or pretendedly found in the Earls Study, the bufinefs
was profecuted by the Attorny General , before fpecial Commiffioners of
Oyer and Terminer, the 24*th.* of *November* 1681, upon a Bill of Endict- 8
ment for High Treafon, againft *Anthony* Earl of *Shaftfbury.* His Grand-
Jury were.

The GRAND-JURY.   9

Sir *Samuel Barnardifton.*	*Thomas Parker.*
John Morden.	*Leonard Robinfon.*
Thomas Papillon.	*Thomas Shepherd.*
John Dubois.	*John Flavell.*
Charles Hearle.	*Michael Godfrey.*
Edward Rudge.	*Jofeph Richardfon.*
Humphrey Edwin.	*William Empfon.*
John Morrice.	*Andrew Kendrick.*
Edmund Harrifon.	*John Lane.*
Jofeph Wright.	*John Hall.*
John Cox.	

---

7. *Hair Trunk:* this document was alleged to have been removed from Shaftesbury's closet and put into a velvet bag when it was removed from the premises.

8. *Commissioners of Oyer and Terminer:* judges of this first and largest of the five
judicial commissions or royal patents, which grant them the power to deal with
"Treason, Murder, and all manner of Felonies and Misdemeanors" (Thomas Blount,
NOMO-EIKON: A Law-Dictionary [1670]).

9. *The GRAND JURY:* the Whig jury selected by Sheriffs Thomas Pilkington
and Samuel Shute. According to K. H. D. Haley, it consisted of well-to-do dissenters,
including some exclusionist M.P.'s (Haley, pp. 675–76).

PART SEVEN

Some Characters

George. Duke. Marquess and Earle of Buckingham, Earle of Coventry. &c.

Portrait of George Villiers, Duke of Buckingham. The frontispiece of Buckingham's *Miscellaneous Works* (1707).

George Villiers, Duke of Buckingham (1707)

One of the fascinating aspects of the history of this troubled time is the emergence of a number of intriguing characters who significantly shaped the events of 1678–1681. Several of them have, of course, been captured with special vividness by Dryden in *Absalom and Achitophel*. Of these people, George Villiers, the second duke of Buckingham (1628–1687), does not seem to have earned the prominence he attained as Dryden's Zimri by his actual role in the affairs of state of this period. During 1678–1679, he did take a leading part in grilling plot suspects, notably Samuel Atkins, in helping to plan the great pope burnings held in London, and in other activities of the Green Ribbon Club at the King's Head Tavern. But he did not support the pretensions of Monmouth, and he did not always get along with Shaftesbury.

After 1680, though he remained a popular, even a notorious, figure, Buckingham's role in public affairs declined. "Worn to a thread with whoring," he was already in poor health and in February 1680, his energies were diverted by an accusation of sodomy brought against him by his enemies, who included a former associate, the infamous Colonel Blood, who had stolen the crown jewels in 1671. A Grand Jury threw out the charges, and Buckingham was able to have his accusers prosecuted for perjury, and convicted, late in the same year. He also sued Colonel Blood for *scandalum magnatum* and was awarded £30,000 in damages. Soon afterward, Buckingham retired to his estate, where he remained in relative obscurity for the rest of his life. At his death, Sir John Reresby wrote of him as "a man of the most exquisite wit of his time, the handsomest, the best bred; but unfortunately given up to pleasures, unsteady in his ways, and, in all respects, an enemy to himself" (Reresby, p. 291).

JACOBUS, Herzog Von Monmuth

Portrait of James, Duke of Monmouth. Printed in "Der um einiger," a 1685 broadside that also contains a drawing of the scene of Monmouth's execution and a portrait of James II.

James, Duke of Monmouth

A True Narrative of the Duke of Monmouth's Late Journey into the West (1680)

James Scott, duke of Monmouth and Buccleuch (1649–1685), the handsome but weak-minded son of the king by Lucy Walters, directed his efforts during the Exclusion Crisis toward undermining public support for his uncle, the duke of York, and making himself appear the best Protestant alternative to him. The apex of his career came in June 1679, with his victory over the Scots Covenanters at Bothwell Bridge, but in the following November, he incurred the king's wrath by returning from Holland without permission. Despite being removed from all court offices and denied access to Whitehall, Monmouth remained in London and became a focus for exclusionist sentiment. In August 1680, he went on his "progress" through the western counties.

For the rest of Charles's reign, Monmouth aided the exclusionists, going on a second progress in 1682 and continuing to plot with Shaftesbury. He played a part in the abortive Rye House Plot of 1683 to assassinate the king and York, but he claimed that he had endeavored to protect his father. He was pardoned and sent to Holland. When James II assumed the throne in 1685, Monmouth led a fatal rebellion against him. In June he landed in the west of England at the head of a small army, but his hopes of uniting the country under his banner proved vain, and within a month he was defeated and captured. On August 15, James had him executed. His fate bears out the warnings directed at him in *Absalom and Achitophel.*

The following tract gives a good idea of the political nature of Monmouth's famous 1680 expedition into the western counties.

A TRUE

NARRATIVE

OF THE

Duke of Monmouth's

Late JOURNEY into the

WEST,

IN A

LETTER

FROM AN

Eye-witnefs thereof, to his Correfpondent in *London*.

S I R,   *3. Nov. 1680*

THAT branch of our conteft (which thefe unhappy times have occafioned betwixt your felf and me, privately) concerning the prefent temper of the people of *England,* as to the reception of Popery, hath now (I think) fo fully been decided, that I fhall no longer differ from you in that point, but with joy acknowledg to you, that I am perfectly convinced, nay fure, that not only the Principles, but even the very *Genius* of the people of *England* will never endure to be again rid like a Hackney of *Rome,* to both the temporal and eternal 1 deftruction of the poor Creature. Of this my eyes as well as my underftanding faw the demonftration, when I faw that incredible (if not univerfal) confluence of people of all Qualities, Sexes, and Ages, meet to welcome a Proteftant Duke into thefe Countries. Now that I have not mifcall'd this a Demonftration, pray obferve this Journal of the Duke's progrefs, and the peoples joy.

On the 24*th* of *Auguft* he came from Efq; *Thyn's* in *Wiltfhire* to 2 3
Efq; *Speak's* in *Sommerfetfhire,* in which Progrefs he had all the way 4

A   been

---

1. *Hackney:* a hired horse.
2. *Esq.:* denoting the courteous title of gentleman.
3. *Thyn's:* Longleat, the famous estate in Wiltshire of Thomas Thynne, known for his wealth as "Tom of Ten Thousand." In *Absalom and Achitophel,* he is ironically called "wise Issachar."
4. *Speak's:* White Lackington, the estate of George Speke in Somerset, near Ilminster.

been careſſed with the joyful Welcomes and Acclamations of the people, who came from all parts, 20 miles about, filling and lining the Hedges with Men, Women and Children, ſome going before, ſome following after for ſome miles in the High-ways, all the way, and inceſſantly with hearty and great ſhouts crying, God bleſs our King *Charles,* and God bleſs the Proteſtant Duke. Some Towns and Pariſhes expreſſed alſo their Country-reſpects in ſtrewing their ſtreets and ways thorough which he paſſed, with herbs and flowers, as was ſeen at *Ilcheſter,* and *Pithyton,* &c. In ſome places where no 5 other better preſent could be expected or made, the honeſt kind Good-women with ruſtick ſincerity preſented to him bottles of Wine, which he courteouſly accepted and taſted. Some of theſe good Dames could not reſtrain their joys, but in their homely phraſe call'd out to him thus, *Maſter, we are glad to ſee you, and you are welcome into our Country.* And then ſome caught hold of his Feet, ſome took him by the Hand, ſome by the Coat, but all cried, **Welcome, welcome, no** *Popery, no Popery,* &c. When he drew near to Eſq; *Speaks* by 10 miles, he was met by 2000 perſons on Horſe-back, who were ſo increaſt before they arrived at Mr. *Speaks,* that ſome conjectured they were in number near 20000, others ſaid, they were many more. At his arrival the Eſq; ſet out ſeveral Hogſheads 6 and Veſſels of Beer, Ale, and Sider, to entertain the people, notwithſtanding that they (to enlarge their paſſage to the houſe) had broke down ſeveral pearch of his Park-pales; and though the hoop- 7 8 ings, ſhoutings, and acclamations of the people had ſo affrighted the Deer out of the Park, that as yet they cannot be got in again (it's conceiv'd that the people did get Veniſon as well as the Duke) yet true, loyal Proteſtant, and *Engliſh* Gentleman thus received the Duke and the people. May he be an Example to all the Gentry for his Loyalty to his King, and love to his Country, for being an Orthodox Proteſtant, and a true hoſpitable lover of our dear true Proteſtant *Engliſhmen.*

On the 26 of *Auguſt* he dined with Sir J *Sydenham* at *Brempton,* 9 where he met ſuch an abundance of people, and ſuch a ſplendid entertainment, that it was difficult to determine which deſerved the greater wonder.

On the 27th of *Auguſt* he dined with that true Patriot *William Stroud,* Eſq; at *Barrington;* whoſe noble Treat to this Illuſtrious Prince and Proteſtant Duke, ſuited thoſe high qualities. Nor was 10 this Dinner without that beſt of Muſick, the joyful ſhouts of thouſands.

After Dinner he went to *Chard,* where was preſented to him a 11 Collation of great variety and excellency, the ſecond Courſe was 12 the hearts and tongues of very numerous people. He arrived there

---

5. *Pithyton:* South Petherton, a town in Somersetshire, near Ilchester.

6. *Hogsheads:* large casks; one hogshead equals sixty-three gallons (U.S.).

7. *pearch:* a measure of length, usually 16½ feet.

8. *pales:* fence palings.

9. *Brempton:* Brympton D'Evercy, near Yeovil, the seat of Sir John Sydenham. The following words are "where he met such."

10. *Stroud:* William Strode, whose Tudor estate at Barrington is near White Lackington.

11. *Chard:* a town in Somerset, near Ilminster and White Lackington.

12. *Collation:* a light meal or repast.

about five in the Afternoon, followed by a Train of 500 Horsemen; but when entred, he was met by a Crowd of Men, Women and Children, not a Mute amongst them all, but all almost made deaf with their own Crys and Acclamations; scarce was there one that drank not the Kings Health, and the Dukes, to which still succeeded their loud Vollies of God bless the King with long Life, God bless the Protestant Duke nis Son, &c.

That Evening he was most acceptably receiv'd and lodg'd by that worthy *English* Gentleman, Esq; *Prideaux*. 13

The next day, *viz.* 28th of *August*, after a great and sumptuous Dinner, he rode to *Ilminster*, where he accepted of a Collation as at *Chard*; from thence to *Whitlackindon*, where was his stated Lodgings 14

On the 29th of *August* (being *Sunday*) he observed it with a due Protestant and Christian respect, and went to *Ilminster*-Church, &c.

On the 30th of *August*, he removed to *Calliton*, and lodged with the most ingenious, loyal, and generous Sir *Walter Young*. 15

On the 31 he lodged with that *English* Worthy Esq; *Dukes*, at *Otterton*, in which and all the other parts, his Treatments were rich and great, and every where his rejoicing admirers numberless. 16

But on the first of *Septemb*, he journied to *Exeter*, where he was magnificently entertain'd at the Dean's house by that Gentleman of unspotted Loyalty, Sir *William Courtney* The Citizens, together with the people of all the adjacent parts, (verily believed to exceed 20000 persons) came all forth to meet the Duke with their Souls and Mouths filled with love and joy, trumpetting forth his welcome, and shouting out thus, God bless our Gracious Sovereign King *Charles*, God bless the Protestant Duke, God bless the Protestant Prince, &c. But that which most deserves remark, was the appearance of a company of brave stout young men, all clothed in linnen Wast-coats and Drawers, white and harmless, having not so much as a stick in their hand, but joining hands, their number was reputed to be 10 or 1200 (the least conjecture of them was 800) these met the Duke within 3 miles of the City, being put into order on a small round hill, and divided into two parts, and so attended the coming of the Duke, who when arrived rode up between them, and after rode round each company, who then united, and went hand in hand in their order, before the Duke into the City. Where when arrived, the great concourse of people, the amazing shouts, the universal joys were such, as are more easily related than can be credited by the absent Reader. I shall only say of it, that it suited (at this time) the reception that a Protestant people was willing to give to an illustrious Protestant Prince. 17

Sept. 2. he returned to Esq; *Speaks*, where again flocked in to meet

---

13. *Prideaux:* Edmund Prideaux, a Puritan lawyer, whose estate, Ford Abbey, is near Chard.

14. *Ilminster:* a town near Chard, also in Somerset.

15. *Calliton:* Colyton, in Devon.

16. *Otterton:* a town in southern Devon, where he stayed with Richard Duke.

17. *Exeter:* Exeter, the city in western Devonshire.

meet and fee him the whole neighbouring Country , as not yet
enough fatisfied, unlefs thus extraordinarily to careffe him in his
return.

Sept. 3. he dined at the worthy Efq; *Harvy's* near *Yeovil*, and after 18 19
rode to Efq; *Thyn's*, the Country ftill waiting in great fhoals to
expect him on *Howden*-hill, from *Crookhorn*, *Yeovil*, and all other 20
circumjacent parts to the number of 4 or 5000 to take their leaves
of him, and to prefent him their thanks for his kind vifit, and his
acceptance of their *Englifh* true-hearted refpects.

Sir, you cannot but with difficulty imagine (except you had been
both an eye and an ear-witnefs, as I was) with what earneftnefs the
people of all forts, all fexes, all ages and degrees came forth to
exprefs their Loyalty to their King and Soveraign in praying for his
long life and happy reign, and in heartily drinking his Health
every where, but efpecially alfo in manifefting their true *Englifh*
hearty love to this Proteftant Duke, having never fince his Maje-
flies happy Reftauration, had the good occafion to fee amongft
them their King, or any of his Royal Family until now. The Country efteeming it a great glory and happinefs to fee one of that flock
to appear amongft them.

Laftly, let us remark, that in all this progrefs were divers perfons of noble as well as gentile quality, *viz.* Lords, Knights, Ef-
quires and Gentlemen, who together with the Duke made a Con-
ftellation of *Englifh* Proteftants glorious in their beams derived
from the Sun of great *Britain.*

God blefs and fave the King.

Printed, and are to be Sold by *Richard Janeway* in *Queens-* 21
Head-Alley in *Pater-Nofter-Row*, 1680.

18. *Harvey's:* Clifton Maybank, in Dorset, the Tudor estate of Michael Harvey.

19. *Yeovil:* a town in south Somerset.

20. *Crookhorn:* Crewkerne, a town in Somerset, also near White Lackington. For
geographical information in these notes, I am indebted to Bryan Little's *The Monmouth Episode* (London: Werner Laurie, 1956).

21. *Janeway:* see L'Estrange's *Observator* (p. 201).

His Grace the Duke of Monmouth
Honoured in His Progress (1681)

During his progress through the West in 1680, Monmouth was hailed as a Protestant hero, and the tale given here of his touch curing the king's Evil (scrofula) suggested that, despite the king's denials of the story that he had secretly married Lucy Walters, Monmouth was authentically royal.

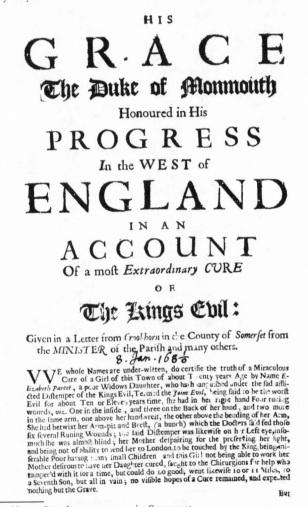

HIS

G R · A C E

The Duke of Monmouth

Honoured in His

PROGRESS

In the WEST *of*

ENGLAND

IN AN

ACCOUNT

Of a most *Extraordinary* CURE

OF

The Kings Evil:

Given in a Letter from *Crookhorn* in the County of *Somerset* from the *MINISTER* of the Parish and many others.   1

8 . *Jan* · 1685

VVE whose Names are under-witten, do certifie the truth of a Miraculous Cure of a Girl of this Town of about Twenty years Age by Name Elizabeth Parcet, a poor Widows Daughter, who hath languished under the sad afflicted Distemper of the Kings Evil, Termed the *Joint Evil*, being said to be the worst Evil for about Ten or Eleven years time, she had in her right hand Four runing wounds, *viz.* One in the inside, and three on the Back of her hand, and two more in the same arm, one above her hand wreit, the other above the bending of her Arm, She had betwixt her Arm-pit and Brest, (a bunch) which the Doctors said fed those   2 six several Runing Wounds; the said Distemper was likewise on her Left eye, insomuch she was almost blind; her Mother despairing for the preserving her sight, and being not of ability to send her to London, to be touched by the King, being miserable Poor having many small Children and this Girl not being able to work her Mother desirous to have her Daughter cured, faught to the Chirurgions for help who   3 tamper'd with it for a time, but could do no good; went likewise 10 or 11 Miles, to a Seventh Son, but all in vain; no visible hopes of a Cure remained, and expected nothing but the Grave.

But

---

1. *Crookhorn:* Crewherne, a town in Somerset.
2. *King's Evil:* scrofula, thought to be cured by the King's touch.
3. *Chirurgions:* surgeons.

But now, in this the Girls great extremity. God the great Phyſitian Dictates unto her, thus Languiſhing in her miſerable, hopeleſs condition; what courſe to take, and what to do for a Cure, which was to go and touch the Duke of *Monmouth*; which the Girl told her Mother that if ſhe could but touch the Duke ſhe ſhould be well, her Mother reproved her for her fooliſh conceit, but the Girl did often perſwade her Mother that ſhe might go to *Lackinton* to the Duke, who 4 then lay at Mr. *Speaks*, for certainly ſaid ſhe I ſhould be well if I could but touch him; her Mother ſlighted the preſſing requeſts of her Daughter, and the more her Mother ſlighted it and reproved her, the more earneſt was the Girl for it; in few days after the Girl having notice that Sir *John Sydnham* intended to Treat the Duke at *white Lodg* in *Henton-* 5 Park, which ihis Girl with many of her Neighbours went to the ſaid Park; ſhe being there timely waited the Dukes coming. Firſt, ſhe obſerved the Perſon of the D. to have knowledg of him as he was paſſing into the ſaid Lodg, ſhe preſt in among a Crowd of People, and caught him by the hand, his Glove being on, and ſhe had a Glove likewiſe to cover her wounds, ſhe not being herewith ſatisfied with this firſt attempt of touching his Glove only, but her mind was, ſhe muſt touch ſome part of his bare skin; ſhe weighting his coming forth, intended a ſecond attempt: the poor Girl, thus betwixt hope and fear waited his motion, on a ſudden was news of the D. coming on, which ſhe to be prepared, rent off her Glove that was clung to the Sores in ſuch haſt, that broke her Glove, and brought away not only the ſores, but the skin: the Dukes Glove, as providence would have it, the upper part hung down, ſo that his hand-wreſt was bare; ſhe preſt one and caught him by the bare hand-wreſt with her running hand; (ſaying, God bleſs your Greatneſs; and the Duke ſaid God bleſs you) the Girl was not a little tranſported with her good ſucceſs, came and told her friends that now ſhe ſhould be well, ſhe came home to her Mother with great joy, and told her ſhe had that touched by the Dukes bare hand (and that ſhe ſhould now be well) her Mother hearing what ſhe had done, reproved her very ſharply for her boldneſs, and asked her how ſhe durſt do ſuch a thing, and threatned to beat her for it, ſhe cryed out O Mother I ſhall be well again, and be cured of my wounds; and as God Almighty the great Phyſitian would have it, to the admiration of all that know of it, or heard of it. Her ſix running wounds in her hand and arm, in four or five days were dried up, the bunch in her breſt was diſſolved in eight or ten days, of which now is no ſign: her eye that was given for loſt, is now perfectly well, and the Girl in good health; the marks of her ſeveral wounds are yet viſible in her hand and arm, all which has been diſcovered to us both by Mother and Daughter, and Neighbours that know her.

Henry Clark Miniſter of the Pariſh, Captain *James Bale*, Captain *Richard Shrlock*, *John Stacky* Clerk, *William Pike*, *Samuel Daubeney*, *George Strong*, *John Greenway*, *Robert Chiſlet*.

Whoever doubts the truth of this relation, may be ſatisfied thereof by ſight of the Original under the hands of the Perſons before mentioned, at the *Amſterdam* Coffe-Houſe in *Bartholomew Lane* near the *Royal Exchange*.

LONDON, Printed for *Benjamin Harris* at the *Stationers Arms* in the *Piazza* under the *Royal Exchange* in *Cornhil*. 1680.

---

4. *Lackington:* White Lackington, the estate of George Speke, in Somerset.

5. *Henton Park:* the estate of John, Lord Poulett, at Hinton St. George, a village in Somerset, only a short distance from Crewherne.

JACOBUS der II itzt regier
ender könig Von Groß-Britanien

Portrait of James, Duke of York. Printed in "Der um einiger," a 1685 broadside that
contains also a drawing of Monmouth's execution and a portrait of Monmouth.

James, Duke of York

James, duke of York (1633–1701), plays a shadowy role in the events between 1678 and 1681, as he does in *Absalom and Achitophel,* where he is given no Biblical name and appears only indirectly. As the target of exclusionist zeal, with a rigid temper that did not win over opponents, he was best kept from the public eye. Though he was exempt from the provisions of the second Test Act of 1678, the king ordered him abroad for most of this period. On March 4, 1679, he left for Brussels by royal command, and remained there until August 23, when he returned upon hearing of Charles's illness. Once that danger was past, he again went to Brussels, then to Scotland, where he remained until the following February. Then he returned once more to counterbalance the defiant return of Monmouth. This time he stayed until October. It was during this period that Shaftesbury and other Whigs tried to have him indicted as a popish recusant. He left the country on the day before Parliament reassembled and stayed away until the spring of 1682, when matters were judged to be well enough in hand to allow his return.

By 1684, the tide of the plot had turned and he was able to sue Oates for *scandalum magnatum* for calling him a traitor in 1680. The court awarded him £100,000 and imprisoned Oates until he paid— which he clearly could never do. And appropriately, just as James ascended the throne, Oates was being tried and convicted for perjury.

Yet for all King Charles's success in preserving his brother's right to succeed him, King James's rule lasted less than four years. After the revolution of 1688, he spent the remainder of his life in exile.

Slingsby Bethel

A Seasonable Answer To a Late Pamphlet, Entituled
The Vindication of Slingsby Bethel, Esq. (1681)

Slingsby Bethel (1617–1697), Dryden's Shimei, like Buckingham, looms larger in *Absalom and Achitophel* than he did in the history of the Exclusion Crisis. He was a merchant with strong republican and Puritan convictions who had written a number of pamphlets, including a violent attack on Oliver Cromwell in 1668, and in 1680 a 357-page book, *The Interests of Princes and States*, which is a collection of his earlier writings in support of free trade and religious toleration for dissenters.

His importance in this period derives from his being elected sheriff of London and Middlesex along with Henry Cornish in 1680. During their one-year term which began in September, these two sheriffs became the first to pack juries in order to thwart the prosecution of exclusionist leaders. Previously, the London shrievalty had been a largely ceremonial office for wealthy merchants who, for the sake of the honor, would pay the expenses of keeping an open table and giving the traditional feasts for the guilds and the aldermen. But as Bethel had sought office solely to aid his party, he had little interest in subsidizing the usual hospitality. This "parsimony," as it was called, along with his truculent nature, earned him considerable antagonism. In 1681, he collected all the charges brought against him and attempted to answer them in *The Vindication of Slingsby Bethel*. About half of this tract is devoted to the issue of his miserliness. But the *Vindication* provoked the *Seasonable Answer* (1681) included here, in which the anonymous author, in addition to ridiculing the *Vindication,* has found a new charge to use against him.

On October 5, 1680, Bethel had been tried for assault and battery upon a king's waterman named Robert Mason. The incident had occurred the previous February during the polling in Southwark to select members of the Oxford Parliament. Bethel was a candidate, and it was alleged that he struck Mason and tried to drive him from the polling place. In the trial, an account of which was soon printed, he was quoted as telling Mason, who wore the king's insignia, "I will have your Coat pluck'd over your Ears!" Mason's pointed answer was, "So you would my Masters too, if you could." Bethel was found guilty and fined five marks (£3.6.6d).

He never held public office again, but he did continue his writing.

In 1691 he published an account of the history of his times, *The Prov-idences of God,* in which he denounced the "barbarous and inhumane Proceedings" against Oates in 1685, when he had been convicted of perjury in the plot trials, and blamed the entire plot on Charles II. To the last he was a narrow partisan, and, as Burnet wrote, a "sullen and wilfull man."

A Seaſonable

A N S W E R

To a Late

PAMPHLET,

Entituled,

The Vindication

O F

Slingsby . Bethel , Eſq;

One of the Sheriffs of *London* and *Middleſex*.

By one who is a Citizen of London, *and an Inhabitant of the Borough of* Southwark.

Neſcis quo valeat nummus ? quem præbeat uſum?
Panis ematur, olus, vini ſextarius : adde
Queis humana ſibi doleat natura negatis.

Hor. Sat. 1.   1

LONDON,

Printed for *C. Mearne.* 1 6 8 1.

---

1. *Hor Sat. I:* Do'st thou not know the use and power of *coyn?*
It buys bread, meat, and cloaths, (and what's more) *wine;*
With all those necessary things beside,
Without which Nature cannot be supplied.
—Horace, *Sermones* (Satires), I, ll. 73–75; translation by
Alexander Brome (*The Poems of Horace*, 3d ed., 1680, p. 193).

A Seafonable

ANSWER

To a Late

PAMPHLET,

ENTITULED,

The Vindication of Slingsby Bethel, *Efq; one of the Sheriffs of* London *and* Middlefex, *&c.*

THE City of *London* is a place of fo great Confideration, and well known to abound fo much with men of True Loyalty, undoubted Integrity, plentiful Fortunes, generous Tempers, untainted Credit, and every way fit to difcharge its principal Offices, that it cannot be under any neceffity of taking up with perfons of *Factious Principles*, Moot Honefty, Invifible Eftates, narrow and fhrivel'd Souls, or Fly-blown Reputations, to difgrace any of the Honourable Employments in it.

And yet to the great furprize of multitudes that did, and that did not know him, Mr. *Slingsby Bethel*, one of the moft Notorious, & moft Obfcure men that ever was made Free of the *Leather-Sellers* Company, was the laft year, by the feverifh Zeal of a boifterous puffing Party of miftaken Citizens, blown up into a Sheriff of *London* and *Middlefex*, though fince that fudden Guft of popular breath is laid, he has dwindled and fhrunk up into a Thing not commenfurate to the Dignity of an *Ale-Conner*.   2

For now that his fond mif-led Friends have had time to confider and underftand him, they have with a Modefty to be encouraged, difown'd the Man and his Manners; and notwithftanding their late Midfummer Complement, upon   3 occafion of Difcourfe concerning him, have been ready to blufh for him fince, as much as they fweated for him at firft.

The Borough of *Southwark*, comparatively with any other Borough, or indeed City in *England*, is much more a Neighbour to the City of *London* in its   4 Trade and Commerce, and in the number and condition of its Inhabitants, than in its Scituation; and was never fo barren of Men, Honeft, and Wife, and Wealthy, as that it needed to crofs the Water for Burgefles to ferve in Parliament.

And yet at the laft Election the fame *Slingsby Bethel* having now gained the Additional Title of Mr. *Sheriff* and *Efquire* to promote his pretenfions, becomes very officious in tendring us his Service in the Houfe of Commons ; and with as little Invitation to our Pockets as ever we had to his Table, over the Bridge come his Horfe and He (the principal Burghers being not yet refolv'd which of the two to make a Senator) and being encourag'd by fome few male-content Renegado's from amongft us, who like Whifflers came juftling and making Elbow-room for him, he fets up for Himfelf, and will be our Reprefentative, and put his hands into our Purfes whether we will or no.

This way of Addreffing the more confiderable fort of our Burghers were fo unacquainted with, that prefently we became curious in fearching into the qualifications of a perfon of fuch extraordinary Application ; and upon enquiry we

received

---

2. *Ale-Conner:* one who tests ale.

3. *Midsummer Complement:* sheriffs were elected for one-year terms each Midsummer Day, June 24.

4. *Southwark:* "The Borough" is just across the Thames from London.

received such a Character of him, as that the least limb of our Body, the Men of *Kentstreet* it self, would disdain to send him up to *Oxford* as a Representative 5 Broomstick.

Indeed he had once the Honour to be return'd by the Ward of *Farrindon Without*, one of the two Commoners, of whom the Court of Aldermen were to chuse the more Worthy to be Alderman of their Ward; but it is to be noted, that he had the Honour likewise to be rejected by that wise and impartial Court; both which put together (especially considering the grounds of his boasted *general Consent*, which, in defence of that Ward, I shall in its due place explain) I am apt to think that the advantage of Credit from that Enterprize is not on his part so great, as to give him any just encouragement of hoping ever to arrive at so high a Dignity; but when *Michaelmas* is come, the Retinue discharged, the 6 Horse sold, and the Gold Chain restor'd, he must sit down content to be *Slingsby Bethel* in *cuerpo* still. 7

Now for a Gentleman born and bred, one so well read and travell'd as he has 8 been, and who is of too great a Spirit to stoop to the Office of Executioner, to serve the Greatest Prince that ever was brought to the Block; for such a Man to be so miserably defeated in his pretensions on both sides the Water, to be so scornfully neglected, and re-buff'd in the Borough of *Southwark*, when he came over, resolv'd to be their humble Servant; to be so unexpectedly Dismounted and Un-Burgessed, when his Confidence of Success had already put 9 him to the trouble of preparing some Speeches for the House: And then in the City to be denied Admittance into the Court of Aldermen; and while his 10 younger Brother, the other Sheriff, is a Member of it, for him to be forced to 11 dance Attendance upon it, to be made a Companion to Foot-boys, and to have no other Diversion than what arises from being Spectator of the *Olympick* Exercise of *Span-Farthing*: These are Indignities which no man of so equal a Mix- 12 ture of Wit and Bravery, can be expected to pass by un-revenged one way or other.

And therefore his Courage and Fancy being hereby raised, in a short time he boldly sets up for an Author; and that he may be even with *London* and *Southwark* together, he at once publishes a Libel upon both, under the Name of *The Vindication of* Slingsby Bethel, *&c.*

But certainly this Man is under an ill Fate; he is not more unsuccessful in his Adventures, than unfortunate in writing their *Commentaries*; he plays Booty with his own good Name, in that which he calls his *Vindication*, and washes, 13 and lathers, and scrubs himself so long to no purpose, that he is such a Picture of the *Labour in Vain*, that no Suburb Sign can match him.

He begins with a precarious Assertion of the Innocence of the former part of his Life, thinking no doubt, that being an Old Man, and having been a Traveller, he might have the Liberty which the Proverb allows him; and hoping 14 probably thereby to bury the Remembrance of his Pranks at *Hamburgh* (and I question not but that, as well as he loves Money, he would be glad to be at the Charge of Five Pound to have it done in Linen) but the mischief of it is, 15 there are several Merchants living, who were Witnesses of his Words and Actions there, that can testifie his first Paragraph to be false. Indeed he speaks with 16 a great deal of Diffidence of himself, and rather like one that desires, than believes a thing to be true; however slily he carried himself in his *Private Station*, and whatever there may be between God and his own Conscience, yet he tells us, that he did not deserve (as he *reasonably hopes*) any Reproach from Man. But to see how credulous Interest will make Men! How could he *reasonably hope*, that none of his Contemporary Merchants at that Staple, should tell his 17 Famous History, and display him in his Colors at their Return into *England*? How

5. *Kent Street:* the road from Kent to Southwark and old London Bridge; in this period it was ill built and derelict, inhabited by the poorest of people.

6. *Michaelmas:* the date, September 28, that would bring Bethel's term of office to an end; then he would pass on the emblem of the office, the gold chain, to one of the new sheriffs.

7. *cuerpo:* body, substance (Spanish); i.e., unadorned.

8. *Office of Executioner:* in his *Vindication* (1681), Bethel reports that he was accused of being one of the executioners of King Charles I; in reply he asserts that he was in Hamburg at that time (1637–1649) and that he is, in any case, "too great a spirit" for such a lowly post.

9. *Un-Burgessed:* i.e., he lost the election for burgess or M.P. from Southwark.

10. *Court of Aldermen:* in his *Vindication,* Bethel bitterly complains of the rejection by the aldermen of his nomination to be one of their number.

11. *Other Sheriff:* Henry Cornish (d. 1685).

12. *Span-Farthing:* a game played with farthings.

13. *plays Booty:* acts falsely in order to gain an objective.

14. *Proverb:* "Old men and far travelers may lie with authority." Bethel was sixty-four at this time.

15. *Linen:* i.e., the graveclothes (for burying the memory of his "pranks").

16. *his first Paragraph:* in which Bethel declares, "I deserve the reproach of no Man."

17. *Staple:* a market town or commercial center.

How could he *reasonably hope* to survive all those who are able to justifie to his Face the Truth of what they had related, when he should have the Confidence to deny it ? How could he *reasonably hope*, that Factious and Turbulent Practices should not deserve to be punish'd at least with *Reproach* and *Infamy* ? How could he *reasonably hope*——But that I may encourage Modesty, especially in such a one as He, for the fake of that blushing Parenthesis, I will spare him at present, till he give me further occasion to deal more roughly with him.

From his private Station, which I cannot allow to extend any farther than to his Continuance at *Hamburgh* : For after his Return into *England*, he himself acknowledges, that he did embrace Civil Offices ; and 'tis well known, that he was always edging himself in to make one in all the late shiftings of the Scene, and the Continuator of *Bakers Chronicle* attests him to have been nominated one   18 of the *Councellors of State*, who were to abjure the Family of the *Stuarts*, and all Kingly Government ; but these things it was his Interest to dissemble and conceal ; and therefore I say, from his *Private Station*, as he calls it, he immediately passes to the time of his being chosen a Sheriff of *London* and *Middlesex* ; and because I resolve to keep up close with him, I must e'en take the same Leap too.

He tells us he was call'd forth by his Fellow Citizens to a Publick Employment, (meaning the Shrievalty) *contrary to his Inclinations and Humor*, which indeed is both true and false : 'Tis very true it was *contrary to his Inclination and Humor*, to be at the Charge and Expence which usually attends the Execution of that Office, as the Event has sufficiently shewn; but that it was *contrary to his Inclination and Humor* to have in his Hands the Power of doing Mischief, which accompanies it, is as false : For otherwise, why should he take the Sacrament, according to the Rites of the Church of *England*, the Oath of   19 Allegiance, *&c.* (about which he and his Conscience were not agreed for Twenty Years before) merely to qualifie himself for that Employment, when 'tis probable the Court of Aldermen would rather have given him Money to be rid of him, than insisted upon any high Fine to excuse him.   •   20

Well, Mr. *Bethel* is Sheriff of *London* and *Middlesex*, and would have been a Burgess of *Southwark* : And what then ? Why then he falls a complaining most bitterly of his hard Fate, that he can no sooner leave his *Private Station*, and stand in Competition for Places of great Honor and Trust, but presently men enquire whether he be fit to be trusted ? and search into the History of his Life, and slander him with all the matter of Truth that they can collect. And is it not a most sad and deplorable Case, that a man of his Bulk and Character, who comes and says upon his Word, that he is as honest, and wise, and every way as fit to be our Representative as any man we can chuse, should be so contemptuously repulsed and baulked as he was by a company of inquisitive and unconfiding Burghers?

And now that by chance I have mention'd Mr. *Bethel*, and Honesty, and Wisdom in one Paragraph, I cannot but take notice of the extraordinary Cast he gives us of both, in his assuming the Honor of being one of our Representatives, and making one great reason of Writing this Vindication of his to be , That those of the *Neighbouring Borough may not be thought to have been mistaken and deceived in the Person whom they preferred to a place of so great Trust*, p. 2. Was it *honest* in him to insinuate to the World, That he had been chosen a Burgess for *Southwark*, when he was excluded by a considerable Majority, and those more considerable for their Quality than Number ? It being highly probable, that the misled men who crowded for him, might as easily have been persuaded to give their Votes for *John Doe* and

B   *Richard*

---

18. *Bakers Chronicle:* see *Vox Populi*, p. 166. In 1660, Bethel was appointed one of the ten non-parliamentary members of the Council of State.

19. *The Sacrament:* Bethel and Cornish were disqualified after their election because, as dissenters, they had not taken the Anglican sacrament within the past year as required by the Test Act of 1673. Subsequently they took the required sacrament and were reelected.

20. *Fine:* if a man elected as sheriff declined to serve, he was fined £400.

Richard Roe. And was it *wife* for him to tell us in Print, that we had elected him, when we knew we had not? No, No, Mr. *Bethel,* such Tricks will not do with us. We that opposed you, are satisfied, that we were not (as you say well) *miftaken and deceived* in you; and Multitudes of those, who through a Blind Zeal appear'd for you, are now enlightened and convinced that they were miftaken : So that I would advife you, as a Friend, that, if when His Majefty fhall be pleas'd to Summon another Parliament, you find the fame hankering after a Memberfhip continue upon you, you would apply your felf to fome other Borough, where you are lefs known than here.

Having acquainted us, to our Amazement, that he was our Burgefs, he proceeds next (with a Confiftency peculiar to himfelf) to let the World know the Obftacles which hindred him from being fo. He fays, That to difable him from holding any Place of fo great Truft, *It was objected that he was a Papift and a Jefuit; and that upon fome Variance happening between him and Dr. Oates, he did declare, that he knew him beyond the Seas to be fuch; that he was a Souldier in the Parliament's Army, in the time of the late Wars, and was moft cruel and unmerciful in the Exercife of Arms; that being at Hamburgh at fuch time as the Late King's Death was refolved on in* England, *he did there fay, That rather than he fhould want an* Executioner, *he would come thence to perform the Office; and that he was not only one of the Late Kings Judges, but one of thofe two perfons in Vizzards, that affifted on the Scaffold at his Death.*

To each of thefe Articles he fays fomething, which he hoped, no doubt, would look like an Anfwer; but the whole amounts only to this, that he ftifly denies 'em all.

But if none of thefe things were true, how comes it to pafs, that after he had boafted under *Article 3. p. 3.* That he has brought his Action at Law for the Vindication of himfelf in that point, he fhould yet drop that Action with two more of the fame Nature; and that the Profpect of 30000*l.* (for fo much he laid his Damage) fhould not be fufficient to encourage him to be at the common charge of the Law to go on with them? Whence fhould arife fo much Smoak if there were no Fire? How did it chance that the reft of the Competitors had not the like Brands of Infamy faftened upon them? Whence did it proceed that all the Dirt of the City and Town fhould be thrown into his Cart? Certainly he is one of the moft unfortunate Men that ever left *Private Station,* if he be innocent.

That he is Innocent, we have only his own Word, and how far that ought to weigh, we may judge from what follows in his next Paragraph, concerning a Paper, Publifhed foon after the Election, entituled , *How* and *Rich,* &c. 21 (which by the way I obferve lies very heavy upon his Stomach) out of which Scandalous Libel, as he calls it, he unluckily felects that Paffage between him and Mr. *Mafon,* one of the King's Watermen, who, when Mr. *Bethel* threatned to *pull his Coat over his Ears,* replied, *Ay Sir, fo perhaps you would my Mafter's too, if it were in your Power.* This Mr. *Bethel* declares to be moft notorioufly falfe, and without any Color or Ground of Truth, *p.* 4.

There lying now fo much Strefs upon Mr. *Bethel's* Veracity, we will bring the Cafe to a fhort Iffue : If no fuch words paffed at the time and place of the Poll between thofe two Gentlemen, then I will take Mr. *Bethel's* bare Denial of the foregoing Articles, to be a juft Vindication. But to fee how Time will bring things to light! It happen'd, that on *Wednefday, June* the 29th. 1681. a General Seffions of the Peace being then holden for the Borough of *Southwark,* at the *Bridge-houfe-hall,* by the Lord *Mayor* and *Aldermen* of *London,* and Mr. Sheriff

---

21. *How and Rich:* an account of the Southwark election hostile to Bethel (1681).

riff *Bethel* being there prefent, an Indictment was exhibited againft him upon the occafion of thefe words, together with the foul Battery that accompanied them; and the Battery and Words were proved by the Oaths of four fubftantial Witnefles, and the Bill accordingly found by the Grand Jury. Now I leave the Reader to judge, whether he that will Print a Lye, to wipe off a fmart *Repartee*, is likely to boggle at faying, or un-faying any thing to bring himfelf off in Matters of fo heynous a Nature as the Articles contain. **22**

Having hitherto put on as good and as bold a Face as the former matters required, he next proceeds to fome Exceptions of a lefs dangerous Nature, that have been made againft him; and expreffing a wonderful Glee, that the Laws of the Land do not make Covetoufnefs a Capital Crime, he becomes now unconcern'd, and cares not much if it be admitted to be wholly true, that he is an Inmate, a Garreteer, and all that: For he hopes this will be no good Exception in the Cafe of a Burgefs to ferve in Parliament; telling us it is a *Maxim, That thofe that are moft faving of their own Eftates, will be moft careful of the Peoples*; thereby unhandfomly infinuating, that a Parliament-Man is only a kind of *Padlock*, for fecuring the Peoples Money, whatever juft occafion there may be to part with it: But pray Mr. *Bethel*, come no more among us with your fordid *Maxims*, 'tis well known, that we have better *Maxims* of our own; and you may fee by all the Papers we have Publifhed fince you gave us the laft Trouble, that this *Maxim* is like to do you but little Service with us. In *How* and *Rich*, you will find, that one part of the Character which recommended thofe Gentlemen to our Choice, was, *That they were Liberal Benefactors to the Poor of our Borough*. In our Addrefs to them at their fetting forth towards *Oxford*, we declare it our Opinion, *That it is highly reafonable that we fhould help to defray the Charge, as well as enjoy the Benefit of His Majefties Gracious Government and Protection*; and in our Addrefs to His Majefty, upon the Occafion of his late Declaration, we humbly affure His Majefty, *That whenever His Majefty in his Princely Wifdom and Providence, fhall fee fit to call another Parliament, we will take all poffible care to chufe fuch Reprefentatives as fhall be ready to prefent His Majefty with fuch Supplies as the Dignity of the Crown, and the Neceffities of the Government fhall require*. By this Mr. *Bethel*, you may judge, that your Temper and ours do not at all agree, and you may reft fatisfied, that the Borough of *Southwark* will never be guilty of fo great a Blunder, as to fend to the Parliament fuch a Mif-reprefentative as your felf. **23** **24**

The Subject of the following part of his *Pamphlet* is very pleafant and diverting; and with (or indeed without) Mr. Sheriff's Leave, that the Reader may know what Entertainment he is to expect, I fhall give him the following Bill of Fare. 1. Here is the Grandeur of living in a Garret. 2. The Hofpitality of keeping no Houfe; and, 3. The Charity of Starving Poor Prif'ners. But you will fay, thefe are all empty Difhes: Why truly if they be, I cannot help it, they are fuch as Mr. Sheriff's Table and Book afford.

For unlefs you will allow Mr. *Bethel* the Titles of Great, and Hofpitable, and Charitable, in fpite of that Contradiction which his Actions give to them all, there is nothing which he fays for himfelf, that can give him any fhadow or color of Right to either.

Indeed, to vindicate his Honor from the Difparagement of living in a Garret, he fays, That to avoid the Trouble and Inconveniency, which commonly attends the Shifting of Lodgings, he took the Houfe he now lives in; but fuch a Houfe it is, as is rarely to be feen in the City of *London*: For this Houfe has neither Garrets nor Cellars, nor Rooms on the firft Floor; fo that either he muft acknowledge himfelf to have taken only fome Rooms of an Houfe, and confe- **25**

---

22. *foul Battery:* Bethel was accused of striking Robert Mason, a king's waterman, and of trying to drive him out of the polling place. He was convicted and fined.

23. *Inmate:* a lodger. Bethel was accused of living in a garret and keeping no table (sheriffs customarily entertained the citizens lavishly, so that they often spent several thousand pounds during their year in office). Bethel denied the garret, describing his lodgings in considerable detail, but he admitted his parsimony and defended it—see below.

24. *late Declaration: His Majesties Declaration;* see p. 205 of this volume.

25. *Rooms:* Bethel reported that he had rented for the past ten years a house in London; he occupied the entire structure except for the garret, the cellars, and one small room on the first floor.

consequently to be an Inmate, or else he must be suppos'd to live in a *Wird-mill*; for there is no other sort of House that I can think of, which answers that Description.

He goes on to tell us what I would not for a World should be omitted by the Writer of his Life; That at the Beginning of his Year, he kept two Feasts, of Famous Memory, to his great Charge: Nay, that he had agreed for a fair large Inn (much better, and more capacious than the *other House*) and had resolv'd to keep a plentiful Ordinary, and for one Year round, to live as merry as mine Host; but, as he says, it fell out unluckily to this purpose, that the Ancient, Wise, Prudent, Sumptuary Laws of the City, lighting hard upon his Conscience, and a Repulse received from the Court of Aldermen, sticking fast in his Gizzard; these two Accidents gave such a Check to his Natural Complacency, that he presently un-resolved all again, and has not been in an Entertaining Humor ever since.   26   27

As for the former of these Accidents, I shall only make this Remark upon it, That of all Laws, Mr. Sheriff *Bethel* has most diligently enquired into, and most religiously obferv'd the Sumptuary Laws, they being (as he obferves) *most wholesome* for the Pocket: Though I cannot imagine those Laws do forbid any Person to exceed a Nine-penny Dinner fo strictly, as not to allow him the Liberty of an *Orange* with his Plate of Veal; and yet this is a Law which a Renowned Citizen (who to avoid the ungrateful Repetition of the same word too often, shall be namelefs) has for a certain enacted to himself.

For the latter, I have obliged my self to give an account of it, fo far as the Ward which return'd him is concern'd, and it is briefly thus: The Alderman of the Ward of *Farindon Without*, dying, the Principal Inhabitants, upon Conference with one another, found themselves divided in their Opinions, concerning the Superiority of Merit between Sir *Richard How* and Mr. *Pilkinton*, and yet resolv'd, if possible, to have one of them. Of this indeed they might have been certain, if they had return'd them two; but it is to be considered, that then there had been no Tryal of Skill between their two Parties; and also that being both worthy Men, either of them which should be assign'd to that Office, would have feem'd to be the Court of Aldermen's Choice, rather than theirs: Hereupon. to leave as little fcope as might be to the Court of Aldermen, for the exercise of their Prerogative, both parties confented to return Mr. Sheriff *Bethel* for one, as knowing him to be a person fo un-acceptable to that Court, that they might be sure of him of the other two, to whom it should fall by the Decision of their own Votes. So that that Gentleman who loft it at the Poll, had more respect shewn him by the Ward, than he who carried it without a Poll; and they unanimously agreed to chuse Mr. *Bethel*, because they knew they were in no Danger of being troubled with him. And now Sir, much Joy to you of the Honor of that *General Consent*, and the *concurrent Votes* which you fo highly boast of.   28   29

Now, becaufe the Court of Aldermen had discovered a Dislike of his Company, he therefore resolves and declaims against House-keeping; and groundlefly mifplacing his Anger, falls foul upon the Innocent; and without any Provocation in the Earth, does vent fuch undeferved Reproaches, and bitter Invectives against all the Dishes of a Generous Sheriff's Table, even from Roft-Beef to Cuftard, that certainly it is his Interest to diffuade all men from reading his Book till they have Dined: For no Hungry Stomach can with Patience bear, to have its good Friends and Allies fo vilely abufed.

He says, that nothing can be lefs Honourable to the Sheriffs than Feasting of the Companies, that good Eating is a great Expence of time, and a plentiful   30
Table

---

26. *Ordinary:* a public meal regularly provided at a tavern or eating house.

27. *Sumptuary Laws:* limiting "Extravagance of Entertainments"; by this time, all such laws in England had been repealed.

28. *Sir Richard How:* sheriff of London in 1678, when he received his knighthood. London sheriffs were normally knighted, but Charles made an exception in the case of Bethel and Cornish.

29. *Mr. Pilkinton:* Thomas Pilkington (d. 1691) was to succeed Bethel as one of the sheriffs elected for the following year.

30. *Companies:* the guilds of London.

an Enemy to that *sober Industry which is the rise and glory of a Trading City*; as if a sober industrious Trader, who intended to thrive and grow wealthy, were obliged now and then to satisfie himself with the refreshment of sucking a Button, and be glad to take up with the smell of a Cooks shop instead of a Meal. Beef and Mutton defend us! say I : If this man were Manciple, he would within the compass of a Week so effectually promote his Landlords Trade, as to deserve to sit Rent-free; for within that time our Bellies would dwindle and grow so lank, that happy were he who could get a Taylor to adjust the Wast-band of his Breeches.

Being destitute of any farther Arguments to put a colour upon his sordid way of living in so publick an Employment, he falls to his Prayers to God, that among other Sins , *Fulness of Bread, which was charged upon* Sodom *and* Jerusalem, *as one Cause of Gods Judgments, may not grow to that height in this City, as to become the Ruin and Destruction of it.* I do not love to jest in Serious Matters, and shall therefore only take notice, that there are certain Citizens under his Custody, who, through his Neglect, are able truly to plead Not Guilty to that Charge. Had Mr. Sheriff *Bethel* fed the Poor, instead of Feasting the Rich; had he supply'd the Defect of Splendid Entertainments by an extraordinary Charity towards his Prisoners, he might have had a fairer Plea: But he himself, without blushing, grants it to be true, that he does not contribute to the Relief of their Necessities, and has so utterly renounc'd all Modesty, as boldly to undertake to prove it his Duty to be unmerciful. For mark you me, by putting a Stop to the usual Payments; If any Prisoners be famish'd this Year, the Court of Aldermen, and a Committee of the City will take care to prevent the like Mischief against the next : And my holding of my Hand, says he, will prevail with others to open theirs, and encourage them to Chrritable Benevolences and Legacies, for the Maintenance of those wretched People. *Heavens* , what Arguments are these! But such a man can never be defended but by such *Logic.*

I shall now trouble the Reader no further, after I have told him that I am a Person not at all delighted in enquiring after, or exposing and publishing the Vices or Follies of any man ; and, as probably I had never known that he has been reported to be a Jesuite, one of the late Kings Judges, *&c.* unless he himself had told me; so the World had never known for me, that his carriage towards his own Company of *Leather-Sellers* has been such, that they have thought fit, contrary to their usual Method of Proceeding, to wave his *Merit of Congruity* in their late Election of a Master, notwithstanding that he is present Sheriff of *London* : That a Person who might have escap'd a troublesome, and (to any but himself) a Chargeable Office, by swearing that he was not worth 10000 *l.* should yet (to come off for a Shilling, at the time of the last *Poll-Tax*) give order to a Maid-Servant, to acquaint the Officers, that he was a *Decayed Merchant*; That when he knew the *Easter* Sermons were to be at S. *Sepulchres*, he should yet perversly make a Ridiculous Cavalcade to the *Spittle* by himself, like the Pied Piper of *Halberstadt* drawing all the Boys and Girls in the Town after him. These things, I say, with all which has gone before, I should not have concern'd my self to Publish, had he not provoked me to enquire concerning him, and by lewdly applying a Text of Scripture to himself, with a seeming, mighty Confidence of his own Innocence, challeng'd all the World *to Come down and see.*

F I N I S.

250

31. *Manciple:* an officer or servant who purchases provisions.

32. *usual Payments:* the sheriffs were expected to give money to aid poor prisoners; Bethel admits that he did not do this. His reason, he declared, was that he wished to stimulate prison reform (*Vindication*, pp. 8–9). However, in October 1681, weeks after his term as sheriff ended, he did contribute, as a private citizen, several hundred pounds for the relief of poor prisoners.

33. *Merit of Congruity:* in the *Vindication* (p. 6), Bethel cites this "Papist Doctrine" to justify his claim that he should have been elected to the Board of Aldermen instead of Pilkington. This scholastic doctrine contends that one's good works oblige God to confer merit upon one in a certain equality of proportion to their performance. Thus Bethel argues that he should have been chosen, not because he was more worthy than Pilkington, but because his nomination made him more naturally fit—or bestowed on him the Merit of Congruity—for the office.

34. *10000£:* if a merchant could swear that he was not worth £10,000, then he might decline the shrievalty without paying the fine.

35. *St. Sepulchres:* the church nearest Newgate prison; there prayers were said and bells rung for prisoners on their way to execution.

36. *Cavalcade to the Spittle:* on Easter Sunday, the custom was for the children of Christ's Hospital for Orphans and Foundlings to follow the mayor and aldermen to Christ's Church, Spittlefields, where a sermon was delivered on charity.

37. *Text of Scripture:* Genesis 18:21. Upon hearing of the sins of Sodom, God says, "I will go down now, and see. . . ." Bethel asks his readers to investigate his case before condemning him.

251

PART EIGHT

Literary Antecedents

Absalom's Conspiracy; or,
The Tragedy of Treason (1680)

By the time Dryden wrote Absalom and Achitophel, the parallel of the Biblical story of David to that of Charles II was already well established in sermons and poems. In 1627, Nathaniel Carpenter's *Achitophel, or the Picture of a Wicked Politician,* three sermons preached at Oxford, made use of the Biblical story to establish the type of the evil counselor. Comparisons of King Charles to David were common earlier in the Restoration, and Monmouth's likeness to Absalom in his rebellion did not escape notice once he began to oppose his father. Richard F. Jones, in "The Originality of *Absalom and Achitophel*" (*Modern Language Notes* 46 [1931], 211–18), has identified many of these references. *Absalom's Conspiracy* (1680), reprinted here, makes a very close analogy in the way Dryden does and for the same political purpose.

₁ˢᵗ.

Abſalom's Conſpiracy;

OR, THE

TRAGEDY

OF

TREASON.

Againſt the   *1ˢᵗ July. 1680:*   *Duke of monmouth.*

THere is nothing ſo dangerous either to Societies in General, or to particular Perſons, as Ambition; the Temptations of Sovereignty, and the glittering Luſtre of a Crown, have been guilty of all the fearful Conſequences that can be within the compaſs of imagination: For this, Mighty Nations have been drown'd in Blood, populous Cities have been made deſolate, laid in Aſhes, and left without Inhabitants: For this, Parents have loſt all the ſenſe and tenderneſs of Nature; and Children, all the Sentiments of Duty and Obedience; the Eternal Laws of Good and Juſt, the Laws of Nature and of Nations, of God and Religion, have been violated; Men have been transformed into the cruelty of Beaſts, and into the Rage and Malice of Devils.

Inſtances both Modern and Ancient of this, are innumerable; but this of *Abſalom* is a Tragedy whoſe Antiquity and Truth, do equally recommend it as an Example to all Poſterity, and a Caution to all Mankind; to take care how they imbarque in ambitious and unlawful Deſigns; and it is a particular Caveat to all young men, to beware of ſuch Counſellors, as the old *Achitophel*, leſt while they are tempted with the hopes of a Crown, they haſten on their own Deſtiny, and come to an untimely End.   1

Abſalom was the third Son of *David* by *Maachah*, the Daughter of *Talmai*, King *D of monm.* of *Geſhur*; who was one of *David*'s Concubines; he ſeeing his Title to the Crown *of m of walers.* upon the ſcore of lawful Succeſſion would not do, reſolves to make good what was defective in it, by open force, by dethroning his Father.

Now the Arts he uſed to accompliſh his Deſign, were theſe: Firſt, He ſtudied Popularity; he roſe up early; he was induſtrious and diligent in his way; he placed himſelf in the way of the Gate; and when any man came for Judgment, he courteouſly entred into Diſcourſe with him. This feigned Condeſcention, was the firſt Step of his Ambition. Secondly, He depraved his Fathers Government;   2 the King was careleſs, drown'd in his Pleaſures; the Counſellors were evil; no no man regarded the Petitioners; *Abſalom* ſaid unto him, See thy matters are good and right, it is but reaſon that you petition for; but there is no man that will hear thee from the King; there is no Juſtice to be found; your Petitions are rejected. Thirdly, He inſinuates what he would do if he were in Authority; how eaſie acceſs ſhould be to him; he would do them Juſtice; he would hear and redreſs their Grievances, receive their Petitions, and give them gracious

A An-

---

1. *Absalom:* cf. II Samuel 13:19.
2. *depraved:* disparaged.

Answers. *Oh that I were made Judge in the Land, that every Man might come unto me, and I would do him Justice.* And when any man came to do him Obeysance, he put forth his hand, and took him, and kissed him: And thus he stole away the Hearts of the People from their Lawful King, his Father and Sovereign.

d Shaftsbury. But all this would not do ; he therefore joyns himself to one *Achitophel*, an old Man of a Shrewd Head, and discontented Heart. This *Achitophel*, it seems, had been a great Councellour of *David's* ; but was now under some Disgrace, as appears, by *Absalom's* sending for him from *Gilo*, his City whither he was in discontent retreated ; because *David* had advanced *Hushai* into his Privy Council ; and no doubt can be made, but he was of the Conspiracy before, by his ready joyning with *Absalom* so soon as the matters were ripe for Execution.

Absalom having thus laid his Train, and made secret Provision for his intended Rebellion, dispatches his Emissaries abroad, to give notice by his Spies, that all the Confederates should be ready at the sound of the Trumpet, say, *Absalom Reigneth in* Hebron ; and immediately a great Multitude was gathered to him: For the the Conspiracy was strong ; some went out of Malice, and some in their simplicity followed him, and knew not any thing.

David is forced to fly from his own Son ; but still he had a Loyal Party that stuck close to him : *Achitophel* gave devilish Counsel, but God disappointed it strangely : For *Hushai* pretending to come over to their Party, put *Absalom* upon a plausible expedient. which proved his Ruine. So impossible is it for Treason to be secure, that no person who forms a Conspiracy, but there may be some, who under pretence of the greatest kindness, may insinuate themselves, only to discover their Secrets, and ruine their Intentions, either by revealing their Treason, or disappointing it ; and certainly, of all men, Traytors are least to be trusted: For they who can be perfidious to one, can never be true to any.

The Matter comes at last to the decision of the Sword. *Absalom's* Party are defeated, and many slain, and *Absalom* himself seeking to save himself by flight in the Wood, is entangled in a Tree, by his own Hair, which was his Pride ; and his Mule going from under him, there left him hanging, till *Joab* came, and with three Darts, made at once an end of his Life and the Rebellion. Thus ended his youthful and foolish Ambition, making him an Eternal Monument of Infamy, and an instance of the Justice of Divine Vengeance, and what will be the Conclusion of Ambition, Treason and Conspiracy against Lawful Kings and Governours ; A severe Admonition to all green Heads, to avoid the Temptations of grey *Achitophels*.

Achitophel the Engineer of all this Mischief, seeing his Counsel despised, and foreseeing the Event, prevented the hand of the Executioner, and in revenge upon himself, went home and hanged himself, giving fair warning to all treacherous Councellors, to see what their Devilish Counsels will lead them to at last: Mischievous Counsel ever falling in Conclusion upon the Heads where first it was contrived, as naturally as dirty Kennels fall into the Common-Sewer.

Whatsoever was written aforetime, was written for our Instruction: For Holy Men of God, spake as they were moved by the Holy Ghost.

F I N I S.

London, Printed in the Year, 1680.

---

3. Hushai: perhaps Danby or Halifax; cf. Dryden, who uses this name for Lawrence Hyde in *Absalom and Achitophel*.

John Caryll's
Naboth's Vinyard:
Or, The Innocent Traytor (1679)

Studies of the poetry occasioned by the Popish Plot and the Exclusion
Crisis should probably begin with volume 2 of *Poems on Affairs of State*,
ed. Elias F. Mengel, Jr. (New Haven: Yale University Press, 1965). This
volume contains a great number of the verse satires that appeared
between 1678 and 1681, together with full commentary and excellent
illustrations. Of the varied productions from both camps, *Naboth's Vinyard*, by John Caryll, is surely one of the most interesting for the study
of Dryden. Like *Absalom and Achitophel*, it uses an elaborate Biblical
parallel in order to criticize Oates and other supporters of the plot.
And like Dryden, Caryll puts his narrative into couplets and combines
dramatic scenes and speeches with satiric portraits of the characters
and the poet's own impassioned commentary.

John Caryll (1625–1711) was a member of the Roman Catholic
gentry, a playwright, translator, and a man of letters. In 1679 he was
committed to the Tower on suspicion of complicity in the plot, but, as
there turned out to be only one witness against him, he was soon freed
on bail. (English law required two witnesses to convict in cases of high
treason.) He may well have written *Naboth's Vinyard* while in prison. At
the Revolution in 1688, he followed James II into exile, and was created
Baron Caryll of Dunford by the Old Pretender, James's son, in 1701.
The John Caryll to whom Pope dedicated *The Rape of the Lock* was his
nephew.

Compared to Dryden's masterpiece, *Naboth's Vinyard* may seem
weak enough, lacking as it does the verbal density, wit, and intensity
of the later poem. Its chief flaw is Caryll's inability to make the political
situation in England fit the Biblical parallel except in a few particulars.
Ahab, Jezibel, and even Naboth himself have no English counterparts.
And it is awkward, considering his Tory sympathies, that in this story
the king and queen are the villains.

Still, the poem is not to be despised. Amid many weak lines, there
are some strong ones; the whole is clear and fundamentally dramatic,
as are the speeches, which are in the style of Restoration heroic plays.
Caryll effectively contrasts the pretended piety of his villains with their
immoral deeds. His use of the imagery of poison, such as line 177,
where Arod "pour'd venom in her ear" (borrowed possibly from Clau-
dius's action in *Hamlet*) is effective—and may have been remembered
by Dryden, when Achitophel "sheds his venom" (l. 229) in Absalom's

ear. In fact Dryden may have taken a number of hints from Caryll, including the device of ending with a prophecy of the doom that awaits the evil-doers, instead of carrying on the story to their actual destruction.

Further, though it is written by an accused Catholic, Caryll's poem maintains a moderate tone. His enmity is directed toward corrupt witnesses (Oates and Bedloe as Malchus and Python) and partial judges (Scroggs as Arod). Like Dryden, he also condemns the "fierce rabble" who are eager for blood. Yet while he lashes "These vipers in the bosom of our law," his poem is free of religious intolerance or fanatic political zeal. He concentrates his attack on corrupt individuals who, for personal gain, condemn an innocent man. His indignation comes through with firmness and dignity.

Naboth's Vinyard:

OR, THE

INNOCENT

TRAYTOR:

COPIED from the ORIGINAL

OF

Holy Scripture,

IN

HEROICK VERSE

Si fractus illabatur Orbis,
Impavidam ferient Ruinæ. Hor.

1

LONDON, Printed for *C.R.* 1679.

---

1. *Hor:* The shatter'd World may strike him dead,
   Not touch his Soul with Fear.
   —Horace, *Carmina* (Odes), III.3.7–8; translation by William Walsh in
   Odes and Satires of Horace (1715), p. 85.

Naboth's Vinyard.

FLY hence thofe *Siren*-Charms of *Wealth* and *Power*,
 Strong to undo, unable to reftore;
At firft they tickle, but at laft they fmart,
They pleafe the Pallat, and corrode the Heart:
To thofe gay *Idols*, which fond men adore,
Our *Chriftian* Mufe all *Incenfe* does abhor :
Idols ! (like hungry *Moloch*) whofe dire *Food*   2
Too often is fupply'd by *Humane Blood !*

 That precious *Juice* which can, with Soveraign Balm,
The War and Ferment of our Nature calm ;
That can the Anguifh of our Minds allay,
Heal Wounds of Grief, and Storms of Paffion fway ;
That generous Off-fpring of the healing Vine,
I'th' Mufes *Temple* may deferve a Shrine.

 But, hold, 'tis not the *Wine* of common *draught*,
Which *Palma* fends, or greedy Merchants *waft*   3
From *Rhenifh* Banks, or from the *Gafcon* Shore,
T'enrich themfelves, and make the Drinkers poor ;
Poor in their wafted 'ftates, poor in their Mind,
Who in a *Brutifh Club* with Swine are join'd,
And greateft joy in ftupefaction find :
No, our exalted Tafte difdains to feaft
On that dull *Liquor*, which turns *Man* to *Beaft.*

B   It

---

2. *Moloch:* a Semitic deity to whom children were often sacrificed as burnt of-
ferings.
3. *Palma:* in the Canary Islands; along with areas noted in the following line, it
is known for the production of wine.

It muſt be nouriſht with ſome ſpritely *Juice*,
Which does our mortal Frame immortaliſe;
Defies the Arrows of malicious Fate,
The People's Fury, and the Tricks of State.

Quickly, ah! quickly then, (my Muſe) diſcloſe
The happy place, where this true *Nectar* grows.
Is it not *Naboth's Vinyard*? Fame ſpeaks loud
Of thee, but louder of thy Maſter's *blood*;
That *Hero's Blood*, fed by thy *vital Juice*,
Which did, when flowing in his Veins, deſpiſe
The Womans Craft, the Tyrants Avarice;
The bloody Oaths of perjur'd Aſſaſſins;
The Frowns of byas'd Juſtice, which inclines
The giddy Rabble to their Natural bent,
With tongues, and hands to tear the *Innocent*.

1 Kings　　Achab had conquered *Aram*; but, alas!　　4
c 20.v.29
v. 42.　His very Conqueſt his Undoing was:
He ſoon forgot the Hand, which did beſtow
Edge on his Sword, and Lawrel on his Brow.
Proud with the Spoils of the ſlain *Aramites*,
v.13.28. The Power, which gave him Victory, he ſlights:
v. 34. He *treats*, and *bargains* with his Enemies,
And all the *Covenants* of his Lord defies.
Achab diſtreſt, bow'd to his Lord, and pray'd;
Achab victorious, proudly disobey'd;
Ungrateful Mortals! whoſe corrupted Will
Turns Grace to Poyſon, and makes Bleſſings kill.
In vain poor Subjects in the Juſtice truſt
Of *Kings*, that to their *Maker* are unjuſt:

The

---

4. *Achab:* Ahab, the Biblical story is in I Kings 16–20.

The Heart once tainted with a *Mafter-Sin*,
All *leffer Crimes* does eafily let in.

   Poor *Naboth*'s *Vinyard* next lies in his way,   *Chap.21. v. 2.*
His covetous Eye had markt it for his Prey :
He parly'd firft ; but what he could not worm
By *Treaty* from him, he refolv'd to *ftorm*.

   " How (Sir!) can you think worthy your large Soul,
" To crave my fpot of Land, my fleeping-hole ?
" (Says *Naboth*) I my felf fhould prize it not,
" Were it not facred made by *Age* and *Lot* ;   *v. 3.*   5
" By *Lot* confign'd to my Fore-fathers hand,
" Who firft with *Jofhua* feis'd this *Holy Land* :
" 'Twere *Sacriledge* in me to give, or fell,
" What to my *Name* by *Heaven's Appointment* fell.
" May *Achab* his large *Kingdoms* long poffefs ;
" Let *Naboth* his fmall *Vinyard* hold in peace.
Achab was filent, but not fatisfy'd ;   *v. 4.*
The covetous Poyfon through his Veins did glide :
And what his greedy *Eye* and *Heart* devour,
He will extort by an Ufurping Power.

   So have I feen the tow'ring Falcon rife,
And next to nothing leffen to our Eyes,
Beyond the Call of any Game, or Lure ;
The timerous *Fowl* fuch diftance can endure ;
But ill they meafure by their own, the fight,
And fharpnefs of their Tyrants Appetite :
She fports and plys her Wings i'th' liquid air,
As if fhe minded Pleafure, and not War :
But when the *Fowl*, betray'd by flattering hopes,
Takes wing, the *watchful Foe*, as *Lightning* ftoops ;
                             What

---

5. *Lot:* inheritance.

What her *Eye* mark'd, her *Talons* make her own;
As Thunder-ſtruck the Quary tumbles down.

But ill did *Achabs* Eyes, with all their Art,
Cover the ſecret rancour of his Heart:
The Wound did feſter, that his Paſſion made,
Which ſoon his Face unwillingly betray'd.

v. 5. Firſt *Jezabel* deſcry'd his ſecret pain;
My Lord (ſhe ſaid) can your breaſt entertain
A Grief or Joy but what I muſt partake?
O, do not this unkind diſtinction make.
Shame to reveal, and greater ſhame to hide
His Soul from her, his troubled thoughts divide:
At laſt he pour'd his Grief into the Ear
Of his too kind, and fatal Counſeller.

In vain (my Dear) our Scepter does command
From the *North-Sea* to the *Arabian Sand*,
In vain the *Kings* of *Aram* are my *Slaves*;
In vain my *Juſtice* kills, my *Mercy* ſaves,
v. 6. If ſtubborn *Naboth* muſt his Vinyard hold
In ſpight of all *Intreaty*, *Power*, and *Gold*;
If a poor Worm of *Iſrael* proudly dares
v. 6. Reſiſt, not my *Commands*, my very *Prayers*.

Tread on that Rebel Worm (ſays *Jezabel*)
The weight of a Kings Anger let him feel;
Cruſh him to nothing; that your Subjects may
Be taught by his Example to obey.

Then *Achab* ſigh'd, and ſaid, That muſt not be,
People and Prieſts would riſe in Mutiny:
Too much we hazard for a thing ſo ſmall;
The *Tyrant-Law*, which *Monarchs* does enthrall,
Controles

Controuls the Execution of my will,
And makes the Slave bold to refist me ftll.

   At this unmoveable ftood *Jezabel*,
Like one faft bound by an Inchanters Spell ;
Her flaming Cheeks had Choller's deepeft dye;   6
And like ftruck Flints fparkled her furious Eye ;
Such heaving, and fuch panting fhook her breaft,
As if fome Spirit had the place poffeft.
Then fuddenly fhe ftarts with a loud Cry ;

   If *Law* muft do the *Work*, *Naboth* fhall dye.
Let not the *Sanhedrim* a *Monarch* awe ;   *v* :. 7
He that commands the *Judge*, commands the *Law*.
Law is a poor, dumb thing, which none can hear,
But by the Mouth of an Interpreter :
And in the Peoples mouth, 'tis the old Plea
For Rebels, when their Prince they difobey.
Fear not the *Law*, but by the *Judge* be fear'd ;
Elfe, as the *Pedants* gravely wag their *Beard*,
Kings muft of their Prerogatives be ftript,
As Children are for breach of Grammar whipt.
Then truft my skill; I'll bring you quick relief,
To heal the wounds of your unfeemly Grief :
Both you, and *Naboth*, your juft Rights fhall have,
You fhall poffefs his *Vineyard*, he his *Grave*,   *v.* 7.

   Thus with her oyly words fhe skins his Sore,
But adds new Poyfon to the ulcerous Core ;
And that falfe Comfort leaves in *Achabs* mind,
Which Villains in their thriving Mifchiefs find.
She fummons then her chofen Inftruments,   *v.* 8.
Always prepar'd to ferve her black Intents :
         C   The

---

6. *Choller:* anger.
7. *Sanhedrim:* the highest Hebrew court and supreme council; parliament.

The chief was *Arod*, whose corrupted youth   8
Had made his Soul an Enemy to truth;
But Nature furnisht him with Parts and wit,
For bold Attempts, and deep Intriguing fit.
Small was his Learning; and his Eloquence
Did please the Rabble, nauseate men of sence.
Bold was his Spirit, nimble and loud his Tongue,
Which more than *Law*, or *Reason*, takes the Throng.
Him, part by *Money*, partly by her *Grace*,
The covetous Queen rais'd to a Judges place:
And, as he bought his *Place*, he *Justice* sold;
Weighing his *Causes* not by *Law*, but *Gold*;
He made the Justice-Seat a common Mart;
Well skill'd he was in the mysterious Art,
Of finding *Varnish* for an unsound Cause,
And for the found *Imaginary Flaws*.

    With him fierce *Jezabel* consults the way
How she for harmless *Naboth* Snares may lay.
Madam (says he) you rightly judge the course
Unsafe, to run him down by open Force.
In great Designs it is the greatest Art,
To make the Common People take your part:
Some words there are, which have a special Charm
To wind their *Fancies* up to an *Alarm*:
Treason, Religion, Liberty, are such;
Like *Clocks* they strike, when on those *Points* you touch;
If some of these unto his Charge you lay,
You hit the *Vein* of their *Tarantala*.   9
For to say truth, the trick did never fail;
Loud Calumny with them does still prevail.

                            I (Ma-

---

    8. *Arod:* Lord Chief Justice Sir William Scroggs; this was written before he became a hero to Catholics after Wakeman was acquitted (see p. 99) in July 1679.
    9. *Tarantala:* a hysterical, whirling dance associated with the bite of the Tarantula spider.

I (Madam) of these means no scruple make;
Means from their *End* their Good or Badness take.
Naboth a *Rebel* to his Soveraign's Will,
By any ways we lawfully may kill.
Whilst thus he pour'd his Venom in her Ear,
A frightful Joy did in her Face appear:
She said, your faithful Counsel I approve,
You have chalkt out the way we are to move:
But still you leave untoucht the hardest part,
Which most requires your Industry and Art;
Where is the *Crime*? where are the *Witnesses*?

It is my Province (Madam) to find these;
(Reply'd the Judge) and that our Project may
Take faster hold, let there a *solemn day*,
To seek the Lord by Fasting and by Prayer,
Be set apart: This will exactly square
With the whole Model of our Work defign'd;
This will the People draw *Body* and *Mind*,
To act their *Parts* in *Naboth's Tragedy*;
This builds the Stage, on which the Wretch shall dye.
As Glasses, by the Sun's reflected Ray,
The silly Lark into the Net betray,
So will the People, by the dazling thought
Of Godliness, religiously be caught.

When the Queen saw that her Design would take,
She with impatient haste the Conference brake;
Of Av'rice and Revenge such is the thirst,
That with the least Delay the Patients burst.
Lose no more time (she cry'd;) with speedy care
Letters and Orders for our Seal prepare,

v. 8.

Such

Such as the Work requires: For 'till I gain
This Point, each Moment is an Age of pain.

    Since first for *acting* God proud Angels fell,
Still to *ape* Heaven has been the *Pride* of Hell:
As the bright Spirits always attend his Throne,
And what he wills, they execute as soon:
Our *Fury* so could not conceive the Fact
More nimbly, than her Agent-*Fiend* did act.

    Stay, Hell-Hounds, stay! why with such rav'nous speed
Must the dear Blood of *Innocence* be shed?
Blind is your *Haste*, and blinder is your *Rage*;
Hell no succefsful War 'gainst Heaven can wage:
You shoot at *Naboth*, but *your selves* you wound
With poyson'd Darts, for which no Cure is found:
The Poyson drawn from a remorselefs Heart,
Baffles *Divine*, much more all *Humane Art*;
What will your Rage effect, but lasting shame,
In this, in the next World Eternal Flame?
With all your subtle Arts of Perjury,
And all the Varnish of your *Bloody Lye*,
To make him Guilty, and you Rightful seem,
Hell for your selves you build, and *Heaven* for him.

    Arod had always *Tools* at his Command,
Of a fit *temper* for his *Work* in hand:
But here no Villains of a common size
In Wickednefs, or Cunning would suffice:
v. 10. Yet two he found, which did as much exceed
All common Rogues, as common Facts this Deed.
Malchus, a puny Levite, void of sence,   10
And Grace, but stuft with Noise and Impudence,

                                          Was

---

10. *Malchus:* Oates.

Was his prime Tool; fo *Venomous* a *Brute*,

That every place, he liv'd in, *fpued him out* ;

Lyes in his Mouth, and Malice in his Heart,

By Nature grew, and were improv'd by Art.

Mifchief his pleafure was ; and all his Joy,

To fee his *thriving Calumny* deftroy

Thofe, whom his double Heart, and forked Tongue,

Surer, than Vipers Teeth, to death had ftung.

Python his *Second* was ; and his alone ;   11

For he in Ills no other *Firft* would own :

A braver Impudence did Arm this Wight ;

He was a *Ruffian*, and no *Hypocrite* ;

And with audacious, and loud Villany,

He did at once *Vertue*, and *Fame* defie.

Thefe two, though *Malchus* wore the longer *Cloak*,

Were *evenly pair'd*, and drew in the fame *Yoke*.

No Forrefters with keener Appetite

In running down their hunted Game delight,

Than thefe the *Slaughter* of the *Guiltlefs* view,

Whom their *Malicious Calumny* purfue.

This goodly Pair were, by their Teachers Art,   *v.* 10.

Fully prepar'd, and tun'd to play their part.

    A Faft is then proclaim'd ; this ferves as *Leaven*

To raife the People's *Lump* with News from Heaven ;

They in the dark, when bid to feek the Lord,

Are fure for His, to take the Preachers word ;

Thefe, when they tole their great *DIANA*-Bell,   12

Look up to Heaven, and do the works of Hell.

Always State-Fafts fome ftrange Events portend ;

And often in a *Godly Mifchief* end.

         D   The

---

11. *Phython:* Bedloe.

12. *DIANA-Bell:* probably for reveille (a morning signal to awaken soldiers); cf. Italian and Spanish *diana*, French *diane*, and English *dian*.

The fair Pretence is, that the Lord may *weed*

v. 10. *Treafon,* and *Blafphemy* from *Abraham's Seed.*

  Great, and juft God! will it be always fo?
When thy Rebellious Creatures here below
Their black Defigns of deepeft Mifchief frame,
Shall they ftill *ftamp* on them thy *holy Name?*
Make thee, *All-good,* a Party in their *Ill!*
Thy very *Word* abufe, to break thy *Will?*
By which their *Leaders* draw the *Vulgar* in,
With *harmlefs Minds,* to perpetrate their *Sin;*
By which the Juft are by the Impious flain,
And *Abel* ftill is facrific'd by *Cain;*
How can thy Juftice, and thy Thunder fleep,
When fuch affronts on thee, and thine, they heap?
How can the Earth forbear with open Jaws
To fwallow thefe Contemners of thy Laws?

  Hold, Mufe! Thy Zeal now grows to *Mutiny;*
Thou doft ignobly from thy *Colours* fly:
Under the *Standard,* of the *Crofs* we ferve,
And from our *Leaders* ways we muft not fwerve.
By *Form of Law* He did fubmit to dye,
Accus'd of *Treafon,* and of *Blafphemy;*
All powerful He, without revenge, or ftrife,
Endur'd the lofs of Honour, and of Life;
This is the way, which he his Followers taught,
Which him to Triumph, us to Safety brought;
Then in this way let us march bravely on,
Which will our *Innocence* with *Glory* Crown;
And let us pity thofe, whom profp'rous Sin
Harden's, and does on *Earth* their *Hell* begin.

          Now

Now comes the Solemn, and the bloody Day,   *v.* 12.
In which all *Israel* meets to faſt, and pray:
But Impious is that Faſt, and Prayer, which parts
From Lips polluted, and from hardned Hearts.

In the firſt rank of *Levites Arod* ſtood,
Court-favour plac'd him there, not Worth, or Blood.
Naboth amongſt the Tribes the foremoſt Place   *v.* 12.
Did with his Riches, Birth, and Vertue grace :
A man, whoſe Wealth was the Poor's common ſtock ;
The Hungry found their Market in his Flock:
His Juſtice made all Law-contentions ceaſe ;
He was his Neighbours ſafeguard, and their Peace.
The Rich by him were in due bounds contain'd ;
The Poor, if ſtrong, imploy'd ; if weak, maintain'd.
Well had he ſerv'd his Country, and his King ;
And the beſt Troops in all their Wars did bring ;
Nor with leſs bravery did he lead them on,
Warding his Country's danger with his own.

Scarce were the Rites, and Ceremonies paſt,
Which by the Law attend their publick Faſt,
When *Malchus* raiſing up his hands and Eyes,   *v.* 13.
With bended knees, thus to the Judges cryes ;
Hear me (great Seed of *Levi*) Hear me all   13
(*Israel*'s ten Tribes) I for your Mercy call ;
Seal me a Pardon, who too long have been
A dark Concealer of a *Crying Sin* ;
Heaven does this day my wounded Conſcience heal,
And bids me the hid Blaſphemy reveal.
Naboth, ſtand forth ; 'Tis thee, of Impious breach   *v.* 13.
Of God's and the Kings Laws, whom I impeach.

      At

---

13. *seed of Levi:* priests.

At this the Tribes a various murmur raife;
His boldnefs fome abhor'd, and fome did praife:
Some would have *Naboth* by a *Publick Vote,*
Without more Fórm, found *Guilty of the Plot.*
Others the Law alledge, that no Offence,
Can be judged fo on fingle Evidence.   14
While thus they waver, *Arod* takes his kew;
Our thanks to Heaven in the firft place are due,
(He faid) which with fuch gracious fpeed prevents
Our Prayers, and all falfe Traytors curft Intents.
Speak *(Malchus)* then, and this Affembly give
Of the whole *Plot* a perfect *Narrative:*
And whilft this fervice you to *Ifrael* do,
Know, that we *hear you, and believe you too.*

    Malchus applauded thus in publick view,
Did now almoft believe, that he fpoke true:
This arm'd his Face with Brafs, his Heart with Steel,
That he no fhame, and no remorfe could feel.
Then he the Story of his Plot at large
Unfolds, and lays to guiltlefs *Naboth's* charge;
How with the *Aramites* he did confpire,   15
His Country to invade, the City fire,

v. 13. The Temple to deftroy, the King to kill,
And the whole Realm with Defolation fill:
He told, how he himfelf the *Agent* was,
In *clofe Confults* to bring thefe things to pafs;   16
Nor did he fail with proper Circumftance
Of Time, and Place, to garnifh his Romance.
The Priefts aftonifht are; the People gaze,
And the dumb Judges horrour does amaze.

                                                         The

---

14. *single Evidence:* under English law, two witnesses were required to prove guilt in cases of treason.

15. *Aramites:* Jesuits (perhaps also the French).

16. *close Consults:* a reference to Oates's accusations about a consult of the Jesuits in April, 1678, where the plot was formulated.

Then out fteps *Python*, and with dextrous Art,
Weaving his Story, feals a Counterpart
To all, that *Malchus* had before depos'd;
And with deep Oaths the Accufation clos'd.

　Now on poor *Naboth* all their Eyes were fet,
Some red with Anger, fome with Pity wet.
But the fierce Rabble gladly would prevent
His *Tryal*, by an inftant *Punifhment*.

　Whence this unnatural Pleafure to deftroy?
From what ill Root grows this malignant Joy?
Beafts worry Beafts, but when their *Hunger* calls;
But Man on Man with a *full Stomach* falls:
'Tis not our Wants of Nature to redrefs,
That we this Rage to our own Kind exprefs;
But for the *Mifchief*'s fake we *Pleafure* find;
It lies not in our *Body*, but our *Mind*.
Our Seed receives a double Taint and Stain,
From Rebel *Adam*, and from murd'ring *Cain*.

　Naboth, thus charg'd, had need for his defence,
Of all his Courage, and his Innocence:
It was a Tryal of no Vulgar Kind,
To fhew th' Heroick temper of his Mind:
But the tranfparent Brightnefs of his Soul,
E'en through his Eyes, their Malice did controul,
For his Accufers, when he fternly view'd,
Their *tortur'd looks* their *rack of Confcience* fhew'd:
But to his Judges, with a manly grace,
He lowly bow'd, and pleaded thus his Cafe.

　My Lords, by thefe falfe Oaths, this bloody Lye,
God and the King are more abus'd, than I;

E　　　　　　　　For

For I (poor Worm) weigh nothing in the Scale,
When their high Wrongs for Reparation call:
When God's dread Name, when his, and the Kings Laws,
Are thus blasphem'd, 'tis their, and not my Cause.
Pharoah, *Goliah*, and that Heathen Brood,
Less impiously blasphem'd our *Soveraign Good*;
They believ'd not his *Being*, nor his *Might*,
And blindly, what they *Nothing* thought, did slight:
These know him, and him knowingly defie;
And signing with his awful Name their Lye,
Make him a *Party* to their *Perjury*.
Nay, in this horrid Enterprise they do
Their curst Endeavour to destroy him too;
For Truth and He in *Essence* so partake,
That when you *make* him *False*, you him *unmake*.

   These Vipers in the Bosom of our Law,
Will eat it through, its very Heart-strings gnaw;
For when with artificial Perjury
They make God's Sacred Name *espouse* their Lye,
Forthwith that Lye *Omnipotent* becomes,
And governs all below; it saves, or dooms;
Disposes of our Honour, Life, and State,
Gives rule to *Law*, and arbitrates our *Fate*.
No rage of Famine, Pestilence, or War,
Can with this *Legal Massacre* compare,
If perjur'd Villains may a Shelter find,
To make their *Inrodes* thus on Humane Kind,
Laws, for Chastisement of the Guilty meant,
Will turn their Points against the Innocent,

(* As

(* As Cannons of a newly enter'd Town   * Poet
speaks.
From their own Walls the Houses batter down.)
My Lords, if you this Villany endure,
Judges themselves will not be long secure:
And so I leave my Cause in your wise breast,
The *Temple* where *Truth's Oracle* should rest.

   Thus *Naboth* spoke, with that undaunted meen,
Which only in *bold Innocence* is seen:
But least the People's Fury should relent,
Arod their calmer thoughts did thus prevent.

   Naboth, what you have said in your defence,
Adds to your Guilt, clears not your Innocence;
When the Kings Evidence you perjur'd call,
Know, that your very *Plea* is *Criminal*.
Shall Malefactors with Reproaches tear
Their Fame, who for their King and Country swear?
What Thief, what Felon may not do the same,
To purge themselves, the Witnesses defame?
Against two Oaths, so positive and plain,
All your harranguing Rhetorick is vain.
Should stout *Denying* pass for *Innocence*,
The Court must be as weak as your Defence.
Less Confidence your bloody Crimes behov'd,
So weakly answer'd, and so strongly prov'd.
Is it not doubly sworn, that you conspir'd
With *Aram's* King, this City to have fir'd,   *v.* 13.
And in that hurry to destroy the King,
And into *Israel Bondage* and *Idols* bring?

   Stung with these dire Reproaches, *Naboth* again
Offer'd to speak, but offer'd still in vain;

For

For when the Bench did thus his Guilt proclaim,
Their Words, like Oyl, inrag'd the People's Flame;
Who hardly ftaying till the Sentence paft,
Like hungry Wolves, they rufh with furious hafte,
Hurrying poor *Naboth* to a planted Stake,
Where in his Death their cruel Joy they take.
Their *Hands* and *Tongues* they equally employ,
And him with *Stones* and *Calumnies* deftroy:
Some gather Flints, and fome the Victim ty'd
Ready for Sacrifice: He loudly cry'd,
Heaven blefs the King! And I forgive ye all;
O! may this Innocent Blood no Vengeance call
On you, my Brethren——Off'ring more to fay,

v. 13. A murdring fhow'r of Stones took Voice and Life away.

  Thus *Naboth* fell----Kind Heaven! fo may I fall;
Rather than ftand fo high, and Criminal,
As *covetous Achab*, and his *bloody* Queen;
Or ferve the *Malice* of fuch *Luft* and *Spleen*;
Or *judge* with *Arod*, or with *Malchus fwear*;
Or with the Rabble oppreft Vertue *tear*.
Naboth! though caft thou art by *Humane Laws*,   17
Heaven's Writ of Errour has remov'd thy Caufe,   18
And judg'd it fo, that it fhall ftand from hence
A lafting Record of *wrong'd Innocence*.
All to thy Afhes fhall their Duty pay,

v. 19. *Friends* fhall their *Tears, Foes* weep their *Blood* away;
For lo! the great *Elijah*, Heaven's Envoy,   19
Has now furpris'd them in their guilty joy,

v. 18. Caught in the very Fact, and Place, where they
Rejoice, pluming, and hovering o're the Prey:
        What?

---

17. *cast:* condemned.
18. *Writ of Errour:* the legal term for a court's order "to redress false Judgment given in any Court of Record" (Thomas Blount, *NOMO-EIKON: A Law Dictionary* [1670], n.p.).
19. *Elijah:* one of the major prophets in the Old Testament.

v. 20. **What?** have I found you in this Field of Blood,
      (For fo thy Title to't fhall be made good,

v. 19. More by thine own, than *Naboth's*) gracelefs King!
      I from thy dreadful Judge thy Sentence bring,
      (Says Heaven's bold Herald.). *Achab* heartlefs grew ;
      And the Queens *Fears* did all her *Pride* fubdue,
      At this loud *Thunder-ftroke.*   Know (wretched Pair)

v. 24. (Continues he) The Vultures in the Air,
      Wolves in the Field fhall be the living Tomb
      Of all that's born from *Jezebel's* curs'd Womb :
      And *Achab's* Seed fhall be the *worthy Food*
      Of Birds and Beafts that live by Prey and Blood.
      Thy Race no more fhall mix with Human Kind,
      But *nourifh* Beafts, and fo with them be *join'd.*
      Thou, *Achab*, here in this ill-purchas'd Ground,
      Shalt bleed thy laft, from a frefh, mortal wound ;

v. 19. Maftifs fhall lick thy Blood ; and it fhall be
      As fweet to them, as *Naboth's* Blood to thee.
      And thou (curft Woman) *Eve*, and *Serpent* too ;
      Caufe of thine own, and of thy Husband's woe,
      Thy broken Limbs, and into pieces rent,

v. 23. Shall be of Dogs the *Food* and *Excrement* :

2 *K.* c·9. *Low falls thy Body*, lower thy *Soul* will fink ;
v. 33.
      Thy Memory ever fhall remain, and ftink.
      And fo he left them Thunder-ftruck and dumb ;
      Stung with their prefent Guilt, and Fate to come.

F I N I S.

Suggested Readings

For primary materials, one might begin with the contemporary accounts excerpted in this book: *The Diary of John Evelyn,* ed. E. S. deBeer (Oxford: Clarendon Press, 1955); Roger North's *Examen* (London, 1740), Gilbert Burnet's *History of My Own Time* [1724], ed. Osmund Airy, based upon the edition of M. J. Routh (Oxford: Clarendon Press, 1897–1900); *State Trials,* vols. 7 and 8, ed. T. B. Howell (London, 1816), and Anchitell Grey's *Debates in the House of Commons, 1667–1694* (London, 1763). Other important sources include Narcissus Luttrell's *A Brief Historical Relation of State Affairs* (Oxford: Oxford University Press, 1857); Sir John Reresby's *Memoirs* [1734], ed. Albert Ivatt (London, 1904) and by Andrew Browning (Glasgow, 1936); and Father John Warner's *History of the English Persecution of the Catholics and the Presbyterian Plot,* ed. T. T. Birrell, trans. J. Bligh (London: Catholic Records Society, 1953–55).

Modern collections of original materials include *English Historical Documents, 1660–1714,* ed. Andrew Browning (London: Eyre & Spottiswood, 1953); *Poems on Affairs of State,* vol. 2: *1678–1681,* ed. Elias F. Mengel, Jr. (New Haven: Yale University Press, 1965; and, in facsimile, *Diaries of the Popish Plot,* ed. Douglas C. Greene (Delmar, N.Y.: Scholars' Facsimiles and Reprints, 1977) which also contains the complete text of Oates's *True Narrative. The Somers Tracts,* ed. Walter Scott (London, 1812), vols. 7 and 8, contain much that is valuable, as do vols. 20–22 of the *Calendar of State Papers, Domestic Series* for the reign of Charles II (London, 1913) and the *Reports of the Historical Manuscripts Commission* (specific references to which may be found in Warner's *History,* p. 559, and John Pollock's *The Popish Plot* [London, 1904], p. 407). Two collections of material related to Dryden are *Anti-Achitophel: Three Verse Replies to Absalom and Achitophel,* ed. Harold Whitmore Jones (Gainesville, Florida: Scholars' Facsimiles and Reprints, 1961) and the Garland Series of Drydeniana, *viz.,* vol. 6, *On Absalom and Achitophel* and vol. 13, *Folio Verse Relating to Dryden, 1681–1699* (New York: Garland Publishing, 1975).

For Dryden's works, the authoritative modern edition is the "California" Dryden, which contains full and expert historical commentary. *Absalom and Achitophel* appears in vol. 2, *Poems, 1681–1684,* ed. H. T. Swedenberg, Jr. (Berkeley: University of California Press, 1972). Volumes 17, *Prose, 1668–1691,* ed. Samuel Holt Monk (1971) and 18, *Prose: The History of the League, 1684,* ed. Alan Roper (1974) are also relevant for this period.

Extensive bibliographies may be found in the histories by Warner and Pollock cited above and in Francis S. Ronalds's *The Attempted Whig Revolution of 1678–81* (Urbana, Ill.: University of Illinois, 1937). Narcissus Luttrell's *Compleat Catalogue of All the Stich'd Books and Single Sheets Printed Since the First Discovery of the Popish Plot* [1680] has been reprinted in facsimile by Basil Blackwell for the Luttrell Society (Oxford, 1956).

Modern Studies

Haley, K. H. D. *The First Earl of Shaftesbury.* Oxford: Clarendon Press, 1968. An unusually thorough and well-written study that makes the best possible case for Shaftesbury.

Jones, J. R. *The First Whigs: The Politics of the Exclusion Crisis, 1678–1683.* London: Oxford University Press, 1961. A valuable account of the parliamentary tactics of the exclusionists.

Kenyon, John. *The Popish Plot.* London: Heinemann, 1972. The standard modern study; strong on the plot trials.

Lane, Jane. *Titus Oates.* London: Andrew Dakers, 1949. The book is weakened by the author's (whose real name is Elaine Kidner Dakers) hatred for Oates.

Miller, John. *Popery and Politics in England, 1660–1688.* Cambridge: Cambridge University Press, 1973. Useful on the anti-Catholic tradition, with valuable analyses of the pamphlets published in this period, and fairest of all modern studies to the parties concerned.

Ogg, David. *England in the Reign of Charles II.* 2d ed., vol. 2. Oxford: Clarendon Press, 1956. The standard modern history.

Pollock, John. *The Popish Plot: A Study in the History of the Reign of Charles II.* London: Duckworth, 1903. Reprinted in 1944 by Cambridge University Press, minus the bibliography and appendices. Though superseded by Kenyon, this is still valuable; it contains a useful chronology of events up to July 1681.

Schilling, Bernard N. *Dryden and the Conservative Myth: A Reading of "Absalom and Achitophel."* New Haven: Yale University Press, 1961. An influential book employing historical criticism.

Thomas, W. K. *The Crafting of "Absalom and Achitophel": Dryden's "Pen for a Party."* Waterloo, Ont., Canada: Wilfrid Laurier University Press, 1978. This uneven reading assembles a good deal of historical information and provides some new interpretations.

Wilson, John Harold. *The Ordeal of Mr. Pepys' Clerk.* Columbus: Ohio State University Press, 1972. A fast-moving narrative of the arrest and trial of Samuel Atkins, based on original sources.

Index

Absalom and Achitophel. See Dryden, John.
Addresses, 200–203, 205, 207
Arundel of Wardour, Lord, 184.
See also "Five Lords in the Tower"
Ashby, Richard, 29, 32, 33, 34, 35, 101, 103, 104, 106–7, 108, 192
Atkins, Samuel, 11, 47, 229

Baldwin, Richard, 202–3
Barrillon, M., 149
Bedingfield, Thomas, 6
Bedloe, William, 3, 6, 34, 47, 49, 57, 81, 82, 92, 99, 105–6, 112–13, 116, 172, 176–77, 181–83, 259, 269, 271, 273
Berry, Henry, 11, 48, 68, 70, 177
Bethel, Slingsby, 11, 203, 214, 240–51
Black Box, 8, 84–85, 125, 155
Blood, Colonel Thomas, 229
Blount, Charles, 85, 186
Blundell, Nicholas, 32, 43, 192
Bothwell Bridge, Battle of, 95, 99, 133, 231
Brudenell, Francis, 45
Buckingham, duke of, 229
Burnet, Bishop Gilbert, 3, 10, 47, 79–83, 99, 126, 241

Capel, Sir Henry, 141–43
Care, Henry, 72–77, 119–21
Carpenter, Nathaniel, 255
Caryll, John, 258–77
Castleton, Lord, 135
Catherine of Braganza, queen, 27, 34, 70, 99–101, 105, 149, 151
Chapman, Mr., 106–7
Charles II, King, 4, 6, 9, 10, 79–80, 99, 130, 149–54, 204–13, 216, 231, 256–57
Clarendon, earl of, 151
Claypole, John, 94
Coleman, Edward, 6, 41, 47, 57–62, 102, 116–17, 177
Colledge, Stephen, 11, 199–203, 214–20
Coniers, George, 39, 42

Cooper, Anthony Ashley. *See* Shaftesbury, earl of
Corker, James, 39, 99, 100, 102, 104, 108, 112
Cornish, Henry, 11, 203, 214, 240, 244
Courtney, Sir William, 234
Croft, Herbert, 34
Cromwell, Oliver, 94, 240
Cromwell, Richard, 200–201

Danby, earl of, 8–9, 27, 156, 158, 257
Dangerfield, Thomas, 125
Declaration of Indulgence, 144
Dick's Coffee House. *See* Richard's Coffee House
Dover, Treaty of, 4
Dryden, John, 1–2, 12, 69, 136, 156, 205, 229, 231, 232, 239, 240, 255, 257, 258–59
Dugdale, Stephen, 81, 176, 215–20
Duke, Richard, 234

Evelyn, John, 115–18

Fenwick, Father John, 32, 33, 43, 101, 104. *See also* "Five Jesuits"
Finch, Daniel, 143
Finch, Henage, 219
Fitzharris, Edward, 11, 68, 167, 199, 202–3, 210–11
"Five Jesuits" (accused by Oates), 7, 79–83. *See also* Fenwick, Father John; Harcourt, Father; Whitebread, Father Thomas; Jesuits
"Five Lords in the Tower," 6, 9, 69, 116–18, 132, 158. *See also* Arundel of Wardour, Lord; Petre, Lord; Stafford, Viscount William
Flatman, John, 203
Fogarty, Dr. William, 41

Godfrey, Sir Edmund Berry, 6–7, 47–56, 64–65, 66–71, 175, 177, 216
Great Fire of London, 1, 4, 5, 9, 22, 35, 88. *See also* London
Green, Robert, 11, 48, 68, 70, 177
Green Ribbon Club, 65, 68, 70, 147, 229
Grove, John, 6–7

Halifax, marquis of, 9, 147, 148, 180, 207, 257
Hampden, Richard, 129
Harcourt, Father, 32, 101–2, 104, 105. *See also* "Five Jesuits"
Harris, Benjamin, 237
Harvey, Michael, 235
Hawkins, Mr., 202–3
Heraclitus Ridens, 202–3
Hill, Lawrence, 11, 48, 68, 70, 177
How, Sir Richard, 184, 249
How and Rich, 247
Hyde, Laurance, 136, 138

Ignoramus juries, 11, 221
Ireland, Father William, 6–7, 32, 101, 104, 110, 111, 121

James II, King, 187, 231, 239. *See also* York, duke of
Janeway, Richard, 200–3, 235
Jeffreys, Sir George, 105, 218
Jenkins, Sir Leoline, 126–29, 132–34, 137
Jennings, Sir William, 216, 220
Jennison, Robert, 38, 111
Jesuits, 4, 5, 29–45, 65, 66, 82–83, 116, 120–21, 185. *See also* "Five Jesuits"
Jones, Sir William, 70, 131–32, 137–38, 145

Keines, John, 37–40
Kirkby, Christopher, 6

La Chaise, Father François de, 6, 34, 44, 59, 104
Lambert, John, 192
Langhorn, Richard, 7, 79, 82–83, 102, 171–85
Lauderdale, duke of, 36, 37
Legge, George, 140–42

L'Estrange, Sir Roger, 9, 11, 17, 48, 186–203
Lloyd, Sir Philip, 108–9
London, 5, 10, 12, 66, 87–89, 155–61. *See also* Great Fire of London
Louis XIV, king of France, 4, 10, 17, 23, 60–61, 156

Marshall, William, 99, 100, 106, 108, 111, 113, 121
Marvell, Andrew, 5, 17–23, 186
Mary of Orange, 8
Mason, Robert, 240, 247
Mazarin, duchess of, 149
Meal Tub Plot, 9
Milton, John, 186, 192
Monmouth, duke of, 1, 7–8, 10, 84–85, 99, 125, 135, 229, 231–37, 239, 256–57
Montagu, Ralph, 8, 27, 128–29

Nijmegen, Treaty of, 4, 5
North, Sir Francis, 99, 103, 109–10, 186
North, Roger, 66–71

Oates, Titus, 3, 5–7, 9, 11, 12, 26–45, 48–49, 57, 69–71, 80, 82, 83, 92, 94–95, 99–100, 101–4, 106–13, 116–17, 172, 173, 175–77, 181–83, 186–97, 202, 215, 216–20, 239, 247, 259, 268–69, 271, 272–73

Parcet, Elizabeth, 236–37
Parliament, 8–10, 17
Pemberton, Sir Francis, 99, 103, 111
Pembroke, earl of, 48
Pepys, Samuel, 11, 47
Petitions, 9, 125, 157, 199–203, 205
Petre, Lord, 184. *See also* "Five Lords in the Tower"
Pickering, Thomas, 6, 27, 29–30, 45, 112–13
Pilkington, Thomas, 221, 226, 249, 251
Player, Sir Thomas, 70
Plunkett, Oliver, archbishop of Armagh, 10
Poole, Matthew, 32, 33

Pope burning processions, 10, 64–65, 229
Portsmouth, duchess of, 125, 149
Poulett, John, Lord, 237
Prance, Miles, 7, 34, 48–49, 176
Prideaux, Edmund, 234

Quo warranto, writs of, 12

Ratcliffe, Sir Francis, 106
Reading, Nathaniel, 176
Richard's Coffee House, 202–3, 218
Roscommon, earl of, 180
Rumley, William, 99
Russell, Lord William, 126
Ruvigny, Henri de Massue, 61
Rye House Plot, 12

Savile, Sir George. *See* Halifax, marquis of
Sawyer, Sir Robert, 99–103, 105
Scott, James. *See* Monmouth, duke of
Scroggs, Sir William, 3, 7, 11, 69, 76, 99–100, 101–14, 259, 266–68, 271, 272, 275
Sergeant, Father John, 83
Shaftesbury, earl of, 3, 7, 10, 11–12, 34, 125, 147–54, 171, 174, 178, 186, 214, 217, 221–26, 239, 256–57
Shute, Samuel, 221, 226
Smith, John ("Narrative"), 216, 218–20
Somerset House, 7, 34, 48, 70, 101
Speke, George, 232–34, 237
Stafford, Viscount William, 9, 145, 214–16, 218–20. *See also* "Five Lords in the Tower"
Staley, William, 2–3, 72–77, 102
Stillingfleet, Edward, 33
Strange, Richard, 32, 35
Strode, William, 233

Sydenham, Sir John, 233, 237

Talbot, Peter, archbishop of Dublin, 41
Tangier, 207–8
Test Act (1673), 4, 23, 246
Test Act, Second (1678), 8, 239
Thimbleby. *See* Ashby, Richard
Thynne, Thomas, 232
Tonge, Israel, 4, 5–6, 10, 33, 42, 43
Tories, 8, 68, 205, 221
Treby, Sir George, 70
Trenchard, John, 144–45
True Protestant Mercury, 202–3
Tuberville, Edward, 215–20

Villiers, George. *See* Buckingham, duke of

Wakeman, Sir George, 11, 34, 40–41, 99–114, 115–18, 119–21
Waller, William, 113
Walters, Lucy, 8, 231, 236
Warcup, Colonel Edmund, 217
Ward, Edward, 101, 103, 105
Whigs, 8, 10, 11, 12, 125, 155, 199–203
White, Thomas. *See* Whitebread, Father Thomas
Whitebread, Father Thomas, 30, 32, 33, 34, 38, 44, 45, 79–83, 102. *See also* "Five Jesuits"
William of Orange (William III), 8, 12, 36, 187
Windebank, Sir Francis, 93
Winnington, Sir Francis, 138–40

York, duke of, 1, 4, 31, 40, 57, 60–62, 99, 125, 126, 151–52, 163, 222–25, 239. *See also* James II
York, Mary, duchess of, 4, 6
Young, Sir Walter, 234